Mari Sandoz

Mari Sandoz

Story Catcher of the Plains

by Helen Winter Stauffer

University of
Nebraska Press
Lincoln & London

Copyright 1982 by the University of Nebraska Press
All rights reserved
Manufactured in the United States of America

The paper in this book meets the guidelines for
permanence and durability of the Committee on
Production Guidelines for Book Longevity of the
Council on Library Resources.
First Bison Book printing: 1982
Most recent printing indicated by first digit below:
1 2 3 4 5 6 7 8 9 10

Library of Congress Cataloging in Publication Data

Stauffer, Helen Winter, 1922-
Mari Sandoz, story catcher of the plains.

Bibliography: p.
Includes index.
1. Sandoz, Mari, 1896-1966 – Biography. 2. Novelists,
American – 20th century – Biography. I. Title.
PS3537.A667Z8 813'.52[B] 81-22014
ISBN 0-8032-4121-6 AACR2
ISBN 0-8032-9134-5 (pbk.)

Acknowledgments for the use of photographs appear on page 312.

ILLUSTRATIONS

Preface

No matter how sedulously writers try to keep the personal element out of their work, their quality as human beings, their
integrity, their passions, and their vision of the world cannot be
effaced from the printed page. Certainly this is true of the work of
Mari Sandoz. Her first and perhaps best-known book, *Old Jules,*
in particular, bears directly on her early years and her crucial
relationship with her father; therefore, I have looked rather
closely at that book from an autobiographical perspective. Some
psychological inferences were inevitable; however, I have tried
to avoid turning this biography into a psychological study. In
addition to *Old Jules* and the twenty-five books that followed,
my prime sources include letters from and interviews with
people who knew Mari Sandoz, material in the Nebraska State
Historical Society, and the author's own letters and files. The
most extensive letter collection is in the archives of the University of Nebraska–Lincoln, at Love Library, where her correspondence of more than forty years, her historical notes, index file,
maps, working library, and most of her book manuscripts are
preserved. I have also drawn on the Mamie Meredith–Mari Sandoz correspondence file at the Nebraska State Historical Society;
the file of the Sandoz Corporation at the home, near Gordon,
Nebraska, of Caroline Sandoz Pifer, Mari Sandoz's sister and
executor; and materials at Chadron State College, Chadron, Nebraska; Syracuse University; the University of Wyoming; the
Denver Public Library; the private museum in the Chamberlain
Furniture Store in Gordon; and the family museum on Highway

26 between Gordon and Ellsworth. I also gained information from tapes and transcriptions of television appearances and speeches.

The Sandoz letter files at Love Library contain both letters she received and carbons of her letters to others. Long before she sold any of her writing, Mari Sandoz believed that her correspondence would be an essential adjunct to the study of her work; her philosophy, in the words of a friend, Dorothy Thomas, was "Goethe's own: 'never be so mad as to doubt yourself.' " According to her sister Caroline, "Few writers have been so purposeful in expecting their letters to become part of their literary heritage." Undeniably, Mari Sandoz was correct in her evaluation of the importance of her correspondence to the biographer, but one can hardly fail to recognize that a woman with so great a degree of self-consciousness will be at some pains to reveal only chosen aspects of her life, to disclose only what she wants known. She permits us to see much of her professional life, but little or nothing of her personal life, particularly before she moved to Lincoln in 1923. Her acquaintances, too, often noted that although they found her friendly, she was extremely reticent about certain aspects of her life. Believing that a writer was a public person in much the same way as any celebrity, Mari created through her correspondence her public image—one not always consonant with the private image her family and close friends recall, or even that projected through her television appearances and taped lectures.

Since the focus of this biography is primarily on the author's life as it relates to her work, the pertinent letters become even narrower in scope; they give only partial—and sometimes misleading—clues to the "real" person. True, the carbon copies of Mari Sandoz's letters somewhat ease the biographer's task, but their very existence is a constant reminder of how early she had her eye on posterity. Similarly, in her autobiographical notes one feels the presence of the self-conscious writer, always with an eye on the audience, as well as the mature individual writing about time past. For some aspects of my study, then, my information has come from interviews with her family and acquaintances rather than from Mari's files. Some of it is privileged information; the sources prefer not to be identified.

Little has been written about Mari Sandoz's life, and important material may yet come to light. At present, it has proved impossible to trace her precise whereabouts and activities during several periods. I have sometimes made conjectures about these periods. In each case the assumptions are my own, validated, I hope, by my symbiotic relationship with my subject— Mary, Marie, Mari Sandoz.

Mari Sandoz in the 1920s

Acknowledgments

This book could not have been written without the help and concern of many people. I can name only a few: first, my family, to whom I owe the greatest appreciation for the sacrifices they made so often for my research; and the Sandoz family, in particular Mari's young relative David Sandoz, who encouraged the idea of writing the biography, and Mari's sister Caroline Sandoz Pifer. She was my hostess whenever I was in the sandhills, located source material, shared family history, drove me to visit her brothers and sister, and was generally interested in my work. My thanks go to all the friends of Mari listed in the bibliography, but a special word is due Thomas Hornsby Ferril for sharing his 1940–42 diaries with me, Caroline Bancroft for her help regarding Mari's Denver years, and Kay Rogers and Polly Richardson for their long and helpful interviews by tape and letters. I had fine assistance from Ron Hull at Nebraska Educational Television; from Joe Svoboda, Archivist of the University of Nebraska–Lincoln libraries; from the staff at the Nebraska State Historical Society; and, in tracking down special important details, from Anita Norman, research librarian at Kearney State College. The Sandburg Family Trust kindly granted permission to quote from a letter written by Carl Sandburg.

Among my colleagues, Bernice Slote, Dwight Adams, and Harland Hoffman gave understanding and assistance; Hazel Pierce deserves a star in her crown for the hours she spent criticizing, suggesting, and editing the work in various stages. I could not have undertaken the research without financial assistance from the Nebraska State College Research Foundation and a grant from the National Endowment for the Humanities.

None of this would have come to fruition without the interest, patience, and encouragement of that superb editor Virginia Faulkner. Her death was a great loss not only to the University of Nebraska Press but to me personally.

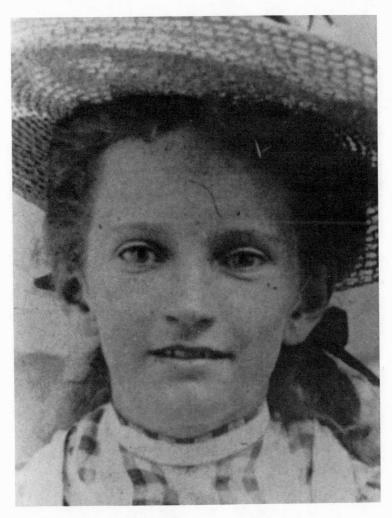

*Mari, perhaps about the time of the
publication of her first short story
in an Omaha newspaper, for which she
was soundly punished by Old Jules*

Mari, Jule, and a neighbor, Mrs. Surber, at the Niobrara River place

Introduction

Mari Sandoz is recognized as a novelist, historian, and biographer, as well as an authority on the Indians of the Great Plains. Her work varies in quality, her novels usually considered least successful, and her histories, particularly her biographies, most trenchant. In the latter she has fused her skill as a writer, her mastery of historical research, and her empathy for her subjects to create works of unique and lasting value.

About some aspects of her writing Mari Sandoz had clear and precise theories; about others she was surprisingly vague. She seldom discussed biography as such, for example, in respect to either genre or technique; she seemed to assume it was something everybody knew about. One of the first books she helped get into print, a biography of Lewis Carroll by Florence Baker Lennon, came out of the writers' conference at Boulder, Colorado, in 1941, but her assistance to the author, apart from moral support, was advice about that particular book; she did not discuss the genre itself. In her lectures, articles, and writing classes she concentrated on the writing of fiction; she seldom discussed nonfiction and biography hardly at all.

Mari seemed to make little conscious distinction between methods of writing fiction and those of writing nonfiction. She spoke of using the same techniques for biography and for fiction, except that in biography one must keep as close to the actual story, the actual people, and the actual times as possible. Her nonfiction written as narrative history used facts and was faithful to them, but she concentrated on specific events and characters to bring out the drama. Mari's interest, and the theme of all her books, was in the relationship of man and the land. "Why doesn't anyone who really understands the farmer's weaknesses, his strengths, his triumphs, and his problems—and appreciates the fierce affection that grows up in him for his not always friendly plot of soil—write of him?" she asked early in her career.[1] In particular, she spoke poetically about the country of the Running Water, the Niobrara River, which would never accept the intruder unless he gave himself wholly to it; no one, she said, who had ever been in that region could forget it. Her concern was not with the history of dates or wars, but with the history of man in his environment.

On her chosen landscape, the trans-Missouri basin, certain memorable men appeared from time to time, and it is their experiences she relates in her biographies and histories. Her subjects are significant because of their unique qualities as human beings, but also because in their individual lives they exhibit certain universal qualities. They respond and react to the force of events on the Great Plains, caught in a historical moment when one culture supersedes another.

Mari Sandoz also felt a strong need to preserve the past, seeing it as a guide to the future. Someday, she believed, man will learn that the same mistakes need not be made over and over, nor will each generation need to learn once more man's goodness, generosity, and courage. Her themes are the working of fate, the re-creation of the past, the importance of nature, the rhythm of life, the strength of evil as manifested in man's inhumanity to man, and, paradoxically, man's essential nobility. These themes shape her writing. Although Mari Sandoz left no written evidence of a consciously formulated philosophy of life, throughout her writing career her epic vision was remarkably consistent. She saw man romantically, larger than life, a creature who could occasionally display characteristics of grandeur. In her biographies, histories, and novellas, Mari Sandoz hoped to recreate the culture and virtues she found in the Plains societies of the past. Her feeling for the fine qualities of the Indian societies of the nineteenth century is evident in her recollection of He Dog, the aged Oglala Sioux chief, once famous companion of Crazy Horse, but in the years that she knew him blind and living in extreme poverty. Once he had stood with Crazy Horse and Sitting Bull and Gall against the power of the United States government, and she had no words to express her sorrow at his fate. It also "broke her heart" to see the young Indians of modern times forced to deny their individuality and heritage, trying to become like the whites so they could earn a decent living.[2] As early as 1932 she regretted the passing of the distinctiveness of communities: "The uniqueness of speech, the attitudes, and the very life of the isolated community are being endangered. The hinterland is trading its individuality for cheap imitations of that which is mediocre, the tawdry of our commercial centers."[3]

However, Mari Sandoz did not allow her sympathy for the cultures and the heroes of the past to stand in the way of what André Maurois has called the "indefatigable search for the truth." She worked constantly to correct false historical notions, as is attested by her frequent arguments with those who venerated such figures as Buffalo Bill Cody. Her quarrel was with history and biography that perpetuated the old, incorrect information. She combined her sympathy for her heroes with solid historical research, much of it in primary scources, some never used by other historians. One of her editors has written that her books are distinguished by "the poetry of structure and style, the combination of first-hand knowledge, absolute scholarship, and creative historical vision."[4]

It has been charged that western writers are too close to their material, that their personal involvement prevents objectivity. On the other hand, these writers have the inestimable advantage of writing from inside their subject, an asset that no outsider, no matter how skilled or sympathetic, can acquire. Although Mari Sandoz aimed for truth and objectivity, she could not, of course, achieve it completely, any more than can any other historian or biographer. Whatever her purpose in writing beyond simply presenting the facts, that purpose directed her use of the raw material. She recognized this when she acknowledged that every event in *Old Jules* could be authenticated but the interpretation of the action was hers, and that she tried to make the book artistically and philosophically as well as historically true.

She agreed with those who believe that writing is both an ethical and aesthetic problem.

Something of a mystic, Mari shared with most western American writers the classical view of myth and tragedy, emphasizing the importance of intuition rather than logic. Relying too heavily on reason could leave one out of tune with nature, she believed; response to the natural environment should be through emotion and the senses rather than through intellect. Her proclivity toward the occult encouraged her belief in fate as a force greater than the individual. She saw the death of Crazy Horse, for example, as fated. In her own life, she commented, it seemed fated that whatever she wanted and worked for seemed to come at the wrong time. Nevertheless, she said, "I am convinced there is a reason for everything."[5] Agreeing with the theory of the collective unconscious, she was strongly attracted to the use of image, myth, and symbol. The concrete images of her childhood included the guns of her father and the cattlemen he opposed; the smoky kitchen of her childhood home, Indian Hill; the Niobrara that flowed past the farm; and the sandhills. There was also, constantly, her intense awareness of nature. Her pulse "leaped to the glory of the spring along the winding Niobrara. She had a song for the shining snow water rushing downstream. She seemed to actually see the stirring roots of grass, flowers, and trees. Because of their awakening Miss Sandoz never failed to rejoice in the re-enactment of one of the fine miracles of this earth."[6]

Later her images included that of the magnificent Nebraska state capitol as she described it in *Love Song to the Plains:* "Around the tower, in bas-relief, march those gone-before ones, the buffalo, the Indian, the fur men, the pioneers. The great figures of humanity, such as law, justice and mercy, stand watching or depict their significant victories, from those of the Old Testament down through the Independence and the Constitution with its freedom of speech, and of the body and the heart."[7] She invested the statue of the Sower at the top of the tower with special significance. She wrote, "There were some who believed that the Sower of the Nebraska capitol should broadcast not only seeds upon the fertile earth but ideas in government as well" (p. 242). She often typed on the front lawn of her apartment house where she could see the capitol tower standing over her, white, with the Sower dark against white clouds.

As a writer, she enjoyed working with both old and new forms. Allegory, one of the oldest and most didactic forms of storytelling, is recognizable in *Winter Thunder, Slogum House, Capital City,* and *The Tom-Walker.* Her nonfiction is less obviously allegorical, but the elements are there, stressing the author's belief in the absolute necessity of development through struggle, and, particularly in the Indian books, the loss the white civilization had inflicted upon itself because of its discrimination. She felt that the United States would always have on its conscience the sin of what it had done to the Indians, and for that reason would never be what it could have been. In her use of allegory she felt close to Faulkner and Hemingway. Faulkner's *A Fable* seized her with an emotion she could not express; she ranked Hemingway's *The Old Man and the Sea* with *Moby Dick* and *Steppenwolf,* two of the world's great allegories.

Mari Sandoz was a loner, a member of no group or school or movement, although during her Lincoln years she knew and talked writing with other young authors, an exhilarating experience for the young woman fresh from the isolation of the sandhills. As she often remarked later, she spent years working out for herself simple techniques and ideas she could have learned in a very short time with the stimulation of other creative minds. She felt it true that in most instances American writers, working alone, miss the spur and prodding that communication between authors stimulates, for in the periods of great world literature there was natural contact and friction between authors.

With the exception of John G. Neihardt, western writers seem not to have influenced Mari Sandoz directly. She seldom discussed them individually in her letters, and when she did, or when she reviewed their books, she judged them primarily on the basis of the amount of research undertaken and the accuracy of their historical re-creation. She approved or disapproved of authors according to how well they presented history, since she thought of herself as a historian. The writers she felt worthwhile were those who had a sense of responsibility to world society as well as to that of their own locale, who understood their obligation to see the present and future implications of their material wholly and clearly and who presented it as honestly as possible.[8] The trans-Missouri region was the one with which she had strong emotional ties and the one she knew best, but her writing was, she hoped, universal in scope.

As early as 1933, in speaking of *Old Jules*, she explained that instead of attempting to write a popular book she was trying to write one showing a way of life, bringing to the readers an experience they could get no other way, a book that would be good even fifty years later. Such books often deviated from the accepted standard for structure and treatment. As to her writing for the future, she stated that the twenty-first-century child would be so versed in psychology and so sensitive to human conflict that even the most elusive of present-day writers would seem obvious. She hoped in her writing not to escape the grasp of her contemporaries and not to be overly obvious to readers of future generations. Since she feared that none of her contemporaries understood her purpose and that very few in the past had been interested in what she thought important, she was forced to look to the future for understanding.[9]

Mari's own literary influences came primarily through her reading and studies. She had read Conrad as a child but was introduced to other major authors later. Hardy, whom she read shortly after she first came to the university, made a profound impression on her; the structure of *Slogum House* was based on that of his novels.[10] Of later discoveries, the Russians strongly affected her, as did Shakespeare and, finally, the Greeks, with whom she saw so many parallels in her Indian heroes. "I've always felt that the underlying theme of Crazy Horse, the destiny fore-ordained for him and the people he led, no matter how great his personal virtue, is Greek in its tragic implications," she wrote to her friend Mamie Meredith in 1957. "I've always felt, ever since my introduction to Greek literature, that the Plains Indians had a close affinity for the Greeks in their sense of honor and honor lost." At some point she read Whitman and was strongly impressed by both his philosophy and his style, as were

so many other western writers. His American romanticism influenced her indirectly as well, through such writers as Carl
Sandburg and Willa Cather. Her reading of Adolph Hitler's *Mein
Kampf* was an experience she never forgot. Eliot's *The Waste
Land* was a major discovery, as was Céline's *Journey to the End
of the Night*. Kafka's *The Castle* she found especially illuminat-
ing of her own occasional sudden sense of being lost in the
world, "a complete unfamiliarity with even the commonest
things." For her, Kafka's book was terrifying and yet one she
returned to every year or so.[11] That she came to so many of the
classics late, when she was a mature woman but while still
formulating her own writing style and ideas, made them especially vivid to her, in the same way that her delayed learning to
read affected her when she was nine: "I learned reading
late . . . learned *cat*—a tremendous revelation—could always
recognize it . . . [as] the greatest gift in the world, and I was old
enough to appreciate it," she told an audience.[12]

By conventional literary standards, Mari Sandoz's nonfiction measures up well. Strongly affected by her sense of history,
of time and of place, she wrote powerful and effective histories
when working with protagonists whom she could identify with
her own region. She mastered the art of recreating a man and his
culture, emphasizing the moral issues involved when one culture destroys another, and illustrating her own romantic view
that man has dignity and worth. She adhered closely to carefully
researched information, and the strength of her artistic imagination lay in creating a verisimilitude of actual events, rather
than in creating imaginary scenes. In her biographies particularly she succeeds in re-creating the living past. She accepted
the artist's purpose: "The crude matter of life assumes
significance from the shaping hand of the artist."[13]

The re-creation of early settler life abounds in Plains literature, but Mari Sandoz's *Old Jules* is so unusual it has few imitations. Her ability to fuse Jules's importance to the region with
scenes from his domestic life, while involving herself, is rare.
(The only biography I know that manages similar emotional
material so unemotionally, achieving aesthetic distance, is Ed-
mund Gosse's *Father and Son*, about life in the 1800s in En-

gland.) In 1935, Old Jules shocked people, not only because of the domestic scenes but because it showed the public a stark, unromantic view of the frontier. The strong language, the sometimes brutal realism, the frankness were all criticized vigorously, but they made the book powerful. The swearing no longer shocks contemporary readers, who are frequently confronted with pungent, and often pointless, profanity, but the realism and frankness are just as gripping now as they were then. The children cowering under the bed, Henriette's fright when a shot breaks the lamp in her hand, Uncle Emile shot down in front of his family by a hired gunman—these scenes as well as the descriptions of the prairie's beauty are still as effective as ever. The conflicts described best in Old Jules, Crazy Horse, and Cheyenne Autumn still hold significance, although the specific incidents are well in the past. The West is now tamed, and the Indians are, legally at least, freer to move about as they please, but the emotions engendered by those conflicts are universal. Mari's people experience love, hate, ambition, jealousy, sorrow, fear, satisfaction and joy. Some are caught by forces too large for them to control—by a government gigantic and relentless and sometimes apparently mindless. Some learn their fate is controlled by men too small for their responsibilities, too ignorant or too greedy to value human life. And some fight back. These things have been going on since long before the Greeks wrote of them, and we see them today. The theme of man and his fate is timeless. Mari Sandoz hoped to match her subject matter with her art. In these three books she succeeded.

Those books of her Great Plains series using an animal as the protagonist and humans as antagonists—The Buffalo Hunters, The Cattlemen, and The Beaver Men—have a less clear-cut focus, primarily because her efforts to cram a large amount of information into them make the works seem disjointed. Although the many minor characters, together with the vast amount of time and space involved, make these books less easily controlled by the author and sometimes a challenge to the reader's memory, they are stimulating, useful, and in most instances well written. Mari uses in these books the skills of the storytellers she heard and admired in her childhood to develop the many and disparate episodes making up the variegated thread of western history.

Mari Sandoz's prose, often lyrical and lovely, appears to be standing the test of time. Much of the timelessness is achieved through her use of images and symbols, the word-pictures by which she describes the geography of the Great Plains. Of special note is the language form she created for her narration of the Indian way of life. While other writers had stressed the Indian point of view, the language of the white author almost always interfered with the atmosphere of the Indian culture portrayed in the story. It is by means of her particular use of language in her Indian books that Mari Sandoz brings the reader to greater understanding and perhaps even identification with her Indian heroes.

It may be too soon to make serious critical judgments of Mari Sandoz's canon, but her work is impressive in both quantity and quality. John K. Hutchens says of it, "Here is a large statement but, I think, a true one: no one in our time wrote better than the late Mari Sandoz did, or with more authority and grace, about as many aspects of the Old West."[14]

The Sandoz homestead in the sandhills

One
The Father, the Family, & the Frontier

Mari Sandoz once remarked that an author's work is determined largely by physical inheritance and by the traditions and the environment into which he is born.[1] Although she was speaking in general terms, she was alluding to her own heritage bequeathed her by her Swiss immigrant parents and to her childhood on the frontier. Both the general reference and the specific intent are of importance to her writing. While her books deal with the universal conflicts of mankind, they are set in the world she knew best, the northern Great Plains, more particularly, the sandhills of the upper Niobrara River region of northwestern Nebraska.

To understand Mari and her work, one must come to know both the region she grew up in and the person who most influenced her imagination; her father, Jules Sandoz. As a youngster living at home and for years afterward, even when she had moved east to pursue an independent life and career of her own, she was dominated by him. The stories she heard over and over as a child from Jules and his friends gave her her first knowledge of the history of her region. She learned of the Indian wars and other events of the area from the people who had participated in the events they spoke of. Her early acquaintance with the old storytellers determined what she would look for and what she would later say about the Great Plains. The tales told and retold about Jules pictured him as a frontiersman rather than a pioneer and illustrated his significant role in developing the primitive frontier into a civilized, productive part of the United States.[2]

Jules's life and his character were the subjects Mari explored at great length in her early writing. He served as the model for the antagonist in her first novel, never published, and she featured him in her first published article,"The Kinkaider Comes and Goes" which appeared in the *North American Review* for April and May 1930. Her first published book, *Old Jules* (1935) carries his name. The writing of that book took many years during which she struggled to come to an understanding of this enigmatic man. It was only after she had resolved this problem that she became a successful writer.

In 1881, the young Swiss Jules Sandoz was one of a vast throng of European immigrants and native-born Americans moving onto the prairies and plains of mid-America to homestead.[3] Jules, a bachelor of twenty-two, took a claim in northeastern Nebraska, near the confluence of the Niobrara and Missouri rivers. Like many others, Jules was running away from problems at home as much as seeking new opportunity. A spoiled, impetuous young man, he had quarreled with his family and had come to the United States to live his life as he pleased.

The Sandoz family had long prided itself on its liberal beliefs, strongly influenced by the Calvinism which had found a home in Switzerland. Sandoz ancestors were religious followers of the heretic Peter Waldo in Italy in the twelfth century who fled religious persecution to France and later to Switzerland.[4] James Boswell, on his grand tour of the Continent in 1764, stayed with innkeepers named Sandoz in the village of Brot while waiting to introduce himself to their neighbor, Jean-Jacques Rousseau. James Boswell wrote in his journal that the Sandoz clan, numbering about five hundred, had set up a fund to help family members, primarily with scholarships. He also mentioned the innkeeper's daughter, Mlle Sandoz, who talked volubly and sang duets with him to entertain the company.[5] Many Sandoz relatives were professional people—doctors, lawyers, and chemists; several had become governesses for nobility and royalty throughout Europe. Jules's Aunt Jeanne came to the United States and was later governess to Franklin D. Roosevelt.[6]

Little Mari often heard her father contrast his home in Europe with his present life in Nebraska. Jules, born 21 April 1859, in

the French-speaking canton of Neuchâtel, in the Jura Mountains
of Switzerland, was the oldest of seven sons and one daughter of
Ami Frederic Sandoz, a veterinarian, and Ida Dousoulavy Sandoz. When Jules was eight, the family moved from their small
village of Fanin to the city of Neuchâtel, but his father sent the
boy back to the German farmers of the Jura in the summers to
learn farming. The family was from the reasonably prosperous
middle class; the mother had property in her own right, and the
father was an officer in the national reserve army.

Jules often referred to his study of medicine at the University
of Zurich and his work during vacations as a clerk on the mail
train running between Zurich and Florence, Italy, and back,
learning Italian on the route.[7] Mari knew, too, about Rosalie, a
young clerk on the mail train with whom Jules fell in love. Her
social position was not good enough to suit his family, and for
once Jules could not win over his mother, though she spoiled her
eldest son outrageously. There had been other serious family
crises as well. Jules had seen the American advertisements en-
ticing Europeans to the rich farmlands of the Midwest. Why stay
in Europe with all its restrictions, its pettiness, its lack of opportunity, when one could go to a land of unlimited possibility?
Jules left for the United States, planning for Rosalie to follow
him.

From St. Louis, Jules traveled by river steamer up the
Missouri River as far as his money would take him. He was a
crack shot, familiar with guns as were most Swiss men, and he
hunted meat for the boat in part payment for his passage. His
journey ended in Knox County, Nebraska, not far south of
Yankton, South Dakota. He took a homestead several miles south
of the confluence of the Niobrara with the Missouri, in rough,
broken, hilly country, near the site soon to be platted as the town
of Verdigre.[8] He began immediately to recruit his young professional friends from Switzerland.

In the mid-1800s the world had westering fever. People
flocked west to try their luck on free or cheap land. The farmland
was often less desirable than elsewhere, but it gave one a chance
to begin again. In Nebraska, the most attractive areas along the
eastern rivers went first, but the frontier pushed west, inexorably

though sometimes slowly. When Jules arrived in the 1880s, parts of Nebraska still had room for settlers.

Jules's letters to his friends back home did not tell the real story. True, Nebraska had some of the most fertile farm soil in the world, but he did not point out that the climate was noted for extremes in temperature, with violent storms and blizzards, nor that in some areas the average rainfall was far short of the thirty inches necessary for good crops and certainly much less than the thirty-six-inch average of his native Switzerland. Here the country was almost treeless; even on many of the rivers it was barren, sandy, and windy.

Jules stayed in Knox County only three years. When Rosalie refused to come to the new country, he married an uneducated young woman, Estelle Thompson, possibly part Indian.[9] The marriage was stormy. One day in early spring of 1884, after throwing their sugar and flour to his pigs in a temper, he left the tiny log cabin, taking the forty dollars he had received for relinquishment of his claim. With two horses and a wagon he headed west once more, alone, following the Niobrara River, which flows across northern Nebraska from Wyoming.

His journey took him through the strange, unique area of the sandhills, which encompass some eighteen thousand square miles in north-central Nebraska. Because of their shifting shapes, treelessness, and sparse vegetation, the hills could appear deadly—and they could be deadly—but they were dotted with clear lakes, and the valleys supported a good grass cover well suited for livestock grazing. But Jules was not interested in ranching; he was looking for farmland. He passed the western edge of the sandhills and, almost 300 miles from Veridgre, came out onto the high plains, level tablelands with occasional deep gullies, that stretched west and north of the sandhills. This was subhumid, short-grass country with an annual rainfall of only about eighteen inches a year. As Jules followed the north bank of the Niobrara, however, he found a place he thought would be fertile, would grow crops. On the only knoll on his land he set up a tent. Later building a dugout, roofed over with ash poles covered with sod, the common building material for this treeless area, he became the first homesteader on what would be called

Mirage Flats. He dreamed of establishing here his own domain, with people settled all around him. Once more he began writing to people in the East and in Europe, offering to locate settlers, to help them find suitable homesteads, to survey boundaries, and to assist them with their filing requirements. He also wrote the government asking for a local post office.

Jules was, indeed, on a frontier. Since the nearest law officer was almost at the Wyoming border, three days' ride away, the young homesteader would have to rely on his own fine marksmanship to prove his legal rights. He would also have to provide for his own basic medical needs; the nearest doctor was forty-five miles west of him at Fort Robinson, established ten years earlier during the Indian wars. The Indian wars had ended well before 1884, and the Indians were now settled on reservations, but the two largest Sioux reservations, the Pine Ridge and the Rosebud, were just over the border in South Dakota, not fifty miles from Jules's homestead, and bands of Indians hunted and visited often in his area.

Jules soon met some of the Oglala Sioux from the Pine Ridge, down hunting in the neighborhood. He spent a good deal of time at their camp, learning their ways, making friends with White Eye, Ghost Bear, and the Man Afraid of His Horses and He Dog families. They sometimes took him into the sandhills, full of lakes and places for good hunting.[10] Jules found that land fascinating; he believed it could produce crops if scientifically handled.

Around their campfires the Indians told Jules their version of the recent Indian wars, particularly of events at Fort Robinson. It was there, in 1877, that their great war chief Crazy Horse had been killed; tricked, they said, into the guardhouse, and then stabbed by a white soldier's bayonet as he tried to escape. And the visiting Cheyennes, friends and relatives of the Oglala Sioux, told him of the Cheyenne outbreak there the following winter. The Indians, trying to return from their hated reservation in Indian Territory (Oklahoma) to their old homeland in the North, had been imprisoned at the fort. They were shot down in an escape attempt. Jules was especially friendly with Wild Hog, a Cheyenne living with the Sioux, who had been in the outbreak.

The two often talked of the Cheyennes' experiences and Wild Hog's belief that the government still intended to destroy the entire tribe.

That autumn, 1884, Jules fell sixty-five feet into a well being dug on his homestead. Eighteen days later, passing soldiers from Fort Robinson found him delirious, one leg badly swollen and infected. Neighbors took him to the fort for treatment. The army physician, Walter Reed (who later became famous for his work on yellow fever) attempted to drain the infection and, at Jules's insistence, to save the foot. He succeeded in avoiding an amputation, but the ankle never healed completely and Jules was a cripple the rest of his life. He was no longer able to travel long distances; he could no longer run away from his problems.

Jules remained at the fort for eight months, from October 1884 through the next spring, while his leg mended. There he heard stories from the army men and interpreters who had been in the recent Indian wars. William (Billy) Garnett and "Little Bat" Garnier told the best stories as they recounted their part in events at the fort. Both had known Crazy Horse and the other Indian chiefs; they knew, too, about the Cheyenne outbreak. These were the stories Mari later heard told and retold.

Jules returned to his claim in the spring of 1885. One of his first acts was to complain to the neighbors who had hauled him to the fort that they stole the feather tick he lay on when they took him there.[11] The tick had been so malodorous they had thrown it in the nearest creek after they had left him at the hospital, but Jules refused to believe they would destroy a mattress for such a reason. Nor did he bother to thank them for their round trip of five days, time they lost for improving their own claims.

In 1885 two new towns were incorporated in the area, Hay Springs, seventeen miles northwest of the Flats, and Rushville, eighteen miles northeast.[12] Jules continued to bring in new settlers, a task more important to him than working his own homestead. Never fond of the physical work of farming, he frequently had his land broken and planted by the men he found homesteads for, using labor in lieu of the twenty-five-dollar fee he charged for locating and surveying for them. He had faith that this land was for the poor, for the farmer rather than the rancher, and he kept up a correspondence about the free land, 160 acres from the public domain for a filing fee of fourteen dollars and the promise to remain on it, adding improvements, for five years.[13] Among the waves of new settlers was Jules's brother Paul, later followed by three more brothers—Emile, William, and Ferdinand—and their sister Elvina and two uncles, almost all of whom settled in Jules's neighborhood.

An increasing number of cattlemen, too, were moving into the country. Using their power and influence to frighten the settlers, they sometimes made life difficult. There were confrontations, threats, political maneuvers, vote frauds, and sometimes killings.[14] Jules ordered guns, selling them at cost to the other homesteaders, and cut gunstocks, repaired guns, and molded bullets. He also practiced target shooting where the ranchers could observe his unerring aim.

In 1890, white settlers in northwestern Nebraska became concerned about rumors that the Sioux, on their nearby reservations just over the state line in South Dakota, were performing a strange ghost dance, threatening danger. Jules, always a friend of the Indians, was not afraid, and when General Miles of the United States Army asked him to help bring the Indians in to the agency, he refused. Then Jules heard of the Wounded Knee massacre.[15] That day he went up to the battle site, forty miles north, and saw the Indian bodies, so many of them women and children, lying frozen in the snow. Years later he told Mari of his sickness at the sight. His anger and sadness for the massacred Indians left an indelible impression on her.

In 1887 Jules had married again; he abandoned his dugout to move to the homestead of his new wife, Henriette, on the east bank of the Niobrara River. Unable to put up with his volatile temperament, after four years of marriage she threw his gear out of her house and filed for divorce. Shortly afterward she began to show signs of insanity.

Jules moved across the river to a claim known as the Freese place, dominated by a landmark called Indian Hill, and built a two-room house with a cellar reached by a trap door in the kitchen and an attic reached by a ladder outside the house. He built it for his third wife, a young Swiss woman named Emelia

Paret, whom he had courted by mail. Emelia stayed two weeks after the wedding, but life with Old Jules was so intolerable that she ran away to friends in Rushville.

Disaster came to the area in the 1890s in the form of a drouth which exceeded all probability. Three years later the nation suffered a financial panic and crop prices fell drastically. Corn, selling at 48¢ per bushel in 1890, sold for 18¢ in 1895 and 13¢ in 1896. Three of Rushville's four banks closed. Money, the most difficult commodity for the homesteaders to obtain, now dried up almost entirely. Farmers, unable to get credit, often lost everything they had and abandoned their homesteads.

Many homesteaders joined the Farmers Alliance, a forerunner of the Populist party, agitating for reforms.[16] Jules was interested in their platform; he shared their bitterness at the monopolistic railroads, whose transportation rates seemed outrageously high to the farmers, and at the excessive loan interest rates charged to homesteaders—10 to 12 percent considered liberal, 18 to 24 percent not uncommon, and 40 percent not unknown. He resented the fact that the big moneyed interests from the East foreclosed and then owned the farms. Over 90 percent of the farmland in some counties in southern Nebraska and in the neighboring state of Kansas went to the loan companies, most of them eastern. When Populists in Nebraska put together their first party platform in 1892, he agreed with many of the planks—the Australian ballot, graduated income tax, and popular election of U.S. senators—though not with the Populist call for woman suffrage. The preamble of their platform expressed Jules's feelings: "Corruption dominates the ballot box, the legislatures, the Congress . . . businesses [are] prostrated, our homes covered with mortgages, labor impoverished, and the land concentrated in the hands of capitalists." Although Jules agreed with the concepts of the Populists, he stayed for the most part comfortably in the Democratic party. He railed against the establishment, but he was more concerned about the physical aspects of farming than taking the time to work actively for the new political party.

By the mid-1890s Jules had established a reputation for himself on the Flats. Improvident, never one to pay his debts, too

busy with lawsuits, fighting neighbors and ranchers, and argu-
ing about post offices to settle down to farming profitably, he
had not succeeded financially. But he had located innumerable
settlers here. It would surprise many to know that the dirty man
with the smelly crippled foot had come from a cultured family
and had a university education. Some realized that he was a man
with a vision, a community builder. As a man of action, he was a
formidable foe of the cattlemen who illegally used free government land, which he felt should be for settlers. As a man of
vision, he was consulted by several scientific and agricultural
societies. An innovator in dry farming, he had also begun his
experimental work with orchards and vegetables. Important
men from the universities and from the government often came
to visit him.[17] In 1895, at the end of those eleven years on the
Flats, Jules married his fourth wife, Mary Fehr.

Mary came from Schaffhausen, canton of Schwyz, a German-
speaking area of Switzerland. The daughter of a butcher, she
counted among her ancestors one who had signed the document
establishing the Swiss Confederation in 1291. On first coming to
the United States she went to the home of an uncle in Arkansas,
but the climate was bad for her health, the dampness danger-
ously irritating to her asthma. Then, during a severe flood, she
contracted typhoid and almost died. Brought to a hospital in St.
Louis, she eventually recovered and remained in the city to work
for a Dr. Geiger, a nerve specialist. She was now threatened with
the possibility of tuberculosis, and Dr. Geiger suggested she
move to a dry climate. She and her brother Jacob, who had been
in the United States for several years, decided to homestead in
Nebraska. He was to meet her in St. Joseph en route, and they
would travel the rest of the way together to establish residence.[18]
Her brother failed to meet her in St. Joseph, however, and she
went on to Nebraska alone, hoping he had preceded her to the
recently built little railroad station at Hay Springs. Instead, she
was met there only by the locator, Jules Sandoz, who did not
impress her at all favorably.

     Jules took her to his place, seventeen miles southeast of Hay
Springs on the Niobrara. Jacob did not come, and Mary, realizing

that as a city-bred woman she could not make a living on a claim or find work in this rural area, accepted Jules's offer of marriage. If she married him she would have "the house to live in, a garden, trees, brush with wild fruit, a team for the heavy work, a big roan milk cow . . . and the river."[19]

Jules took Mary across the state line to South Dakota to be married. She thought it romantic until she found out that Jules was already married, for his divorce from Emelia was not final. He told Mary about Emelia just before his brothers and families came to visit, knowing he could not keep that information secret once they began to talk to her. It was a blow to Mary, a strict Lutheran, concerned about morals and her reputation. She found out more: he had been married, not once, but three times before, first to Estelle in Knox County; then to Henriette, now a crazy woman living across the river; then to Emelia. He was deeply in debt, and he was a permanent cripple. Mary, who prized neatness and cleanliness, also now learned his unchangeable habits: he would not wash, shave, or change his clothes; he cleaned his game in the kitchen, leaving the entrails for her to dispose of; and he spit tobacco on the floor. She had no friends; because of his feuds with the neighbors he would not let her associate with them. Then there was the language barrier. Jules could speak Mary's Swiss German but she could not understand his Swiss French. He was old, too, almost eleven years older than she.

By the time Mary realized her situation, she had given Jules her savings and was completely dependent on him financially. They had sent for her widowed mother and younger sister, Suzie, to come from Switzerland to live with them. And she was pregnant; she could not leave.

Mary soon learned the hard lot of the frontier wife. The housing was miserable. Because of the scarcity of cash, families often lacked even the most common amenities in clothing, shelter, and food. Living in sod houses or drafty frame shacks, homestead wives worked hard trying to keep their families clean with a minimum of water, often hauled several miles from a well or the river. They cooked on smoky stoves using buffalo or cow chips for fuel and learned to substitute for sugar, coffee, lard, even flour. They made children's clothing from those of adults, underwear from flour sacking. And they suffered from the heat of summer, the blizzards of winter, and the eternal wind that blows harder and more constantly on the high plains than anywhere else in America except at the seashore.

Jules aggravated the situation with his self-centered belief that others, particularly women, were created for his benefit, an attitude extreme even for that rough time and place, and inexplicable in relation to his family background; other men in the family treated women with consideration.[20] To Jules, women were intended to bear children and to wait on him. Mary soon learned that if any work was to be done in the fields or garden, she would have to do that too. It often entailed hauling water from the river to keep the garden alive. Jules had little feeling for either animals or people. He had been known to run a horse to death, and he was sometimes brutal to Mary.[21]

Jules and Mary's first child was born in May 1896. The baby was named Mary but was called Marie (which she later changed to Mari) to distinguish between mother and daughter.[22] Mary was small-boned and had a difficult labor, but hospitals, doctors, or nurses were not thought of on the homesteader's frontier. A neighbor woman, whose rough hands finally brought relief, served as midwife. Jules could ease the pain a little with morphine, which he kept to doctor animals or humans. When Mary awoke, she saw Jules leaning in the bedroom window with a bouquet of wild plum blossoms. Quite possibly this was the only romantic gesture he ever made toward her. Mari never saw her mother and father kiss each other, nor did she remember receiving a hug or kiss from either of them. The little girl grew up in a family that had no use for physical affection.[23]

The birth of her baby ended any notion Mary had of escape from her marriage and life on the prairie: she was trapped. With her duties in the house, garden, and fields, she could give no more time than absolutely necessary to care for the baby; she was too busy, too harassed, and perhaps too resentful of the additional responsibility to give her daughter any cuddling, and Jules was even less likely to show love to a baby who interfered with his life. When Mari, allergic to her mother's milk and ill with "summer complaint," woke Jules with her crying, he beat her until she was blue and trembling. Her mother finally had to rescue her by carrying her out of the house. The effect never wore off; the little girl was always fearful, hiding away within herself, never aggressive, hating even arguments. The beating contributed to Mari's strong feeling of alienation from her family during her childhood.

A second child, Jules Alexander, was born seventeen months later. Because Mary had been caught in the rope of an eight-hundred-pound calf and dragged across the prairie late in this pregnancy, "Jule" was born prematurely, a frail baby, and was given to Mary's mother, "Grossmutter," to care for. He became to all intents her baby until she fell ill several years later. Then, less than two years after Jule's birth, James was born, in September 1899.[24] He was a sunny, happy, healthy child, and quickly became Mary's favorite. As Mari saw, her mother could show affection for this baby.

Mari learned early that she must assume responsibility. Until she was six, Grossmutter was there to take care of Jule and help with James, but then the grandmother became ill with cancer. Suddenly the little girl became the babysitter for her two small brothers, caring for them alone all day while her mother did the outside work. In 1903 the grandmother died, and shortly afterward the third brother, Fritz, was born. For Mari at seven, life now became serious. In addition to her other duties, she was given Fritz to care for when he was two weeks old, to keep him quiet in order to escape Jules's fierce temper and heavy hand. Fritz was a large, demanding baby with a loud cry. Because he had a hernia, Mari placated him whenever he made his first whimper, spoiling him badly. She carried him everywhere, riding on her hip, his head soon higher than hers. She sometimes cared for the boys alone for two days and nights at a time when the parents went to town on business.[25]

By the time she was ten, she was expected to clean the house, cook, do dishes, and could bake up a forty-nine-pound bag of flour each week. Her hardest problem, however, was her mercurial father, who had at times in the past seemed to favor her, but who now switched favorites, ostentatiously choosing Fritz, so that any special attention she had had from Jules was gone completely.

A young Swiss, Max Rothpletz, stayed with the family for several months one winter. His letters give an intimate view of the family. They were living in the one room, which was furnished with a dilapidated armchair with newspapers, magazines, and catalogs strewn around it, and with a work bench covered with guns, rifles, and ammunition at one side of the room. The visitor slept in a large, heavy, home-made feather bed with Jule and Marie. He became quite fond of them, finding them intelligent, talkative, and kind. They would climb on his knees after his daily hunting trips for ducks and geese and ask him questions, but not in an annoying fashion. Their mother had no time for them; she was too busy with housework as well as with taking care of the cow, catching the horses, and other outside chores. To the father, the children hardly existed unless they got in his way; then he treated them roughly. Jules allowed his guest no chance to get acquainted with anyone in the neighborhood and warned him that Henriette, living across the river, was crazy.

Rothpletz soon learned of Jules's aversion to work: when the weather warmed, Jules, Mary, the visitor, and the children went out to clear the land between the house and the river to plant an orchard. For two days Jules went out to blast the stumps, then he remained in the house. Mary, Rothpletz, and the children did the rest of the work in readying the land for the new trees.[26]

The day after Mari's eleventh birthday, in May 1907, a sister, the fifth child, was born. Jules was gone; he was off in the sandhills locating settlers. Once again Mary had a difficult labor. The little brothers were sent to bed. They were to know nothing of this birth, but Mari was with her mother and assisted the neighborhood women who were called in to help.[27] Although Mari never forgot the experience, shocking to a girl of her age, she felt especially close to the little sister, whom she was allowed to name. She chose the name Flora, from a story she had read about a girl in Scotland who had gone out to search for a lost lamb. Again Mari was given complete charge of the infant, but she did not find her the difficult baby Fritz had been; Flora seemed to Mari like her own little girl.

Throughout her childhood, Mari both sympathized with and resented her mother. She understood that Mary worked very hard, but she could not understand why her mother would endure a situation in which the father did so little physical work while the rest of the family did so much.[28] Starved by the lack of any physical sign of affection from her mother, which emphasized her own sense of her unattractiveness, Mari felt her mother to be tactless, even cruel, in continually reminding her that she was scrawny and sharp-faced, in contrast to Mary's ideal of feminine beauty, a plump, fair-haired girl with nice, young-lady manners. Her mother's insistence on cutting Mari's hair short for the sake of convenience, when other little girls wore theirs long, and her forthrightness in pointing out her daughter's physical inadequacies left psychic bruises.[29] Not realizing that Mary's behavior toward her was inevitably a reflection of her difficult relationship with her husband—her resentment and fear of Jules—as well as her lack of time and money, Mari saw only that her mother did not love or cuddle her as she desired. Nor did she recognize Mary's attempts to show her affection in other ways, such as cooking favorite dishes, cutting out a dress for her, or encouraging her achievements. She felt she was less loved and more overworked than the other children, and was alienated from both parents, an outsider in the family.

Apparently there was no affection between Mari and Jules; she was too afraid of him to express either approval or surprise when he said anything. Whenever any of the children did something wrong, Mari was punished for it. Furthermore, whenever Jules was angry about anything she was usually nearest, in the house and easy to reach.[30] He sometimes banished her to the fearsome darkness of the cellar or beat her; once he broke a bone in her hand, leaving a knobbed scar she carried the rest of her life.[31] She saw him lose his temper with others as well. Once he struck her mother with barbed wire; more than once he pointed a gun at someone who angered him. She knew he had been jailed on the complaint of neighbors because he had started quarrels—sometimes just for the drama of it—a fact which caused embarrassment for his family. Because he was so often embroiled in battles about the local post office or similar issues, Mari was not considered a fit playmate for the girls in the neighborhood.

Her world was a narrow one; Jules seldom allowed his women to leave the farm. He never permitted Mari social visits as a child. She went to town at most twice a year. But Jules had a vast store of esoteric knowledge and had many interesting experiences and acquaintances during the settlement years, and he shared his knowledge and experiences with her. And the world came to her in many ways. Indians were frequently about the place. They knew Jules as a friend, and the farm lay by an ancient river crossing on the Niobrara; often five or six visitors' tipis were set up across from the house.

Jules's Dutch and Anglo-American neighbors did not want anything to do with the "dirty Indians," but Jules had nothing against dirt, so little Mari played occasionally with the Indian children, learning their ways. One of her earliest memories as a toddler was being carried on the neck of Bad Arm, a member of the Man Afraid of His Horse family of the Oglala Sioux.[32] Once she saw a Heyoka, or mystery man. The Cheyennes also camped nearby, the men still wearing beaded moccasins and other remnants of their old-time costumes. The Indians did not speak English, but neither did Mari. She especially liked to listen to Old Cheyenne Woman, who told her wondrous stories in pidgin English and sign language. As her friend the writer Marguerite Young later expressed it, "She grew up with the relics of Stone Age man as her next-door neighbor, a little tottering. This was her childhood, the immensity of an unwritten history."[33]

Jules's location on the river drew many other visitors—old trappers, traders, gold miners from the Black Hills, and army men. "Big Bat" Pourier, the scout and interpreter, came, and others with names such as Ecoffey, Provost, and Charbonneau. They would sit around the stove in the smoky kitchen and yarn for hours. Jules let Mari stay up and listen as long as she was quiet, and she often sat in the wood box by the stove, listening to their adventures.[34] Many of their names would be unknown to historians, but occasionally someone famous came by. She first met Buffalo Bill Cody, with his beautiful flowing hair, when he came for a hunting trip with Jules. It was through him that the little girl learned the difference between appearance and reality. Sent to awaken Buffalo Bill the morning of the hunt, she found he had already gone, leaving his beautiful hair—a wig—on the bedpost.[35] She never forgave him for her disillusionment.

A solitary, lonely, shy, inquisitive child, Mari would sit on the gatepost by the road that wound past the house from the Niobrara to the old military trail into the sandhills, the only road in the neighborhood, watching travelers go by and imagining their stories. Or she would explore the world of nature, for even as a small girl she loved the earth and had a strong sense of belonging to it. She loved to walk barefoot in the dust or mud, to feel she had the right to this direct contact with the land. She formed close emotional ties with the prairie, the bluffs, and the river and was often drawn to the high chalk cliffs along the river to watch the birds and wildlife there. With an intense interest in and observation of the minutiae of nature, she learned the names of the local plants, along with the folklore and home remedies connected with them.[36]

Indian Hill, east of the house and farm buildings and over-looking the river, was Mari's favorite spot. Sometimes the Polish boy from across the river came to play with her there. If she was alone, she would hunt for Indian artifacts on the hill, which was still black from Indian signal fires of the past. Often she sat imagining that the Indians of olden days were camped nearby. When she learned from the old Indian storytellers that Crazy Horse had been in the vicinity as a young boy, she could picture him at this very spot. Not far from the hill, near one of their cherry trees between it and the house, the burial scaffold of Conquering Bear, an important Brulé Sioux treaty chief, had once stood. Occasionally she saw old Indian men stop by the spot to do a few dance steps in honor of his spirit, and she understood the importance of the chief and the place. The fact that the scaffold had been here on their farm was important to her. The river, the gatepost, the hill, the burial spot—these were the boundaries of Mari's world. In these places she could find romance, history, and a retreat from the quarrels and unhappiness of the household.

Her physical world was small, her emotional world unhappy, but Mari knew no other world, so she did not find the situation strange.[37] Her early experiences—the beating as a baby, her father's heavy hand whenever something displeased him—and perhaps her own nature as well caused her to withdraw from the center of action, but she was a keen observer of it. Her world was full of drama, emotion, and violence, and it was also full of the mystery of nature; she watched it all closely.

It was when Mari was almost nine that her boundaries expanded to include country school and formal learning became the most important aspect of her life. Someone had turned Jules's name in to the truant officer, and both Mari and young Jule had to go to school in spite of Jules's contempt for the American educational system.

Jules had good reason for his low opinion of the country schools. People in newly settled areas often regarded formal education as less important than matters of physical survival or seasonal chores. In Nebraska, country school teachers often had minimal education and school terms frequently lasted only three to five months (Mari's first year encompassed only six weeks).[38] Jules felt American teachers were too ignorant to educate his children. But he did not bother to instruct them in reading or writing himself, although he had learned to read and write English within six months of his arrival in America. Instead, he taught them such practical skills as hunting grouse and ermine, coyotes, or eagles; removing and curing pelts; and retrieving birds when he hunted.

Mary had been reluctant to send the children to school for another reason. The family could not afford shoes, and she was too proud to allow them to go barefoot. But once the truant officer called, the money for the shoes was found somehow, and the children were sent to the school closest to them, the Peters School (so called because of the several Peters families in the neighborhood), although the Sandoz homestead was actually not in that district. School districts often covered large areas in that sparsely settled country; the school the children should have attended was miles farther away.

School was both a joy and a torment for Mari. She felt the social stigma of being Jules's daughter. Jules had quarreled with various Peterses; one had him jailed at the time Mari and Jules started school. On occasion, even a teacher added to the misery. Mari was once required to recite a piece called "My Father" extolling the virtues of godliness and cleanliness and kindness, knowing all the time her father had none of these qualities.[39] At one time, because of the antagonism toward Jules, the children were told there was no longer room for them at the Peters School, but Mari's tears so touched one of the school board members that they were allowed to return. To be sure, it was an uncharacteristic victory, the only time in her life that she would get her way by crying, for she did not believe in using tears as a weapon.[40] The tears were sincere; Mari wanted desperately to learn and school was the most interesting place in the world.

Teased about their father's behavior or appearance, their own poor clothes or foreign accents, further ostracized because they were non-Catholics in a strongly Catholic neighborhood, the children often felt persecuted and miserable. Both were undersized and thin, easily bullied. Sensitive to the daily taunts, Mari cried herself to sleep at night, but each morning she was determined to go to school. She suffered frequently from the migraines she had had since early childhood, and once a severe attack of jaundice kept her from school for weeks, but she returned as soon as she could. Not all the other children were cruel. Sometimes the older Peters girls or a teacher came to Mari's aid. Mari liked to watch Mae and Celia Peters in their pretty dresses, picnicking on the hill by the school. They often sang while walking home together, the Peters girls praising Mari's high notes when they sang "Annie Laurie." They envied, too, the good lunches Mary packed for her children, even individual pumpkin pies. But Mari, plagued by her feeling of inferiority, was not aware of their admiration of anything that was hers.

Learning to read was a true epiphany for Mari. She never got over the thrill of discovering that those little black marks always meant the same thing and could always unravel the mystery of words.[41] Having to learn to speak and understand English at the same time she was learning to read and write it was no handicap. Although she entered school late in the term and schoolmates her age were already in the third reader, she quickly memorized words by sight, hurrying through the primer and Baldwin's first three readers. By the time spring came and she had to stay at home to take care of the little brothers, she had mastered the reading of newspapers. Striving for praise from her family, she found she could get recognition through her learning, that her quick mind made the family proud of her.

Mari entered school speaking the Swiss German of her mother, mixed with a few words of French and Polish, with an accent so thick she could hardly make her name known to others. She spent her evenings and summer vacations learning to speak and write English and working on correct spelling and the rules of grammar. Others in the neighborhood spoke foreign languages, too, but she wanted to learn English well enough to write her own stories, for there were not enough books available to satisfy her.

Once Mari had learned to read, she avidly absorbed whatever she could find. All the pamphlets and newspapers that came into the house, all of Jules's government agriculture bulletins did not satisfy her. She surreptitiously borrowed books and magazines from anyone who had anything to lend. She read *Toby Tyler* with the same enthusiasm as the Socialist newspaper *Appeal to Reason*. Although Jules disapproved of fiction of any kind for his family, she smuggled books in the baggy blouses she wore at that time and carried them up the outside ladder to bury in her lumpy straw mattress in the attic, where she slept with the current baby. No one would discover them there. Jules could not climb the ladder, so she could read undisturbed at night by lantern light. Some of what she read was trash, but some was excellent, and her taste for good literature developed quickly. Her favorite books were those of Joseph Conrad.[42]

Mari enjoyed storytelling, both written and oral, and found in it a way to attract favorable attention from her schoolmates while developing her own imagination. Soon she was writing little stories. When she was almost twelve, one of them was accepted for the Junior Writer's Page of the *Omaha Daily News*.[43] Delighted at seeing her name in print, she showed the story to the family. Jules was enraged; fiction was only for hired girls and hired men. Jules forbade all the creative arts to his children. They were not to write or draw or play a musical instrument. Now Jules beat his daughter and put her down in the dreaded cellar, where there were mice and possibly snakes, a punishment she never forgot. Never again would she make it possible for her father to punish her for her writing, although she continued to write.[44] The thrill of seeing her name in print was too great for her to stop. She continued to send in her stories, using a series of pseudonyms. With that first children's page story, her writing career began.

Mari's book and newspaper reading and her observation helped to stretch her boundaries beyond the Niobrara place, even though she herself did not venture farther away than the two miles to school. She became even more aware of the realities of her world with the shocking news that her Uncle Emile had been shot down in front of his family by a rancher's gunman. When a hired killer came to their place one night but was scared off by Jules's Winchester, she realized that the cattlemen were really after her father. She knew he was deeply involved in the continuous rancher-homesteader quarrels as the cattlemen fought to keep their free range and the settlers pushed onto it. In 1905 and 1906 Jules served as a witness in Omaha, when the government brought fraud suits against the big ranchers. She saw him as a leader and something of a hero to the settlers.

Mari's emotional attachment to the sandhills, so important to her later writing, began when the family moved into that region from the Niobrara in 1910. For some years, Jules had been locating settlers on formerly fenced range land in the sandhills and had himself been contemplating a move into the land southeast of the Flats. The settled river area was getting too crowded, the amount of land on his farm suitable for cultivation was rather small, and, as usual, he was on bad terms with his neighbors. He put a notice in the *Rushville Standard* describing the farm and his reasons for wanting to sell:

We offer our ranch on Niobrara River for $10 an acre, 640 acres deeded land with house and all fenced and cross-fenced. . . . 6000 fruit trees and shrubbery. . . . Terms cash. Possession given any time. Reasons for selling: Can't get mail service nor school for our children, and the county authorities have refused for years to protect our property, lives, and liberty.

Jules A. Sandoz
Mary Sandoz[45]

In the sandhills, land was available now, freed by government action from illegal grazing use by the ranchers. Through the Kinkaid Act of 1904, the government allowed a homesteader to take out a claim of one section, 640 acres, of nonirrigable land in any of the thirty-seven counties of northwestern Nebraska. The Kinkaid Act was based on the recognition that a farmer could not make a living on a 160-acre homestead in that area. But the premise that this was rangeland and not good for intensive cultivation of crops was not an idea Jules agreed with entirely. He had his own theories about what would grow in this treeless, sandy area.

Jules located on a spot with a small lake on it. His claim was completely surrounded by the huge Springlake and Spade ranches. The large ranch owners sometimes held their land by filing claims on strategic neighboring sections. They used the Forest Lieu Act of 1897, which permitted the exchange of privately owned land in government forest reserves for "in lieu" selections elsewhere.[46] This allowed the cattlemen in the sandhills of Nebraska to carefully choose land controlling water and attractive hay meadows. Sometimes a rancher could completely surround unowned areas with his own sections, making access by others difficult; he would thus have use of the unowned sections. The government wanted to put a stop to such practices, and it was on one of these unowned sections that Jules filed.

In 1909, Jules and young Jule took their small herd there to pasture. The several thousand head of Texas cattle grazing on the neighboring Spade ranch lands pushed down all the Sandoz fences and grazed that land too. The Sandozes had to return to the Niobrara place with the remnants of their herd and with no feed provisions for the winter. But Jules planned to return the next summer.

In May 1910, Caroline, the last baby, was born, and Mary was not ready to move. To protect his claim, Jules sent Mari, now fourteen, and James, ten, to live in the large shack that served as both store and home. They lived in the thirty-six-foot-square building, which had no windows, door, or floor, through the late summer.

For the two children this was a time of enchantment. Mari now had the time and freedom to explore this new country intimately; for the first time in her life she was free of adult supervision and demands and had few household duties and no little brothers and sisters to care for. She and James managed the little business of the store; otherwise they could do as they wished. It was a dreamy, happy time of roving the sandhills and getting acquainted with a physical world quite different from that of the Niobrara place. Here there were no trees at all, no river, no bluffs. Mari had always been aware of the sandhills on the horizon, sometimes frightened by, sometimes attracted to them.[47] She now observed the subtle details of their flora and fauna, their colors and contours. She and James made a pet of a little muskrat that moved into the shack with them and she saw an unforgettably dramatic prairie fire.[48]

The physical world was harsher here than on the Niobrara. The scarcity of trees, for instance, meant they had to burn cow chips for fuel. It also meant scorching hot days in summer, bitter cold in winter, with no shade or windbreak. Mari found that the sandhills represented the isolation and harshness of life, but she also saw their beauty. Her move strengthened her love for and identification with the land. Perhaps because of that first idyllic summer, she could accept the sandhills joyfully.

There were new social experiences for Mari when the rest of the family moved to the hills in the fall and the children started to a new school where they were no longer social outcasts. The Sandozes were no worse off than the other Kinkaiders in the neighborhood. Mari was no longer an ugly duckling; here men outnumbered women by a large majority. At the age of fifteen she was allowed to go to her first barn dance, wearing a blue chambray dress. Young men came to work in the hay fields in the summer from faraway places—New York, Boston, Texas.

The move, however, was not a happy one for her mother. Mary had made a life for herself; she had found friends on the Flats in spite of Jules. The new house was wretched—a series of lean-tos with a flat roof, no more than seven feet high, freezing cold in winter, baking hot in summer. Out of doors, there was not a tree to break the horizon, although Jules immediately started a new orchard. She knew no one. And Jules soon started a feud with his nearest neighbors.⁴⁹

Mary took complete charge of Caroline, the newest and last baby, relieving Mari of that responsibility, but she was now expected to do more of the outside work. That spring there was a late May blizzard and next day she and young Jule were sent out on horseback to find and bring back the cattle that had drifted away. They returned that evening with most of the herd, but the glare of the sun on the snow throughout the long day brought on a raging headache and excruciating pain in Mari's eyes; she could not see. Eventually the pain abated and she could tolerate some light. By the end of six weeks, the sight returned to her right eye, but she was permanently blind in her left eye.

The snow and freeze ruined the fruit on the river place, still not sold the spring of 1911, but the next year the plums, cherries, and apples bore. James and Mari were sent there that summer to care for the stock and orchard. The customers picked their own fruit, so the two had only to oversee the orchard and keep the cattle from straying. They spent another happy summer together, Mari often reading to James from books like *Sinbad the Sailor*. They also spent the summer of 1913 at the Niobrara farm. It was the last summer that Mari's relationship with her world would be unchanged. In the next years she would take her first steps toward independence.

Mari when she was teaching in the sandhills

Two
Breaking the Ties

The decade from 1913 to 1923 was marked by pivotal events in Mari Sandoz's career. During these years she first attempted to break away from her father's domination and make a life of her own—as a schoolteacher, a married woman, a self-supporting student in Lincoln, and a beginning writer. Unfortunately, these years are perhaps the most difficult to reconstruct, for she left few letters of consequence and few other clues for the biographer. We can know with some certainty where she was and what she was doing, but of her personal life, her ambitions, her dreams and plans, there are only faint hints.

We do know that world events during this decade made a permanent impression on Mari. While she was engaged in her personal odyssey from childhood to adulthood, farm and ranch life was changing rapidly. Mechanization of farm machinery, the shift from the horse to the tractor, brought about larger farms and ranches. New varieties of seed and new methods of growing and harvesting—always of primary interest to Jules—produced larger yields and more dependable harvests. Automobiles began to be seen more frequently, although even the famous Tin Lizzie (the Model T Ford) could not travel all the roads in the sandhills. It would be years before the sandy trails could be graded for dependable travel. In the towns, gaslight gave way to electricity. Rushville's main street was electrified, with fitting ceremony, in 1914, although country dwellers would not have electricity until the 1940s.

Political concerns also shifted. The issues of Populism were replaced by those of woman suffrage, prohibition and the United States' entry into World War I. The war, with its accompanying social, economic, and technological changes, reached even the comparative isolation of the sandhills, causing Mari to recognize that the world around her was changing drastically. She could see that the frontier as her parents knew it, and even as she herself remembered it, was disappearing forever.[1] The war also disclosed a sharp philosophical difference between Mari and her father. She was staunchly pro-Ally. Jules was at first a pacifist, as were many of the old Populists; then, when he saw that war was inevitable, he favored the German cause, loudly and vociferously. The difference in point of view perhaps helped Mari to extricate herself from her father's influence. The war was the first major stimulus which impelled her to write on serious themes.

In 1913, when Mari, at the age of seventeen, passed the county eighth-grade examination, it did not occur to anyone in her family that she might go into Rushville or Gordon to high school; it was taken for granted that she had finished her formal education. But one day in July she sneaked into Rushville from the family farm on the Niobrara, riding the eighteen miles on horseback, to take the rural teacher's examination.[2] At that time, Nebraska issued a so-called third-class certificate for teaching in rural schools to persons who passed this test, even if they had less than high school education. It was possible to upgrade the certificate to second-class or even (though it happened rarely) to first-class by taking sections of the test until an applicant's score was raised to the designated level.

For Mari, the decision to try for a teaching certificate was a momentous act of independence. Already frightened by her own daring—she knew Jules would be furious—she felt her old sense of inadequacy return when she saw the other candidates. They seemed so grown-up and sophisticated, while Mari, weighing only seventy-five pounds and wearing a childish gingham dress adorned with cross-stitching, looked like a little girl. She still felt conspicuously immature and unattractive. Nevertheless, she passed the test, and once she announced her success the family was proud of her. In fact, Jules even bragged about her accomplishment to others. She was a year under the legal age for teaching, but that was not unusual on the frontier.

But being a teacher did not remove her from Jules's domain. She taught at District 163, a new school split off from District 140 in her own neighborhood—a split that had resulted from a fight between Jules and other District 140 members. Jules was a director of the new school, and Mari lived at home. Her school was in the Sandoz barn.

In addition to teaching school, she had another new interest, a serious suitor. He was Wray Macumber, a young bachelor living on his claim a few miles north of the Sandoz homestead. Wray had come to the sandhills from Iowa in 1909. Although his parents had also moved to the vicinity, he was baching on his ranch and was lonely. He was at the Sandoz ranch so often Mary thought of him as one of the family. His attentions to Mari were noted and to some extent approved, for the Sandozes, in the tradition of other families from the Old World, believed it a girl's duty to marry and have children. Although Wray was not quite the suitor they would have liked for their daughter—he was Irish and they preferred a Frenchman or Swiss—Jules was friendly with him, did business with him. Wray was one of the petitioners for the new School District 163, and Jules was a witness when he proved up on his claim in May 1914.

We have few details of the courtship. There was an active social life on the frontier: spelling bees, box socials, square dances, play parties, literaries, sewing bees, Sunday schools, and occasional shivarees for newlyweds, but Mari did not participate in these gatherings. Her father seldom allowed the women off the place for any reason. Mari attended her first social function alone at sixteen, when she was allowed, as bridesmaid for her friend Martha Fisher's wedding, to attend the wedding dinner at her home nearby. She was not permitted to go with the wedding party to town for the actual ceremony. Jules did, however, believe in having people come to his place, and often fifteen to thirty guests would show up, with or without invitations, for Mary's big Sunday dinners.

As Mari's brothers grew up they often got together with others in the neighborhood for "ranch Sundays." Sometimes it was at the Sandoz ranch; once in a while Mari managed to join her brothers at a neighbor's. Almost every ranch with young people on it could find a bronc or two for the daredevils to ride. Too small and informal to be called rodeos, the gatherings served the same purpose for the participants: a chance to try their skills, show off, and enjoy the fun.

Barn dances were big events. After Jules built the huge barn at his ranch, he held dances there every month or so. Mari loved to dance, and Wray was a fine dancer also. These barn dances were long-lasting and energetic affairs. The host might put an announcement for a house party in the local papers: "Dinner from one to seven. Beds and breakfast for all. Everybody welcome."[3] Sixty to eighty people might come from as far as thirty to forty miles away, dance until sunrise, and sleep on any available space well into the next day. The Sandoz youngsters eventually were permitted to attend some of these house parties.

There was nothing cosmopolitan about them. The music was whatever was available—usually a fiddle and drummer or folding organ. Refreshments, served around midnight, were dishpans full of hearty sandwiches and coffee boiled in wash tubs. Someone with a thirst for more potent liquid refreshments could usually find whiskey outside by the wagons or in a secluded area of the barn. Extra entertainment was provided by such activities as chapping contests. Two young men separated a pair of chaps, then took turns swatting one another's buttocks with the leather chaps until one admitted defeat. The winner could choose the girl he wished to take home from the dance.[4]

Wray and Mari apparently attended some of the dances. They knew each other for several years, and it was no surprise when the *Rushville Recorder* published the following item in its 29 May 1914 issue: "Married: Miss Marie S. Sandoz and Wray Macumber were united in the bonds of holy matrimony by Judge Edmonds on the 27th inst. The bride is the daughter of Jules Sandoz. The Recorder joins friends in congratulations." Their wedding picture shows a pretty, almost plump young woman. Mari was eighteen that month, Wray was twenty-seven.

During the next five years Wray and Mari lived on the Macumber ranch and Mari taught intermittently in various

nearby schools, periodically renewing and upgrading her cer-
tificate.⁵ Then, in the spring of 1919, Mari filed for divorce,
charging extreme mental cruelty. It is hard to say just what
brought her to this decision. In later years she seldom spoke of
her marriage, although she confided to a few friends that it had
been a mistake, that she had been "blighted early" and that Jules,
anxious to get rid of her, coerced her into the marriage. She
sometimes implied that Jules was also involved in the divorce
and took her to the courthouse to file for it. The divorce was
granted 30 August 1919.

The years of Mari's marriage correspond with the years of
World War I, which affected the lives of many in the community.
In Nebraska, a large percentage of the population were immigrants or first-generation Americans with close ties to the Old
World. When war was declared in Europe, there were corre-
sponding tensions in Nebraska. Although the majority of Nebraskans were sympathetic with the Allies, there was a heavy
German population, many of whom tried to convince their
neighbors that there was something to be said for the German
side of the argument. The Czechs, the second-largest foreign
element in the state, together with the Poles, French, and English, argued for the Allies. Originally, a third sizable faction felt
that the United States should remain neutral. Woodrow Wilson's promise in his 1916 presidential campaign to keep the
United States out of the war played a significant role in his
election victory. Nebraska's William Jennings Bryan, Wilson's
secretary of state, resigned because he disagreed with the president's actions regarding the sinking of the *Lusitania*.

Even before the United States declared war in April 1917,
there were those who acted with vigor against suspected German sympathizers. Some used the opportunity to pay back old
scores; others were carried away by patriotic enthusiasm. Tempers ran high. People in the panhandle town of Minitare attempted to lynch a fellow townsman who made pro-German
remarks.

Jules, who for years had written fiery letters to the local
papers, saw no reason to refrain from expressing his unpopular
views. In 1914, denouncing the Democratic party for failing

to get him a local post office once more, he had sputtered: "I am ready to help the Japs, Germans, or English to do it by force, even if our confounded liberty has to go." (The next year the editor chortled that Jules had got the post office where he wanted it but did not succeed in getting the appointment of postmaster.) Later, in a diatribe against woman suffrage, Jules warned, "Woman suffrage will destroy what there is of home and leave this country prey of an invader, and the American men . . . leave [it] to their women, who will flock to the uniformed invaders, after the American male dishwashers have all been killed off. I am thoroughly disgusted with the American system and figure on emigrating to South America."[6] As the United States was drawn into the war, Jules's opinions caused great difficulty for the family.

In 1918, the state legislature passed vigorous laws to back the prosecution of the war. In Nebraska, aliens were deprived of the right to vote, to hold office or any official position, or to teach in public, private, or parochial schools. The teaching of any foreign language in school below the ninth grade was forbidden, and church services in German were prohibited. American women married to German men were obliged to carry cards denoting them enemy aliens. County Councils of Defense, appointed to check on pro-German subversives, were authorized to enter and inspect homes of suspected food hoarders. People who failed to contribute to the Red Cross or to buy liberty bonds might find *slacker* painted across their fences or buildings.

The war brought a dramatic change in the economy and life of the area, too. Farmers, responding to the great demand for foodstuffs and the attractive prices, expanded their operations and put hitherto unbroken rangeland into active cultivation. Even more spectacular was the discovery by two young chemists that the potash needed for munitions and fertilizer, which was once imported from Germany, could be supplied by minerals from the sandhill lakes. The stinking alkali lakes were suddenly valuable. Antioch, a tiny hamlet about forty miles southwest of the Sandoz ranch, quickly grew to a population of 2,500 and had five huge potash plants operating twenty-four hours a day. Within two years, however, the demand for potash disappeared, and so did Antioch. The town dwindled to fewer than 150 inhabitants, most of the buildings were dismantled, and only the skeletons of the factories remained.

In the midst of the patriotic fervor, Jules, always the iconoclast, continued to express his outspoken views. He was convinced, at least in part by his German-speaking wife's diligence and that of the hard-working German-Swiss immigrants in his neighborhood, that the Germans were far more industrious and therefore more worthy of support than the French. Admiring Germany's strong central government and efficient army, he could tell stories from his European youth to back his opinion. One battle of the Franco-Prussian War, he recalled, had ended with the surrender of the French near his home town in Switzerland. After the French soldiers had stacked their weapons in the town square, Jules and his brothers had stolen some rifles and discovered the bullets had so little powder they would not shoot to the top of the trees. He claimed, too, to have met the kaiser in Switzerland when he was a young man, the two exchanging stamps for their collection.[7] Inevitably, Jules was investigated by the county Council for Defense, but though his family was embarrassed by the notoriety, no action was taken against him.

Mari's philosophical difference with her father was further exacerbated by Mary's disapproval of her daughter's divorce. While divorce was more common in the sandhills than in more settled communities, and no scandal attached to Wray and Mari, Mary could not overcome her distress at the failure of the marriage. To avoid facing her mother's tears, Mari did not return to the Sandoz home when she left her husband in the spring of 1919. She went, instead, to stay on Pine Creek, near the old Niobrara place, with the orphans of her Uncle Emile, taking her clothes with her in paper sacks.[8] She had a contract to teach at the nearby District 112 school that fall, but she was there only briefly.[9] In September she and her cousin Rosalie went to Lincoln, over four hundred miles east at the opposite end of the state, to attend the Lincoln Business College.[10]

She was leaving a part of the country that was still rough and primitive in many ways. Most rural western Nebraska homes had no indoor plumbing, unless it was a cold-water pump in the kitchen, no electricity, no central heating. Many homes lacked carpets on the floors, decorative pictures, or even wallpaper. Major purchases were made from catalogs. Everyday clothes were cotton print dresses and overalls. Distances were important; travel was still often by horse and buggy or wagon on unpaved roads, many only trails through the hills. The Sandoz ranch itself was thirty miles from the nearest railroad, seventeen from Ellsworth, the nearest hamlet.

Lincoln, a city of fifty-five thousand, was almost another world to the woman from western Nebraska. It had wide paved streets, beautiful parks, department stores with elevators, a building eight stories high, cosmopolitan hotels, fine restaurants, public transportation, and five railroads. It was a bustling city, expanding rapidly, as it would all during the 1920s. There was a great deal of new building, several structures to be from twelve to sixteen stories high. Out west, few people could go to concerts, operas, or symphonies; in contrast, Lincoln's own junior symphony orchestra gave performances, or Mari could hear some of the many traveling musicians stopping there. The Nebraska Art Association had started its collection in the university's Morrill Hall as long ago as 1881. Amateurs acted in the community theater, and touring theatrical companies visited the city regularly. Wesleyan University and Cotner and Union Colleges as well as the university offered interesting programs.

There were other attractions. Mari learned of several municipal innovations made by the mayor, Charles W. Bryan, brother of William Jennings Bryan and later governor: a free legal aid department, an employment bureau, and later a municipal coal yard and gas station. She enjoyed the city newspapers and came to know A. L. "Doc" Bixby, columnist, and Frank L. Williams, one of the editors of the Lincoln Journal. The libraries and museums drew her, and the bargain basements of the big department stores, Miller and Paine's, and Gold's, had wonderful sales. Here she could indulge her one extravagance, hats. Her mother had taught her that no self-respecting woman ever left home without a hat. This was one subject on which the two agreed.[11]

Although she found much she liked, there was much she

disliked. She had moved from an elevation of about thirty-two hundred feet to a flood plain of about one thousand feet. In the lower altitude the heat and humidity of the summers aggravated her migraines and increased the possibility of tuberculosis for lungs inherently weak. To counteract the heat in those days before air conditioning, people put wet sheets over doors or windows to cool any stirring breezes, and at night some slept on lawns.

Mari observed how dependent Lincoln was on government—city, state, and federal. From its beginning, it had been designed to be the capital of the state. In addition to the capitol, here were located the state university and agricultural college, the men's reformatory, the penitentiary, and a state mental hospital. During her years in Lincoln, she saw a regional veterans' hospital built to serve four states, and Lincoln win a fight with Omaha to retain Nebraska's Federal Relief headquarters. Even though the city had a number of insurance companies, wholesalers, and retail stores, its business was primarily government. It sometimes seemed to her that the governmental bodies lived off the rest of the state.

Mari was absorbed by her new life. If she had already determined to write about the history of man's incumbency on the plains, as she later stated, she put the idea aside temporarily.[12] Her cousin Rosalie, who roomed with her while they attended the business college, never heard her speak of it; indeed, Rosalie did not see her do any writing during that time. Mari listed her occupation as teacher.

She took the secretarial course at the business college from October 1919 until April 1921, acquiring practical skills in shorthand, spelling, composition, and typing. She earned good grades—A's in spelling—and became a good enough typist to type a book manuscript for Lucius A. Sherman after he retired as chairman of the English Department at the university. She also was able to take dictation verbatim from almost any speaker in Lincoln, but she seldom used shorthand in the thousands of holograph notes she later made for her historical research.[13]

After finishing at the Lincoln Business College, Mari worked for a short time in the courthouse in Osceola, Nebraska. She also upgraded her teaching certificate to second-class and in the fall of 1921 returned to teaching, at the Dalton School in Cheyenne County near Sidney. Located in the Nebraska panhandle, it was about eighty miles southwest of the Sandoz ranch, another country school in ranch country.[14]

The Daltons, with whom Mari boarded, thought her an alert, energetic young woman, adventurous, full of questions, a capable school teacher. She was able both to maintain discipline and order and to keep friendly relations with parents, a problem other teachers had found difficult. In that horse-riding community she was noted for her love of riding, and she frequently attended house parties. She quizzed the settlers about the history of western Nebraska, eager to know their part in settling the country. She was willing to tackle any job, including attempting to fix farm machinery or anything else that had broken down. Miss Macumber, as she was known there, was popular and had a serious romance with the son of an influential family. No one knew she had been married.[15]

In the summer of 1922, Mari returned to Lincoln, this time planning to attend the university. If she continued to teach, she needed more education; if she hoped to write, she needed writing skills and humanistic knowledge. Since she had few, if any, high school credits, she was not eligible to matriculate at the university, but she called on various officials until she finally wore down William E. Sealock, dean of the Teachers College. Observing that she could do no more than fail, he allowed her to enter Teachers College as an adult special. She filled out the required form for college entrance, claiming two years' attendance at Sheridan County High School and two years at Chadron Normal College, but there never was a Sheridan County High School and her attendance at Chadron consisted of one short, summer teachers' institute. The four mythical years of education were a hedge against university requirements. She also gave her name as Marie Alice Susetta Macumber; the *Alice* was her own addition.[16] Even though she preferred to use the name Macumber instead of her maiden name, her title was *Miss*. She enrolled in education and methods classes for both summer sessions—music, drawing, reading, and junior high administration—and she had no difficulty in keeping up with the classwork.

Mari returned to the Dalton School in the fall of 1922, but one day the students were surprised to find a note on the door, "No school. Teacher gone." They never knew the reason for her leaving. Her romance had ended; perhaps that was the cause. She returned to Sheridan County and finished the year at the Hunzicker School, boarding in that district since it was too far from the Sandoz ranch for her to live at home.[17]

That summer of 1923 Mari returned to Lincoln and summer school at the university. Her courses were now related to sciences: introductory psychology, elementary geology, general physics (electricity and light), and field geography. The Lincoln summers were hot, the classes often boring, the teachers sometimes uninterested and uninteresting; nevertheless, she stayed. Lincon would be home for the next seventeen years.

The young woman who moved to Lincoln to become a full-time student at the university carried with her the psychic scars of her youth; her childhood feelings of alienation from her family, community, and schoolmates made her at times self-pitying and frustrated. She still felt strongly the lack of parental love, of physical attractiveness, and of social status. She carried with her her young memories of being set apart because of the language barrier, her father's restrictions on her social life, and the old family stigma.[18] A friend remembers seeing Mari at dances in the sandhills and feeling sorry for her because no one paid her any attention: "They didn't want to have anything to do with the family of Old Jules."[19] Her marriage had ended in divorce and caused a severe rupture with her mother. On the other hand, Mari had achieved some success, primarily through her own efforts. She had taught school for several years, finished business college, and created a place for herself in other communities through her own ability.

She expected to do more: by the time she settled in Lincoln in 1923 she had determined to be a writer. Although all that remains of her early writing are a few scraps such as the little story published in the *Omaha Daily News* in 1908, her brother James remembers her writing or reading constantly and being angry when her stories on the children's page did not win a prize. She later told a friend that when she was teaching she had often stayed after school to write, particularly if things were going badly at home.[20] She recognized that the evidence of the social and ecological changes in the sandhills were easily traced, and she was doing some research on Wild Bill Hickok and Buffalo Bill Cody while she taught there. During the winter of 1923–24, Mari and her father worked on a map called "Old Jules Country," identifying more than ten locations important to history and science. She had already found in her country a wealth of material as well as an emotional identity.[21]

Mari's early years on the turbulent Nebraska frontier had shaped her political beliefs. She had witnessed the struggle between ranchers and homesteaders, knew of people run off their farms or even killed. The lack of ready money needed in any new developing region was one cause of her family's poverty. The Populist movement that involved so many of the region's farmers in the 1890s, as well as her father's own interest in socialism, contributed to her resentment of eastern financiers and the railroad monopoly that determined the farmers' ability to market their products.[22] The liberal political heritage she brought with her was opposed to the concentration of too much power or wealth in the hands of the few. Brought up on free or cheap government homestead land, and remembering the cattlemen forced to obey the law only through federal intervention, she welcomed government aid on behalf of its citizens.

A teacher both by profession and by nature, Mari was a moralist, with a strong sense of social ethics and a sense of mission. She naturally loved to share knowledge, even when not in a formal classroom. To Mari, giving information was almost a crusade. A friend, remembering her from this time, describes her intensity: "Marie thought, 'I must reach a high plateau. I must straighten things out, I must guide and inspire and lead and *compel!*' If people weren't compelled, 'off with their heads.' She could teach you, but the minute your attention slid and the minute you began to get a little sloppy, she dumped you."[23]

Many forces drove her at this time. She desired to be independent, away from family and home, but at the same time to bring the stories of her region to the attention of the world. She wanted to prove she could be somebody important, to show that she was intelligent despite her father's belief that women were inferior. She wanted to teach, to influence others, and to write.

A less obvious side of this energetic, enthusiastic, pragmatic young woman was her mysticism. Interested in the occult, the unexplainable, even in astrology, she was adept at reading palms, although she did not take her skill as seriously as some of her friends did.[24] She had come to the concept of a controlling fate—her "nemesis," as she called it. She often felt out of balance with the rhythm of circumstances and once kept a diary to prove that she was.[25] Her later studies of Greek tragedy only emphasized her belief that the law of nature demands compensation for all things. Although her moral code was influenced by the Calvinism of her parents, she was nevertheless not an orthodox Christian and did not believe in an afterlife. Attracted to the Plains Indians' concept of man attuned to nature, man as a part of the natural world, she especially respected the northern Plains Indians' religion because it did not encompass the idea of the Christian hell, nor did it include satanic or witch figures among the supernatural powers. She was drawn to the great Sioux war chief Crazy Horse because he was a mystic. Although she herself apparently did not have dream visions, she believed others did, and she herself experienced extrasensory perception.

Mari's ability to separate her life into segments, to divide it into compartments that had little apparent relation to one another, doubtless helped her to ovecome her self-pity and to achieve a fine detachment about events in her childhood. This proclivity for eliminating parts of her past from her memory accounts for her vague or contradictory recollections of certain happenings in her early life. Always publicly silent about the five years of her marriage, she also frequently omitted mention of her attendance at the Lincoln Business College and was vague about when she taught school or attended the university. As a historian she was meticulous in establishing dates in her works, but she was not at all averse to telescoping or erasing events in her own life.[26]

In Lincoln, at the Boston house on J Street

Three
New Horizons

By the time she came to Lincoln in 1923, Mari had formed most of the attitudes that would appear in her later writing, but Lincoln determined her career and the form and direction of her writing. Her goal, to write, had already been established in the sandhills, but not the means by which to reach that goal.

The years to come brought challenges and trials as difficult in their way as any she had faced before. She was influenced by her college classes and her instructors to a far greater degree than many of her younger classmates. Seldom has an apprentice writer been so persevering in defeat as Mari. In spite of extreme poverty and years of rejection slips, she dedicated herself to her writing. In the past, Mari had not hesitated to withdraw from unsatisfactory situations: she had left two schools in mid-semester, and she had ended her marriage and had left the sandhills in part because her mother was so upset by that divorce. But she was persistent in her determination to achieve recognition through her writing.

The fall of 1923, when Mari enrolled for the regular term at the university, the subject matter of her classes changed from education to the arts and sciences: Latin, English composition, algebra, and geology. The reason for the shift in curriculum is unknown; she may have wished to broaden her cultural background. Whatever her purpose, her experience that year in the Department of English influenced her plans for the future, because her instructors recognized her talent and encouraged her dream of writing. Mari had always felt compelled to write,[1] but she had never before had an English composition teacher to evaluate her work.

Her own attempts to publish had met with meager success. She was therefore encouraged when her professor, Lowry C. Wimberly, submitted her short essay, "Prairie Fire," to the *Freshman Scrapbook* published by the English Department the spring of 1924. Public recognition of her achievement was important to her throughout her life, a validation of her accomplishments. Now it solidified her purpose, and she established her method to reach her goal. Her priorities would be, first, to write whenever possible; second, to attend the university whenever she could, to learn more about the subjects she wanted to write about; and third, to work only as much as necessary to pay her expenses. Everything else would be subordinated to these aims.

That spring semester, a history professor, Fred Morrow Fling, exerted a lasting influence on Mari. She already had a great deal of informal and general historical knowledge; now she learned the skills to adapt her knowledge to her work. An expert on the Napoleonic period in European history and a graduate of the University of Leipzig, Fling had pioneered in the source approach, the examination of historical proof. He was particularly concerned that his students learn to separate fact from hearsay. Although Mari probably took her European history course under Fling's assistant, Laura B. Pfeiffer, she knew him at the university; the man and his methods inspired in her a passion for accuracy, a preference for primary evidence. To her, he was one of the "henniest and fussiest" men imaginable, but his approach to historical fact was impeccable.[2] She learned his methods of evaluating conflicting and contradictory eyewitness accounts, which she used for her later research and writing.

She also used his elaborate filing system. As her three-by-five-inch cards carrying information from printed sources, from archival materials in various repositories, and from private journals and interviews grew into the thousands, she kept her material organized through an elaborate indexing system based on the one worked out by Fling. Keeping her notes from each

individual source together so that she could evaluate the quality
of information or spot any gaps or contradictions within the
entire account, she would cross-index the material, sometimes
making as many as thirty or forty cards for a note page, a tedious
process but worth it, because she could get at her information
immediately. She began this system with newspaper articles on
such general topics as Indians, prairie fires, cattle, or incidents
involving wells even before she had started research for any
specific book. Some notes provided pertinent information for
book after book.[3]

Another history professor influenced her in quite another
way. She studied Greek history under John Andrew Rice, a
classicist whose methods and personality were in sharp contrast
to those of Fling. The two men, in fact, would stop in the hall and
yell insults at one another. Rice was given to broad, flamboyant
statements, and Mari began to check his sources by reading the
Greek tragedies and the comedies of Aristophanes. From this
reading came a lifelong interest in Greek drama; Aristophanes,
in particular, was a favorite.[4]

At the time Mari began the regular fall term in 1923, she found a
part-time job at the Smith Dorsey Drug Laboratory, filling capsules. She liked the pharmaceutical work and eventually was
given the task of mixing formulas under the eye of a chemist. She
wrote in one of her college essays, "One must fill many, many of
these bubbles [capsules] at 25¢ a thousand to pay the fees, pay for
books and have something left for a room and a 'tater a day
and a glass of milk. Many girls fill a thousand in forty minutes,
but I never got to that stage. It takes dogged drive to do twelve
thousand capsules in an eight hour day but even with less,
college can be made. There are always Saturdays, holidays,
summer vacations."[5] The style of the essay is sometimes labored
and amateurish, indicating that it was written early, but the
writer's affection for the work and her fellow workers is evident:
"To every graduate comes the moment when the little car-
tilaginous ring in the throat contracts and an exquisite, deep
pain suffuses the whole being. Well, I have mine for a group of

girls in gingham aprons with green, yellow, black smudges on their noses, rubber gloves on their hands, gathered about a long table. Slangily speaking. 'Them were the days.' "

Working half-days and Saturdays, she earned about thirty-five dollars a month; extra earnings during college vacations helped pay her fees. She also borrowed fifty dollars from the Scottish Rite Education Fund, although her family was not associated with the Masonic Lodge. The debt was incurred for dental work, and she was not able to repay for many years because she used all her extra money on stamps to send her stories around to magazines.

Mari did not attend the university in the fall of 1925, and her activities that year are not certain. She seems to have continued to work at Smith Dorsey; undoubtedly she was also writing. According to her sister Caroline, when she had a stack of stories in what she thought to be acceptable order, she sent them out to a list of publishers she found in A. S. Burack's *The Writer*, sending them from one magazine to the next in alphabetical order. The stories all came back, again and again. Since the 1924 stories no longer exist, what they were like cannot be determined. The author herself commented that her stories from 1924 to 1926 were all very abbreviated, the only detail she offers.[6]

The austere life that Mari led in these years soon affected her appearance. Always slender, she became painfully thin and unhealthy looking, simply because she had too little to eat. An acquaintance recalled that Mari could often be found in the dining hall of the old Temple Building at the university, a place usually swarming with students grabbing a snack between classes, as it was the only place on campus to eat. Sugar and crackers were on the tables at all times, and were free. Her friends suspected that Mari lived on tea, sugar, and crackers. "It must have been pretty rough on her, who had nothing, to see the hordes flooding the place, all very careless with their nods in her direction, and when the class bell rang rushing away leaving more food than she saw in weeks. But she looked on with that pinched, sardonic half smile, I think counting the time when she would show us all up," the friend speculated.[7]

That one could live in poverty during the affluent twenties

seems paradoxical, but the fact that Lincoln was a college town, with 80 percent of the men students and 40 percent of the women students earning their way through college and willing to work for almost nothing, had a good deal to do with it. Although Mari found work when she wanted it then, the pay was always low, seventeen cents to thirty cents an hour.

Lincoln itself was not experiencing the general prosperity of the country, because farm prices had taken a drastic fall early in the decade while the cost of living remained high. Nebraska was dependent on its major source of income, agriculture. When farmers could not pay for their seed or keep their mortgaged land, they could not pay their taxes either; the state government, and the city so dependent on it, suffered as well. The Midwest anticipated the Great Depression by several years. Nebraska banks began to fail early in the twenties, farm prices dropped, local demand for labor declined, and wages fell, while migration from the state increased.[8] In those depressed years, Mari herself, writing at every opportunity, worked only enough to earn the minimum she felt she could survive on. Sometimes she underestimated or circumstances interfered; then she was truly hungry.

Although of average height, five feet, five inches, she seemed taller because she was so thin. She often wore long-sleeved dresses to cover her matchstick arms, and her face, already angular, became a series of sharp planes. Her clothes did not help her appearance. At a time when the difference between country and city attire was easily recognized, the woman from the sandhills was odd-looking in Lincoln. The cotton clothes she wore were often drab, mismatched, and threadbare. Her campus costume consisted of a shirtwaist and skirt and almost invariably a quaint hat. Her addiction to hats was noticeable, and often the hat did not seem to relate in any recognizable way to her dress. Except for her vibrant loping walk and her good humor, according to one friend, she looked like the stereotype of the old-maid school teacher. She sped along, clutching an enormous pile of books under one arm and trying to stick her hair under her hat with the other hand. People noticed her, wondering about her even if they did not know her. Her eyes were particularly compelling, at times hazel, at times green. Intense and bright, they had an unusual flash, sometimes of compassion. Her glance could stop someone in his tracks if he attracted her attention.[9]

Although it was not true, as some thought, that Mari was unaware of her difference in appearance, she had neither time nor money during her early student years to do much about it. Actually, even though she had no clothes sense that her friends could see, she was interested in fashion and attempted to learn about it, often designing and remodeling her clothes. She was not hesitant to try various combinations and styles, but as with so many other things, she had to learn through a long period of trial and error what suited her.

Mari's most noticeable attempts to change her appearance were her experiments with hair coloring. Although she sometimes had her hair washed and dried at a shop because the lack of proper facilities made it difficult to do in her apartment, she set her hair herself. She also colored it herself. Her efforts to bring a reddish cast to her rather mousy blonde hair were occasionally spectacular if not successful, at times resulting in a scarlet color. Once her hair actually turned purple. Eventually she worked out a successful formula and for a time her hair was dark red. Later she subdued it to a very attractive red-gold, sorrel, or auburn, and wore it long, in a French knot or bun, its luxuriant growth a sharp contrast to the short-cropped wisps she hated so in her childhood.

Her acquaintances of this time found Mari an enigma. Because of her early experiences and her great desire to learn and to create, she appeared a woman at once hostile and friendly, a loner. None from this time on ever felt they knew her intimately. By the time she moved to Lincoln, she had encased herself in an apparently impenetrable armor of self-protection. The hurts she had suffered as a child and in her marriage she would not allow to happen again.[10] She could not bear intense emotion or contention, nor would she allow personal probing. Sometimes she almost hated music because it affected her emotions so strongly. During her early years in Lincoln she wrote out her feelings in a poem:

Why must there be music
To awaken all my soul
From deepest stupor
Of mock contentment;
To fling me upon the wrack of reality,
To tear me with hot tongues of longing;
To awaken the cry for unrealized dreams,
Aspirations;
To fill my quivering flesh with arrow,
Filter salt into my wounds of pride,
Until I hate it all;
The world, myself,
My very soul.

God! Why must there be music?[11]

Her friends knew her to be infinitely patient and encouraging to young writers; in fact she helped aspiring writers long before she herself was published. With something close to a maternal attitude toward these neophytes, she gave far more time and patience than seemed worthwhile to some of her friends. She was full of energy and enthusiasm in pursuing knowledge, happy to share her discoveries. But if someone tried to overstep the bounds of personal privacy, to penetrate the mask of good humor, she withdrew. Sometimes she could be brutal. "One might just as well have tried to befriend a porcupine," one acquaintance later commented.[12]

On the other hand, Alberta Sheehan, who lived in the same house as Mari and attended summer school in 1925, recalls that the two had great fun, being silly, laughing at almost everything. Mari did not talk about her family, nor did Alberta know she had taught school. Mari read her short stories to Alberta, and the two swam and went to occasional movies together. Mari and a boy friend would take Alberta to dances at one of Lincoln's popular large ballrooms or they would spend Sunday at Alberta's parents' nearby farm. But, Mrs. Sheehan says, "We didn't tell each other anything. We didn't have any past or future—we just enjoyed each other. She could forget her troubles and just laugh and act silly and talk about nothing. I just knew one side of her."

Mari was friendly to many, but wary of close ties. Although

she was eager to see her friends, there was no show of tenderness toward anyone. Her friends did not think her cold, but they did not ask questions. She could be expertly detached and, as in the case of her name, she could be devious or use subterfuge. People who thought they knew her quite well supposed that Marie Macumber was her maiden name. Others believed she had chosen Macumber as a nom de plume. She did not bother to disabuse them, although to a few she spoke rather freely about her marriage as well as other aspects of her early life. Her eventual complete obliteration of her marriage could be due to compartmentalization, to sealing off and expunging experience, but her explanations of her use of the name Macumber had to be deliberate obfuscation. She often told people she used Macumber as a pen name because she wanted to protect the Sandoz family women from her father's disapproval of either her writing or her college attendance. In fact, it was her legal name from the time of her marriage in 1914, the name she kept after her divorce, and the name she was known by in the sandhills, at the university, and in Lincoln. In 1929, at an agent's urging (reinforced by a numerologist's prediction that the change in name would bring good luck)[13] she changed it to Mari Sandoz.[14]

Nor did she tell anyone her true age. She felt the pressure of time, certainly. She was twenty-six in the summer of 1922, when she first attended the university, twenty-seven when she enrolled for the regular session the fall of 1923. She was driven by her schedule, too, interrupting both her jobs and college work in order to write.

Mari's sense of isolation, which she felt strongly as a child, continued to some extent into her Lincoln years, but for different reasons. Now she was always in a hurry, driven by her ambition to write. On campus, her age, her lack of money and of time, the fact that her living quarters were some distance from the campus, even her writing talent, set her apart from the student body more than she wished. But she could tolerate the isolation now because it was one of the costs of reaching her goal. She was aware of what she was missing, but being alone was the habit of a lifetime. She did not mind it so much personally, but she felt that the quality of her writing suffered from her lack of stimulating contact with other creative people.

Apparently still writing and working during the daytime, Mari took four extension (night) classes at the university the spring of 1925: a course in history (under another of Fling's associates), a course in foreign relations, and two English classes. One of these was on the English contemporary novel; it was here she first read Thomas Hardy, another milestone in her intellectual growth. Next to Conrad, Hardy had the strongest influence of the contemporary writers on her. At first she thought him profoundly depressing, but she felt also a strong sense of recognition. In his characters, people caught in circumstances beyond their control, she saw a parallel with real life in the sandhills.[15] She also saw his landscape as significant to his people in the way that her own landscape was to her.

That spring of 1925 she took a class in short story writing under a young man just come from the University of Iowa, Melvin Van den Bark. She considered it the most important experience in her writing career. Now at last she learned what to do with her story material, how to organize and manage it. Here she learned her theory of structure and developed her method of composing a single declarative sentence to encompass the entire thesis of each article, story, or book and typing the sentence and putting it above her typewriter before she began the writing itself. For her, the class was electrifying, a true epiphany, an experience comparable in its way to her first learning to read. She had had the material; now she learned the skills to put it together.

As a result of her work in the class, Mari was offered a job at the university reading freshman English papers and helping in the preparation of an extension course in short story writing. It brought in only thirty to thirty-five dollars a month and the checks were sometimes held up for ten days or so, but she felt the lean times were worth it because she was working with a man who understood the creation of literature. Van den Bark's courses and the extension work gave her experience and confidence; she was grateful to him throughout her life for showing her a method that would succeed.

In Van den Bark's classes Mari met a group of gifted people; she found it exhilarating, for as she later wrote—"when one does not have anyone to sharpen the steel of his creative mind" he finds it hard to drive himself.[16] The friends she made now shared their work and criticism, lent one another money and encouragement. They and others interested in the arts often met to talk about their craft. Lowry C. Wimberly's office at the university was one gathering place. Here Mari first met and became a lifelong friend of Rudolph Umland, whose work was eventually published in many journals. In the thirties he became assistant director of the Nebraska Writers Project and subsequently was for many years literary critic for the *Kansas City Star*. Here, too, she first met Dorothy Thomas, one of a large and talented family, who was a poet, a prize-winning short story writer, and who later published two well-thought-of novels, *Ma Jeeter's Girls* (1932) and *The Home Place* (1936).

Members of the group would often drift into the bus depot at Thirteenth and M Streets, not far from the campus and open all night, to drink coffee and talk about the art of writing; to gossip about the battles between the university faculty and administration and the rigidity of the college rules; or to complain about the narrow, stodgy, churchy atmosphere of Lincoln. It was the heyday of H. L. Mencken, and his iconoclasm appealed to many in the group. Several faculty members knew Mencken. Wimberly, for one, had published articles in his *American Mercury*, and Mencken's ideas of the "boobus Americanus" were elucidated and applied to local situations. The group included lively, talented, and sometimes quite unconventional people: short-haired women poets, long-haired men essayists, and "artistic" playwrights of both sexes.[17] Although the university had its share of Big Men and Big Women on Campus, maneuvering for positions of distinction, these young intellectuals were not often among them. Their concerns were with their art and fellow artists. Weldon Kees, from Beatrice, was a painter as well as a poet; Mabel Langdon, also a poet, later married a fellow poet, Loren Eiseley, who became a distinguished professor of anthropology and the author of such well known works as *The Immense Journey* and *Darwin's Century*. Pan Sterling, Tuck Stanley, and Jim Van Lieu, all Van den Bark's students, discussed their own short stories. Others who joined the circle were Gretchen Beghtoll Lee, an aspiring journalist, and artist Leonard

Thiessen.[18] They discussed successful regional writers such as Willa Cather and Dorothy Canfield Fisher, and talked of problems of technique, hopes of publishing. Most of them were first published in Wimberly's *Prairie Schooner*.

There were moments spent on other interests too. Lincoln *was* stodgy: there were Sunday blue laws for stores and places of amusement. Movies could not be shown on Sunday; downtown Lincoln was quiet as a tomb on that day. Lincoln residents tended to be of "Republican faith and the Methodist persuasion" and assumed God was too, according to Lowry Wimberly.[19] But on occasion Mari dined at Le Petit Gourmet, a small restaurant run by her friend Sarah Deutsch, who was widely traveled and knew French cuisine. Mari loved to dance and went often to one of several large ballrooms that attracted big-name bands. There were the popular roller skating rinks. Lincoln's salt-water lake at Capitol Beach helped to beat the heat of the summer evenings, or Mari and a girl friend would go to the municipal pool, saving money by sharing the fifteen-cent basket rental for their clothes. Mari's love of fun and her friendly interest in others made her popular with both men and women. She had many dates and several proposals but would not let fun, romance, or love interfere with her writing.

Until 1925 Mari lived in a series of dingy, cheap, uncomfortable rooms; then she moved to living quarters she liked so well she remained at the same address, 1226 J, for the next twelve years, although she occasionally moved from one room or apartment to another in the house.[20] The house was in an older part of town, near the commercial district, a neighborhood once elegant but by the 1920s largely made over into apartments and boarding houses. The Boston family, the owners, lived on the first floor; the second floor had been converted into rental units. The location suited Mari: she was only a few blocks south of the business district (for Lincoln was still small enough that the business district was the center of activity in the city). She could easily walk to whatever central gathering place she wished, to find people to talk to. The walk north to the university was longer, about ten blocks or so, but still a reasonable distance. Then, too, the mother of Mari's landlord, a Christian Scientist, had a philosophy Mari liked; she would "hold the right thought" for the success of the young woman's goals. Mari believed that this kind of general good will, directed on the part of someone who would not benefit from the result, was a strong force in bringing about beneficent events.[21]

In addition, she was just two blocks west of the state capitol and could watch the construction of the tower and, later, after the Nebraska State Historical Society was moved into the capitol building, do research there. The building was a matter of great interest to her. It was financed on a pay-as-you-go plan, and construction was halted, sometimes for months at a time, whenever the state ran short of money. The architecture of the building was also unique. Designed by Bertram Grosvenor Goodhue, it was one of the first public buildings of its kind in the United States—a series of low rectangles built around inner courtyards and surrounding a tall white tower with a gold dome surmounted by a statue of a man sowing grain. Some people considered it too unusual and freakish, but Mari liked its appearance, agreeing with those who believed it had a beauty that affected both Lincoln's skyline and its spirit. She was proud that Nebraska had dared to build something so unconventional. She watched the tower from its beginning in 1922 until its completion, and saw the statue of The Sower raised to its place in 1932. The tower became a symbol to her, both as a monument worthy of the state and also, ironically, as a symbol for what she thought the state should stand for but often did not.

Mari's first room at 1226 J was small—only space for sleeping, with a tiny cupboard for a kitchen—but she enjoyed fussing with it, painting, rearranging, or decorating it. It was often filled with friends and prospective writers, many of whom she advised on their work. Her desire to help others write was the one impulse she had trouble disciplining. Her schedule was hectic because she took on so much of this in addition to her own strict regimen of writing, attending college, and working. On occasion she refused to see anyone, sometimes because she did not want them to see her poverty, sometimes because she needed writing time. Whenever she put a "Busy" sign on her door her friends respected it.

Mari managed a great deal of writing in 1925, submitting work to *Harper's, Dial, Adventure,* the *Saturday Evening Post, Atlantic, Bookman, Scribner's, Cosmopolitan, Forum,* and *Parents Magazine,* among others. They all returned the stories, often with regret; for one reason or another her work was not suitable for their public. Sometimes she revised a story according to an editorial suggestion, only to have it rejected once more. The rejection slips eventually filled a scrapbook. None were helpful; they only angered her, undoubtedly contributing to her later irritable relations with publishers.[22] She kept right on writing in spite of the implied and outright advice to the contrary.

Magazine readers wanted simple plots, escape and romance. Her work was too gloomy and realistic, in the pattern of Hamlin Garland and Theodore Dreiser. She wrote of depression conditions in city and country, of bootleggers, dance hall girls, and people whose dreams or ambitions were destroyed by forces of society over which they had no control. The editors wrote her (as they were writing young William Faulkner in Mississippi) that her stories were almost always too unpleasant or too morbid.

A further drawback was her choice of locale, almost always the sandhills of western Nebraska, although Lincoln was sometimes the background. Contending that eastern publishers detested her region, Mari attempted to come to terms with the situation, recognizing that if she could not make her land beautiful or significant enough to sell in spite of eastern prejudice, she should not expect to be heard.[23] This problem of apparent eastern indifference to the area she thought so important—the sandhill region of the Great Plains—was a factor more formidable than she could realize at that time. It took her many years to overcome it.

Early in her Lincoln years Mari became acquainted with the Nebraska State Historical Society and its director, Addison E. Sheldon. The society lacked a permanent home in the 1920s. Its collections were scattered about Lincoln, moved from one building to another downtown and on the university campus. The newspaper collection was kept for several years in a leaky, unheated, unlighted basement at Sixteenth and J Streets. In these unprepossessing quarters, the society had its large collection of Nebraska newspapers, some dating from their beginnings to the current issues.[24] Recognizing that the old papers could give her unequaled source material about life in the state, Mari began culling them for background information for use in her future writing. She learned quickly that public repositories held valuable information free for the taking.

Fascinated with the details of frontier life in the panhandle, Mari spent hours and hours in the basement, wearing her coat for warmth and galoshes to protect her feet from the wet cement floor, using a flashlight when the natural light from the windows was not adequate.[25] Eventually her material, copied onto two-ring, ruled paper, filled three of the two-ring black notebooks used by students. In addition, she found other rich historical sources in the society's collection of private papers, published works, and artifacts.

In the newspaper accounts, particularly, Mari found confirmation of incidents involving her father. Since Jules's violent disapproval of writers was too well known to her, even at this distance, to use him as a central character in work intended for publication; and since she could not write of her own experiences without including him, she could not make immediate use of her research as she would like. But she could share her discoveries with her friends. A superb storyteller, Mari kept them enthralled, sometimes bringing them to tears or laughter with her stories of Old Jules and his idiosyncrasies as reported in the old local papers.[26]

In the fall of 1925, Mari returned to regular daytime classes at the university, concentrating again on education courses. The first semester she took four classes in education and only one in English literature. The second semester she studied city and village school administration, along with sociology, philosophy, and two English literature classes. She took no history at all. Her concentration once more on education courses may have been due to discouragement because her stories were not selling. She had sold nothing and, much as she disliked to commit herself to a contract, if she went back to teaching she could earn money to support her writing.

Fate, however, took a hand, or at least she interpreted it that way. In the spring of 1926, Mari won honorable mention in the *Harper's* intercollegiate short story contest with "Fearbitten," a sandhills story. As *Harper's* reminded her in their congratulatory letter, the contestants had been carefully screened by their individual colleges before being entered in the national contest, so the recognition was a high accolade.[27] When Mari saw her name in the magazine, she felt the same thrill she had felt as a youngster when her story appeared in the *Omaha Daily News*. No money was awarded, nor was her story published in the magazine, but seeing her name in print was still magic. Once more an outside validation of her talent spurred her on.

Her father, too, reacted predictably. Although he could no longer inflict physical punishment, when he learned of the award he sent her a short, sharp note: "You know I consider writers and artists the maggots of society." It was signed a curt "Jules Ami Sandoz."[28] But this time he could not stop her; there was no real conflict in loyalties. She would write. Her fall 1926 curriculum once more emphasized the humanities. Mari had a wide variety of courses to choose from in the English Department. Among the faculty were several outstanding professors whom she knew or from whom she would take classes.[29] In addition to Lowry C. Wimberly, there was Lucius A. Sherman, head of the department, who lived not far from her on J Street, and for whom she later typed the manuscript for a book he was writing; there was also Prosser Hall Frye, who taught Greek tragedy; Frederick A. Stuff, who taught Shakespeare; and Sherlock Bronson Gass, who taught a class in magazine article writing. Hartley Burr Alexander, chairman of the Department of Philosophy, had an office in Andrews Hall, where Mari worked. He was interested in poetry, anthropology, and architecture as well as philosophy, and had worked out the inscriptions and art symbolism for the state capitol building. A student of American Indian culture as well, he would occasionally call Mari from her theme grading to admire some new Indian artifact sent him.

Her schedule included advanced composition, public speaking, beginning German, and Old English, the last under Louise Pound, one of the university's most distinguished faculty members, a scholar of international reputation, an author, musician, and athlete.[30] A pioneer in the study of folklore in the United States, she was among the first to bring American literature into the university curriculum. A member of the eminent Pound family—her brother Roscoe was dean of the Harvard Law School and her sister Olivia also a respected educator—Louise Pound linked town and gown, encouraging social and intellectual interaction between the university and the townspeople. She was most interested in her graduate students, encouraging them to do research and to publish in the relatively new field of American literature and folklore. Because of her wide reputation, she was in touch with scholars, writers, and editors throughout the country, including H. L. Mencken, who admired her work in philology. They corresponded regularly and she recommended the work of more than one professor or student to the editor of the *American Mercury*.

Louise Pound strongly encouraged and deeply influenced Mari. It was she who told her to stop trying to write in absolutely correct "Barrett Wendell English." Anyone in Lincoln could do that; Mari should stick to her own pungent idiom, the tangy language of the sandhills. Louise Pound believed, as did other faculty members, that this young woman was a writer who would bear watching. At Sunday afternoon meetings of Chi Delta Phi, national honorary women's writing society, at the Pound home, or occasionally at tea in the home of someone interested in the arts, Mari was one of several asked to read their own work. When she read, her audience was aware that every sentence, every phrase, had been given time and thought.

Although the two came from such diverse backgrounds, Louise Pound, who had a Phi Beta Kappa key and a doctorate from Heidelberg, admired and respected the young woman who from childhood had had to fight for the right to live as a thinking female person. Mari's admiration for her teacher may have extended into other areas as well. Her decision to become a redhead may have stemmed from this acquaintance, for Louise Pound's red-gold braids were famous, and she once organized a club for red-haired women on campus. Although Louise Pound's traditional costume, a tailored tweed, was considered less than chic on campus, in later years Mari, too, often dressed in tweedy suits, although she took care that they were well cut and elegant.

Mari also took, in the spring of 1927, Sherlock Bronson Gass's class in writing feature articles for magazines. Although Gass was often critical and biting in his remarks to her in class, she wrote for him at least two articles that she later developed for publication. One, a lengthy first-person narrative recounting events from the time her family moved to the sandhills, she called "The Kinkaider Comes and Goes" and subtitled "Memories of an Adventurous Childhood in the Sandhills of Nebraska." The other was more general and used an impersonal authorial voice, without referring to the Sandoz family by name. This she called "Sandhills Sundays." Material from both later appeared in *Old Jules*.

In February 1927, Wimberly and members of the Wordsmith Chapter of Sigma Upsilon, a national literary fraternity, launched a new quarterly, the *Prairie Schooner*. Intended at first as an outlet for literary work at the university, it soon attracted regional and national recognition. The first story in that first issue was "The Vine" by Marie Macumber. Although the *Schooner* did not pay for the work it published, the prestige Mari received locally was pleasing, as was the fact that the editorial staff thought enough of her short story to make it their lead offering.

"The Vine," which had been rejected by eastern magazines (one editor noted that he had received a surprising number of works that year featuring a woman from the prairie who went mad), is a well-balanced study of two young homesteaders living in the arid, sun-burned West. The theme, as would be true for almost all of Mari's works, was that of man's relationship with the land. Although the story is bleak, the style is restrained and spare and the characters and background are described with economy and detachment. The points of view of the two protagonists are contrasted so effectively that the reader can sympathize with both. The story earned a three-star rating in Edward J. O'Brien's *Best Short Stories of 1927*. Although "The Vine" was not one of the twenty short stories published in the volume, which included such authors as Owen Wister, Ernest Hemingway, Sherwood Anderson, DuBose Heyward, Oliver LaFarge, and J. P. Marquand, it won important national recognition.

Important as recognition was, however, it did not help pay the bills. In the summer of 1927, Mari accepted a job on the *School Executive Magazine*, a national journal for school principals and superintendents published in Lincoln. Working on the editorial staff at the respectable salary of seventy-five dollars a month, she continued to spend time on research at the Nebraska State Historical Society and to write outside her working hours. She continued to send out her short stories, which were still being rejected. At this time she began her first novel, "*The Ungirt Runner*," later retitled "*Murky River*," using as an epigraph lines from Walt Whitman's "Song of the Open Road":

(Still here I carry my old delicious burden,
I carry them, men and women, I carry them with me wherever I go,
I swear it is impossible for me to get rid of them,
I am filled with them; and I will fill them in return.)

"Murky River" deals with a woman called Endor. The four-part structure covers her sandhill childhood in a violent river-rat family, her struggles as a poor but intelligent college student at the University of Nebraska, her marriage to a man who idolizes but cannot understand her, and her finding of her true ancestral roots at the conclusion. Many of the characters prefigure those appearing in later works, particularly *Old Jules*. Endor is easily recognized as the author herself; Jock, the father, is clearly modeled on Jules, though in this book he has no redeeming vision to offset his grossness. The mother is recognizable as Mary in many of her characteristics. She is unloving, often hostile. The little brothers are much like Mari's as she described them.

Scenes, too, foreshadow those appearing in *Old Jules* and other autobiographical works. The family haphazardly farms their little patch of corn. The huge garden is the mother's responsibility; the father spends most of his time hunting. Jock enveighs against Endor's reading of fiction, something no one in his family is allowed to do. Many details of Mari's growing up appear here: Endor's constant house chores and duties as babysitter for the little brothers; occasional summer evenings when the family sits outside on boxes and talks of the stars, floods, or northern lights; Endor's love of books and fear of her father's whippings, all appear in greater detail in later work. Especially graphic is the scene in which Endor is locked in the cellar for punishment, recalling Mari's own experience when her father discovered she had sent her short story to the children's page of the *Omaha Daily News:*

There was no comfort in the knowledge that the snakes weren't poisonous, that they sought only milk or mice. It was their horrible bodies, their swift-forked tongues that demoralized Endor so completely.

When the door banged to, shutting Endor into darkness almost sensible to the touch, terror descended upon her like a writhing sheet. Afraid to move for fear of stepping on a snake with her bare feet, afraid to stand still because one might slip down her neck from the log, she hunched over, grasping the collar of her dress tightly about her throat and screaming at the top of her voice until they let her out.

Endor's experiences at the university often parallel Mari's own. Endor appears on campus tall, gawky, her red wrists showing below her sleeves, in ill-fitting clothes obviously not originally hers. She has lied to get into the university, just as Mari did. Her first classes are dull, but eventually she finds two that fire her imagination, just as Mari did. The description of Endor's joy when told she has a gift for writing reflects the author's own emotions:

The university campus lay tucked into the eiderdown of a November fog the morning Endor hurried to a conference with her English instructor. When she emerged from the damp basement a new world confronted her. Under the old suit coat the blood sang through the girl's arms, calling her hands to the skies, her feet to a pattern of light steps upon the frosted walks.

But the exaltation Endor felt lay deeper, much deeper, than the external world. Miss Black, the English instructor only one year removed from studenthood and not yet afraid to play God with young destinies, had just suggested that Endor, if she studied and worked hard, might write. She might write, not only well, she did that now, but unusually well. Her papers had been discussed with the department head; there could be no doubt about it. She had talent.

The character Miss Black was based on Mamie Meredith, the

young English instructor at the university whom Mari met very early in her Lincoln years. Mari was never her student, but Mamie Meredith encouraged and believed in her from their earliest acquaintance.

The book has major flaws, as the author herself eventually realized. She was later glad it was not published for people to hold against her as a writer.[31] This work shows both the strength and weakness of her later fiction. When she worked with actual events and people, she could use her imagination to create a believable story, but when she went into the realm of pure imagination she faltered. Even in this early work, which is not avowedly didactic as is much of her fiction, her people become two-dimensional in the later sections; motives are not clearly established, and the writer resorts to an improbable resolution of the novel's plot.

An even more serious flaw was Mari's inability to achieve detachment from her heroine. Her sense of drama was too strong. She identified too closely with Endor's sense of alienation, persecution, and frustration. Overwriting appears often. The author had not yet learned her craft well enough to veil her own emotions from the public.

The *Prairie Schooner* published a second short story by Mari in 1928, "Old Potato Face," about two youngsters whose scheme to get rid of an unwanted old ranch hand works only too well. The most significant feature of the story is the language; the narrator, an unnamed observer, speaks in the idiom of western Nebraska. The tone is breezy, friendly, interested but unemotional, that of a neighbor, perhaps. Eventually Mari used variations of this narrative style in many of the vignettes interspersed throughout her histories.

That year, too, she won honorable mention in the Omaha Women's Press Club short story contest for "The Smart Man." Considerably longer and more detailed than her earlier stories, it too is a bleak tale set in the sandhills. Because the author takes the time to develop details carefully and slowly, she succeeds in creating a believable ironic hero. Plot and chronology are worked out successfully to reinforce the character development, but eastern publishers refused it, although, unlike most of her short stories, "The Smart Man" has a happy ending.[32] It was one of the few stories from this period she did not destroy.

In November 1928, Jules died in the hospital in Alliance. Mari was with him just before he died, and his last words to her were, "Why don't you write my life some time?"[33] This was the permission she so badly wanted. If he had not made that request, she would have had a very bad time with her conscience. She had lost much of her fear of her father in the years since she moved to Lincoln. She had returned only for brief visits, although she kept up a regular correspondence with the family and Flora had lived with her in Lincoln part of one year and attended the university. Jules's ill health had brought both younger daughters close to home, since the brothers were now married and living on ranches of their own. Mari, far away in Lincoln, did not feel it her duty to give up her studies, job, or writing to come home to help. Nevertheless, Jules still had a strong hold on her emotions. His request came as a great relief. Mari had been gathering information for a long time. Now she could write without guilt.

She had been writing regularly, of course, and at this time she became a member of Quill, a women's writing group in the city, begun in the 1920s by a few women who felt they would be more productive if stimulated by semimonthly meetings. Here they read their works and made periodic reports on their efforts to publish.[34] Mari joined Quill in 1929, submitting "The Smart Man" as evidence of the quality of her writing.

She formed lasting ties with several members of Quill; if anyone could claim to be a close friend, it would be from this group. Dorothy and Kenetha Thomas, poets and short story writers, belonged, as did Anna Longman, often a winner of the Omaha Women's Press Club awards and a feature writer for the *Lincoln Journal*. Helen Mary Hayes, another feature writer for the *Journal*, became a special friend, their mutual interest in modern art a particular bond between them. Others included Pan Sterling, whom Mari already knew through Van den Bark's short story class, and Marie Dugan and Mary Jeffery, both of whom lent her practical support during her coming years of struggle. A frequent guest was Mignon Good Eberhart, author of best-selling mysteries; another was Bess Streeter Aldrich, from nearby Elmwood, famous for such popular novels as *A Lantern in Her Hand, A White Bird Flying, Spring Came on Forever,* and *Miss Bishop.*

One of Mari's closest friendships was with Eleanor Hinman, the daughter of the chairman of the Department of Philosophy at the university. Eleanor had graduated in 1920 and gone east, hoping to make a career of writing, but had returned to take graduate work. She had been on the staff of various newspapers in Omaha and Lincoln, including the *Omaha Bee,* and in November 1921 had achieved a journalistic coup by interviewing the formidable and usually reticent Willa Cather for the *Lincoln Sunday Star.* Interested in all forms of writing, she attempted both the short story and the historical novel, had won first prize in poetry in the Omaha Women's Press Club contest in 1923, and published other poems. Eleanor was convinced that Mari's talent far surpassed her own, and became one of her staunchest boosters. Mari's Quill experiences were instrumental in setting her on the next step of her career.

Four
Discouragement
& Success

There were two disparate but significant influences on Mari's career at the end of the 1920s. One was her father's death, which released any restraints she felt about writing of his life and times. The other was her membership in Quill, which encouraged her in her intent to break into the eastern publishing market, led her to acquire an agent, and indirectly influenced her choice of a new professional name.

Several members of Quill were publishing. The work of both Dorothy and Kenetha Thomas, for example, appeared regularly in national magazines as well as local journals, but not all had found a major outlet. One of the speakers at Quill suggested the possibility of a New York agent, Margaret Christie, who was just getting started and willing to work with unknown authors. Mari had been considering just such a move. Earlier, in fact, she had written an agent her own estimate of her situation. She had around thirty stories completed, ranging from fifteen hundred to twenty thousand words and varying in tone from flippant to acutely painful. She also had several essays on widely assorted topics and her novel in an early stage, "embryonic and cynical." Nothing came of that contact, but in June Margaret Christie agreed to work with her.

The agent's most notable contribution to the writer's career came almost immediately, for on 26 June 1929, in answer to a question about a suitable pen name, she said, "Now, about your name—Mari Sandoz is by long odds the best writing name. I am inclined to feel that the transition [from Marie Macumber to Mari

Sandoz] could be made at once better than at any other time."[1] Mari took her advice and used the latter name from then on. The spelling of her first name is unusual, but the pronunciation, with an equal accent on both syllables, *Ma-ri*, is the European version of Mary, the way her father pronounced the name. Returning to the name *Sandoz*, she used it both professionally and personally from that time on. Symbolically, she was once again a Sandoz. Her marriage, which she never discussed in public, was now, as far as she was concerned, annulled. The Sandoz family ties, both those of her own lifetime and those stretching far back to the family history of the Middle Ages, were important to her. She had finally reached a stage of detachment, thanks to her father's death, her age, and her distance from the family, at which family ties were positive rather than negative.

Margaret Christie began to make editorial suggestions at once. Sometimes Mari attempted to follow them, sometimes not. Both the agent and her reader thought "Fearbitten," the *Harper's* award winner, far too good not to be made perfect, and she made suggestions for changes. Mari had no objections to making minor changes in any of her stories if they promised a sale, but she was not always amenable to major revisions and refused to revise "Victorie," a long short story based on an incident in her neighborhood, which won the 1929 Omaha Women's Press Club state contest award.[2] Full of violence, of improbable, exaggerated, or unclearly motivated events, the story seemed to the agent to be a desperate tragedy, not good for the author's mind or for her reputation, although it did suggest that Mari would do well to write longer works. She refused at the time to change the story or put it aside, declaring it the most powerful thing she had written. She continued to work with it for several years, eventually ridding it of its violent denoument. Much that was good in the work appeared in later writing. Several of the characters emerged in the Polish wedding chapter of *Old Jules*; another version of the story is found in "River Polak."

Margaret Christie gave explicit criticism: when Mari had an idea clearly in mind and knew exactly what she wanted to attain, she could write vigorous, interesting, integrated, and arresting material. In purely fictional tales her structural line was not clear; she had a tendency to digress, to give importance to description or other matters that slowed the tempo or distracted the reader. Characteristically, Mari bristled. She wondered if the agent wanted her to give up the subtlety which she felt was her only artistic virtue. Margaret Christie persisted that she should not confuse that quality with good construction—recognizing and respecting the line between subtlety and ambiguity was the mark of a careful craftsman. The agent point out, too, the difficulty easterners would have with Mari's language. " 'Twin Mills' will be a magnificent story when it becomes a straightforward, coherent tale. You see, no one here is familiar as you are with the characters and background. The point is, whose story is this anyway? The real point, actually, is that you are entirely familiar with matters about which you write and we are not."[3] Margaret Christie's consultant commented that the author presupposed knowledge the average reader did not have, so the story was meaningless and a reader would take no further interest: "One is constantly balked and confused by not understanding words and expression." The consultant asked for definitions of *nester, settler's price,* and *hazer.*

Although Mari was still concerned primarily with the short story, Margaret Christie constantly encouraged her to write longer works. Mari told her in the summer of 1929 that *Murky River* would be ready in October or November, but in late September she decided she did not like the tone and began to rewrite it from beginning to end. By late October she was filled with a sense of futility concerning the book. It was too stark and bitter, but she felt she could not write it any other way. She admitted to the agent, too, that she was seriously thinking of writing a biography of her father. Margaret Christie agreed that he sounded like excellent material for a book.

That fall, Mari quit her job in order to devote full time to writing. The spring issues of the *School Executive Magazine* identify Marie Macumber as assistant editor on the masthead, but she was not happy with the editorial policies of the magazine and did not feel the job was leading her in the direction she wanted to go. She began in earnest the life of a writer. Always an avid reader, she now read "violently" in the first weeks of what she considered a utopian existence. Only a few friends were allowed past the "Busy" sign on her door. She dreamed of studying in Heidelberg in the next few years and talked of learning from masters of style, in the same manner that a painter or musician would learn from famous masters in his field.[4] She worked steadily on her novel, following her lifetime habit of breaking off periodically to write short stories when she became too bound by a longer work, and she continued to gather information for the serious writing of the biography.

In September, Mari went back home to ask for her mother's help with the facts of her father's life. She, her mother, and her sister Flora took a short trip into the Black Hills—surely the first real vacation for all three of them.[5] But if Mari thought the trip would make her mother more amenable to her purpose, she was mistaken. Mary brusquely refused to talk about Jules. She also refused to give Mari access to those of Jules's files that she had kept. It was less than a year since his death, and Mary had no desire to share the family's intimate life with the public.

Frustrated and bitter, Mari was nevertheless unwilling to give up her plans; she would have to reconstruct what events she knew about from her own memory. Her mother had wasted no time in getting rid of her husband's trash. Most of his accumulated records of years of feuding and business she threw into the meat house, which was cooled by running water from the windmill. By the time Mari rescued them, they had largely molded into illegibility. She mourned especially an ancient book of pharmacy and medical recipes that had come down in the family for generations, the pages now almost dissolved by the dampness.[6] But she found approximately two thousand items, valuable documentation. Among them were early drafts of letters sent by Jules to Europe and letters from his family and friends in Switzerland, often in either Swiss French or Swiss German. She copied pertinent information into the three black notebooks already containing material from the state newspapers, textbooks, and personal interviews. The original letters she took with her to Lincoln for translation and study. Eventually some were sent to publishers to prove the authenticity of her story.

Some of the long-suffered frustration Mari felt in her relationship with her mother is revealed in a short story accepted by the *Prairie Schooner* that year, "Dumb Cattle" (awarded two stars by Edward J. O'Brien). The background is the Niobrara River place in northwestern Nebraska. The protagonist, a little girl named Sue, feels she is ugly, queer-looking, and unloved by her mother. She overhears her mother tell a neighbor that she was not wanted when she was born. The story is concerned with Sue's misery and her attempts to come to terms with both her ugliness and her unwanted status.

Told from the point of view of the seven-year-old girl, "Dumb Cattle" is of interest primarily because of what it tells us of the author's own emotions. Mari herself admitted that her early stories often had much of her own youth in them. This work is particularly revealing; much of it is intimated elsewhere in autobiographical material. The protagonist, with her "pinched little face, freckle spattered, and her mouse-blond hair that stood straight up in a roach all over her head," and whose face, small as it was, "was mostly forehead, with cheeks that had the sunken look of a starving Armenian," closely parallels Mari's description of herself at that age. Sue looks after a little brother whom she carries on her hip, as Mari carried her little brothers. Sue envies a girl with pretty, stretchy curls, just as Mari envied her pretty neighbors. Even Sue's unwanted birth is suggested in the actual events surrounding Mari's birth in *Old Jules*. The mother's calling the little girl a witch and an ugly "bawly calf" appears also in "Murky River."

Mari Sandoz always had subject matter for her writing. She now outlined for Margaret Christie a series of personal narratives she had in mind, each two thousand to three thousand words long, listing, among others, accounts of a gorgeous prairie fire, a hailstorm that ruined their young orchard and pounded the rye just ready to be harvested, and the time her infuriated father aimed a rifle at his neighbor and Mari jerked it from his hand. But when the agent asked to see the story of her father, she replied that she had conveyed the wrong impression. *Old Jules* was just a sheaf of notes.

Mari quickly became impatient with Margaret Christie's inability to place her work. In July, only six weeks after engaging her, the writer complained she was losing contact she had made with editors through the use of much time and money; even though her stories were always rejected, she had made her name known to several publishing houses and often received personal notes of criticism from the editors. The agent's critical evaluations were similar to those of others working with Mari then. Benjamin A. Botkin, a friend from university days who by 1929 was at the University of Oklahoma and the editor of *Folk-Say*, a publication devoted to folklore, wrote her, "The stories you gave me are not quite what I want and I'm going to work on you until I get it."[7] Lowry Wimberly rejected a story for the *Prairie Schooner* on the grounds that although it was beautifully written, there was too much experimentation with words and image building.[8] Mari herself was beginning to admit that the short story was not her forte, that her strength lay in longer works.

Several turning points came for Mari in 1930. The year started out inauspiciously enough, since she had no job and, in the wake of the October 1929 Black Tuesday stock market crash and disastrously falling farm prices, her bank had failed, leaving her with $1.83 in her savings account. Without train fare to Nevada for a promised teaching job, she reluctantly borrowed from several friends in Quill—Helen Mary Hayes, Mary Jeffery, and Eleanor Hinman—stayed in Lincoln, and continued to write. In a letter full of dramatic metaphor she thanked Eleanor for the "rope" thrown her, drowning in misery, but she, Mari, had already suffered all the misery of drowning and arrived at such a blissful state of semiconsciousness that being dragged back to hard reality was not particularly agreeable.[9] She was pessimistic about the future; chances would probably compel a drowning sooner or later anyway. She was unhappy, too, because her debts gave her such a sense of obligation; she wished to be free of a sense of responsibility to anyone.

It was a very bad time to be jobless. During the 1930s more and more people were unemployed and the salaries of those who managed to keep their jobs were cut 10 to 15 percent or more. It was not many years since the Lincoln newspapers had reported

Lincoln families relying on the city dump for their food, and people in the northern counties were rumored to be on the verge of starvation in the face of continued drouth and crop failures. Mari had earlier watched the months-long Burlington Railroad shopmen's strike, which was unsuccessful. Many people, like Mari, lost their savings when the banks failed. And in the farm belt, the weather made things even worse—searing heat and drouth continued to bring crop failures year after year. The midwestern farmers were losing everything to the wind, the drouth, and the mortgage companies. At every county courthouse one could see sheriffs' auctions, at which the mortgaged farms, livestock, and machinery were sold to satisfy debts or taxes. In Lincoln, young out-of-work farmers pulled up crabgrass on the state capitol lawn to earn a little money. Angry, desperate farmers marched on the state capitol seeking a moratorium on farm mortgages but were given no help by the state legislature. The farmers organized farm strikes; they dumped surplus milk and destroyed excess grain to call attention to their problems. The little central Nebraska community of Broken Bow even had a Communist rally, attended by the famous Ella ("Mother") Bloor, who was arrested and hauled off to jail in Grand Island. The dust storms of the 1930s hit especially hard in the sandhills region, where the soil is so light that the wind constantly reshapes it. The sandhillers, who in many cases had even less than others because their one crop was cattle, shut off their electricity—those few who had it—disconnected their telephones, used horses to pull their cars, and returned to making underwear and dresses from flour sacks. Some people built houses of hay bales; one sandhills rural community, unable to send its teenagers to town, built a high school of sod.[10]

Mari's bitterness was not for herself alone. The plight of the dispossessed, particularly those who had to give up the farms their own families had homesteaded, called to mind the agrarian revolt and the Populist party of the 1890s. Surely the government owed its people help to keep what was theirs. Her own poverty was to some extent her own choice; she could blame fate and the obtuse eastern publishers. But she could not accept the fate of others with equanimity. The misfortune of the destitute farmers and laborers she blamed on powers closer to home: the state legislature, local and state politicians, and the politically powerful families of Lincoln.

Still, good things happened for Mari in the 1930s. Quill honored her at their annual banquet in January 1930, giving her a laurel wreath (from the table decorations) for winning the 1929 Omaha Women's Press Club short-story contest with "Victorie." (At the same banquet, Mignon Eberhart was honored for receiving the five-thousand-dollar Scotland Yard Award for *While the Patient Slept.*) In April, Mari saw the twenty-seven-foot bronze statue of the Sower, designed by Lee Lawrie, raised to its position atop the state capitol dome, outlined against a blue spring sky.[11] The publication in the *North American Review* of the two-part "Kinkaider" article, based on an assignment in Sherlock Bronson Gass's journalism class in 1927, briefly helped her morale. Nebraska newspapers, already friendly and eager to publicize her success, noted the article. An editorial in the *Omaha Bee News* strengthened her determination to write her father's biography: "Students of the University of Nebraska history group who are searching far for ample facts for their present day annals, will do well to read the article by Mari Sandoz. No need for the historian to go far for ample facts for his record, or for the romanticist to invent situations, when the story of Jules Sandoz is yet untold in its fullness. The history of Jules Sandoz should be recorded without delay. His daughter has shown its value."[12]

Margaret Christie had sold the article to the *Review*, but Mari was unhappy with excisions made in it and dissatisfied with the agent's inability to place more of her work. When the agent suggested that Mari tie half a dozen stories together to enter the Scribner's novel contest, she replied it would take two full months of time and several thousand dollars' worth of material, all on a risky gamble, and terminated their relationship. She would not have another agent until after her first major publication.

In the spring of 1930 Mari returned to the sandhills once more, to Rushville, Hay Springs, Chadron, and Pine Ridge, collecting material from the old-timers through interviews and questionnaires. The Rushville banker, Johnny Jones, was helpful, as was her old neighbor Charlie Sears, the only one of fifty people to return the questionnaire she had sent out. And now Mary relented, agreeing to share her recollections. Mari's notes filled more and more of the black notebooks.

Then, in July, Mari took a trip that opened a hitherto unexplored aspect of history and literature to her. With her friend Eleanor Hinman, who was interested in Indian anthropology, she traveled over North and South Dakota, Wyoming, and Montana, exploring the Indian reservations and interviewing Indians. The two women made their three-week, three-thousand-mile jaunt in a Model T Ford coupe, stopping frequently to repair it, for they had to be their own mechanics. They took along a tent and camped out on the reservations during their stay. Another university friend, Helen Blish, was already on the Pine Ridge Reservation. She was interpreting the symbols and rituals portrayed in a pictographic history of the Oglala Sioux drawn by a Pine Ridge Indian, Amos Bad Heart Bull. Because of their interests, knowledge, and work in their field, these two young women served as catalysts, clarifying Mari's purpose to write Indian history.

Although she had known Indians since her childhood on the Niobrara, Mari had not used them as subjects for her writing. She now realized she was in the unique position of knowing the plains culture of the Indians as well as that of the white settlers, that she could view their culture from the inside, as a native of the region, as well as from the outside, as a scholar, and thus could present a valuable insight into their past.

Eleanor's contribution to this purpose is already evident. Helen Blish helped in quite another way, sharing her contacts and special knowledge with the others. The daughter of an Indian Bureau employee, she had spent most of her life on reservations, including ten years at the Pine Ridge. She knew the Indians, administrative officers, interpreters, and agency personnel there. In the summer of 1927, she persuaded the owner of Bad Heart Bull's pictographic history, Dollie Pretty Cloud, to let her rent the book of drawings. Helen Blish returned to the reservation often to consult with the old-timers, particularly the artist's uncles, for explanations of the drawings, since the artist himself was dead.[13] These old men included Short Bull and He Dog, the warrior friend of the famous Sioux war chief Crazy Horse. (Mari had seen the pictographs when Helen Blish was working with them in Lincoln and thought them to be of prime historical importance.)

Helen Blish helped her two friends with their itinerary, providing them with the services of an excellent interpreter and the necessary credentials and introductions to the elderly survivors of the Indian wars who, they hoped, could solve some of the mysteries surrounding the death of Crazy Horse, the primary purpose of the trip.

Mari had heard about Crazy Horse since childhood, from Indians, Indian fighters, her father's cronies, and her father himself. She had also read the available literature about him, including the 1929 issue of *Nebraska History*, which was devoted entirely to this chief and brought together a great deal of material not in official reports of the last few months of his life. It included an account of his coming in to Fort Robinson with his people in May 1877 and details of the intrigues that led to his death there in September 1877. The old men that Mari and Eleanor Hinman hoped to see on the reservation were battle comrades of the martyred chief.

Before the trip, Mari wrote the editor of *North American Review*, among others, proposing an article based on their experiences, called "Stalking the Ghost of Crazy Horse in a Whoopee" (the Model T Ford).[14] After stopping on the Rosebud Reservation to visit with Father Eugene Buechel, an elderly priest who was writing a dictionary of the Lakota language, and at the Pine Ridge to visit with Crazy Horse's old friends, they intended to go to Sheridan, Wyoming, then to the Custer battlefield and the locale of the Battle of the Rosebud in Montana.

No editor seemed interested, but Mari hoped the trip would provide her with many subjects. She saw in the Indians a magnificence she felt should be preserved. The family she admired most was the Man Afraid of His Horse clan of the Oglala Sioux, relatives of Bad Arm, on whose shoulders she had ridden as a toddler. She was also interested in learning what she could about the flight of the Cheyennes under Dull Knife and Little Wolf from an alien reservation in Indian Territory to their old home in the north, and about the capture and slaughter of the Dull Knife group at Fort Robinson in 1878.

From the Indians the women learned at first hand much about the personal life of Red Cloud and Crazy Horse not known to white historians, and what the Indians themselves thought about those responsible for the death of Crazy Horse. They also began identifying the complex interrelationships of various Indian families. This effort eventually led Mari to develop Sioux and Cheyenne genealogy charts that she asserted were the most complete in the world. It was at this time that the women first learned of Crazy Horse's love for Black Buffalo Woman and its importance to later events—his injury, his loss of honors, his betrayal, and finally his defeat and death.

They learned, too, how the differences in culture and language can cause difficulties. Mari's first impression of old He Dog and his friends, the men who were her chief sources of information, was not that of the kindly old grandfathers she later wrote of. The atmosphere was decidedly frosty at first.[15] He Dog was confusing, perhaps deliberately obtuse about relationships. And because they had consulted He Dog and his friends, the women were refused information by another group, including Black Elk, a relative of Crazy Horse. Black Elk would have nothing to do with the other group because, although He Dog and his brothers were close friends of Crazy Horse, they were related to Red Cloud, whom Black Elk held responsible for his cousin's death in 1877. In 1930 the division in the tribe still existed.[16]

Crazy Horse and his story had a strong effect on all three women. Just before Mari and Eleanor left for their trip, Helen, already at the Pine Ridge, sent a letter: "I have been finding out things about CH that may not be so welcome to you. Our hero had been divested of the honor of the chieftainship some time before the surrender of the band. You remember that I told you at one time that several of those last shirt-wearers had lost their shirts because of unworthy conduct. Well, CH was one of them, and it was all on account of a *woman*! But details later. Much mystery seems to enshroud the character in whom we are interested."[17] On the chief's own ground, Mari was affected emotionally. When she slept out in the sagebrush under the stars at the historic sites, she thought about this war chief, silent, powerful, handsome in a way not typically Indian, who had reportedly never allowed his photograph to be taken. She considered, too, the battles in which the valiant chief had bested Generals Crook and Custer. Physical contact with the region was essential for her creativity. Seeing the places and being on the Indians' land helped her to begin recreating in her mind the actions that had taken place there.

When, after the trip, Eleanor sent sections of her Crazy Horse manuscript to Mari for criticism, Mari, usually so patient and tactful with apprentice writers, was often harsh. Obviously she cared that the hero be given a literary treatment she considered worthy of him. Eleanor took the suggestions with good grace, and detailed discussions of the appropriate mode for the novel continued intermittently for several years. In about 1934, Eleanor wrote to thank Mari for information about Oglala Indian relationships, mused on possible ramifications of those relationships, and indicated she was still developing and revising her material.

During the jaunt Mari kept detailed notes and a sort of journal, a habit she often followed; from this and her Indian interview notes she compiled a list of possible subjects for later writing, "all with illustrations available." The trip engendered such diverse topics as a Pine Ridge sun dance, prairie fires, buffalo hunting, early settlers, summers and winters, blizzards, beef issues to Indians, wild game, massacres, army worms and grasshoppers, busting broncs, bone pickers, cowboys on holiday, the curiosity of the antelope, Hay Springs on the map "now has a well giving gasoline!," sea serpents in Nebraska not limited to the western part of the state, mad dogs, and dog days. Every one appeared in her later writing. The trip also inspired a short story, "Reservation," with a heroine named Marie—one of the few extant with a romantic theme—but it was never completed.

After her return to Lincoln in August 1930, Mari was writing, revising, and preparing "Murky River" to send to a publisher, working on *Old Jules,* and sending out, as always, a series of short stories and articles. She had no regular job and attended only one university class that fall, a night class in philosophy taught by Professor Edgar L. Hinman, Eleanor's father. She placed her long article, "Sandhill Sundays," originally written for Professor Gass's class in 1927, in *Folk-Say.* She also began to experiment with Indian material, attempting to arrange her words in a rhythm based on the Indian locution. The long interviews with the Sioux and Cheyennes, although she could understand them only through an interpreter, made an indelible impression on her. Using the dramatic events of a treaty council between United States commissioners and the Sioux at Fort Robinson in 1875, she tried various presentations, sometimes casting the story as fiction, sometimes as historical narrative.[18]

Although she met with no success in this subject matter either, she nevertheless persisted in her writing. In 1929 she had had forty short stories in her files; in 1930 she had sixty and by early 1931 sixty-five. She sent out "Murky River" four times, completely revising the manuscript each time, but it was rejected by all four publishers. In the summer of 1931 she returned to the sandhills and the Indian reservations for a short period of interviewing, this time with her younger sister Caroline to drive. Otherwise, she spent her time in Lincoln, writing, sending out material, and getting it back. She sent "Stalking the Ghost of Crazy Horse" to the *Saturday Evening Post* and the *American* and to some newspapers—the *New York Times,* the *Omaha World-Herald,* the *Chicago Tribune,* the *Portland Oregonian,* and the *Boston Transcript*—attempting to reach outlets other than the magazines that could be expected to be interested in her subject. But it did not sell, nor did her versions of "The Great Council" or "Spent Storm," an article based on her father's final few years and death.

Now desperately poor, Mari worked at whatever she could find.[19] She tried to earn her board and room as housekeeper and cook for Louise Austen, a young artist and teacher at the university who lived in the same house, but Mari was too interested in writing to concern herself with mundane domestic chores. Nonetheless, the two remained friends and talked optimistically of taking a trip to Mexico to study art there.[20] Mari found work as a part-time proofreader for the *Lincoln Journal and Star*, working nights and weekends, but the pay was not enough to live on.

The long period of poverty was beginning to tell on her, mentally and physically. Friends tried to help, but her fierce independence made it difficult. One invited her regularly to dinner on Sunday; others slipped money under a couch or chair when they left her apartment. She once accused Eleanor Hinman of putting her under a moral obligation to hurry through the book she was writing. On another occasion she gave Eleanor an IOU, promising, in her stiff pride, to pay 10 percent interest and thereby hurting her friend's feelings. She asked a department store to which she owed a small bill if she could work it out by clerking.[21] To other creditors she could only apologize for delayed payments, promising to pay as soon as possible.

At a time when so many were unemployed that the churches in Lincoln offered ten-cent dinners to the poor, merchants were not always sympathetic or patient. When Mari asked for credit at a store where she had been a customer for eight years, they sent the credit bureau to her landlady, Mrs. Boston, to check on her financial reliability. Mari was furious and promised the credit bureau she would never trade with that store again under any circumstances.[22] Fortunately, she told them, a small check had come in the mail or she would have starved right into the hospital. Friends noted that these times of actual hunger, of loneliness brought on by her working by day and writing half the night with no publishing success, embittered her. She often lived on stale buns bought at reduced rates in quantity, until she eventually became allergic to wheat flour. Her migraines continued to plague her, and the terrible heat of the Lincoln summers of that period was also debilitating, the temperature hovering over the one-hundred-degree mark for days.

Things began to look up in the fall of 1931, when Mari was hired by the Nebraska State Historical Society, which had just moved into its new quarters in the state capitol. She was to assist the superintendent of the society, Addison E. Sheldon, in research for a book on the Oglala Sioux chief Red Cloud. Sheldon was acquainted with Mari because of the many hours she had spent in the society archives; he was interested in her career and encouraged her, always sure she would succeed. His western background gave the two much in common. Sheldon had homesteaded in western Nebraska in 1886, edited a Chadron newspaper from 1888 to 1898, and been elected to the state legislature from that district on the Populist ticket.[23] Although he had not known Jules personally when he lived in the west, he had since exchanged letters with him. In one, Jules remarked that he was one of the last of the old French trappers in the area and, at sixty-seven, could still kill flying geese and eagles with an army rifle but had not yet learned to drink water, use soap, or shave. Sheldon suggested that Jules write his autobiography, but Jules replied that he was too busy making history to write it.[24]

Earlier, Sheldon had obtained for the Society the Eli Ricker Collection, an extensive archive of miscellaneous materials concerning the Indians: letters, documents, newspaper articles, government treaties. Of special interest were Judge Ricker's personal interview notes with people of northwestern Nebraska and surrounding areas involved in events of the late 1800s and early 1900s. These included survivors of the Indian wars, participants in the Wounded Knee episode, and Indians who had settled on the reservations and were attempting to adjust to that life. Mari went through the entire collection, categorizing the information and taking notes for both Sheldon and herself. She later incorporated parts of the interviews into her own writing almost verbatim.

Mari continued to work on *Old Jules*. By January 1932 she had already been advised that the book should be classified as fictonalized biography, since the material was "too strong meat" for convincing nonfiction.[25] Just what her critic had in mind by this cannot be determined, because all the early versions of the manuscript have been destroyed. Apparently from the first she used factual material but the technique of the novelist.

In January 1932, while continuing her research work for Sheldon, Mari registered for her first regular classes at the university since 1927. In addition to an education class and one in

German, she took two English courses (one under Lowry Wimberly) and John D. Hicks's "History of the Frontier since 1829." Hicks, a disciple of Frederick Jackson Turner and author of *The Populist Movement*, was as insistent upon the importance of primary sources as was Fred Morrow Fling; he was particularly interested in material peculiar to the frontier. It was in his class that Mari worked out the chronological table for frontier history that she used for all her historical books. But it was Hicks's philosophy of history that was most important to her. Although by the time she took his class most of *Old Jules* was done, he verified her own ideas about the history of the region. She had known of John D. Hicks long before 1932. As the head of the Department of American History, he was an ex officio member of the board of the Nebraska State Historical Society, and his article, "Our Pioneer Heritage," in the *Prairie Schooner* (Winter 1928, pp. 16–28), offered ideas she stressed throughout her life. In it Hicks restated Turner's theory that the American continent was conquered by successive waves of population reaching ever farther west, that until recent years there had always been a frontier. The frontier, he felt, was the most important single factor in the making of the United States. Mari particularized several of Hicks's ideas in *Old Jules*: the pioneer was the original radical; schools along the frontier were of little consequence, since the education that counted came from experience. Even late in her life Mari, when stating her accomplishments, included roping, riding, vaccinating calves, cooking, washing, sewing, and baking bread. Hicks may not have given her a new view of the frontier, but he certainly reinforced the concepts she had.

The university classes and work at the historical society took only part of Mari's time. She was also working nights and week ends as a proofreader for the Lincoln papers, reworking her short stories, sending out "Murky River" once more, and experimenting with her Indian material. She began an Oglala book, probably the biography of Young Man Afraid of His Horse.

The manuscript of *Old Jules* went out twice early that year and was twice returned. Mari rewrote the entire manuscript each time, doing much of that work in the popular Cornhusker Hotel coffee shop at Fifteenth and M streets, because she had found very early in her writing that she could revise best when there was talk and action going on around her. The Cornhusker was particularly attractive because it was one of the first places in Lincoln to install air conditioning. Mari would buy an occasional five-cent coke to pay for the booth she used, sipping it slowly. Often, late in the afternoon or at odd hours, friends would stop by and appropriate one corner of the coffee shop as their own.[26]

Mari entered Old Jules in the Atlantic nonfiction contest in October 1932. The Atlantic Press held the manuscript eight months, considering it as one of five finalists.[27] When the manuscript was finally rejected and returned the following May, Mari found a penciled note in it saying that it was a dull book about a dirty old man. She vigorously defended her work. However, that spring of 1933, when the book was rejected by Atlantic Press after being held so long, Mari reached her nadir, ill, discouraged, and penniless.[28]

The job at the Nebraska State Historical Society had long since run out. She was no longer attending college and could get only odd jobs. She put away her first novel, "Murky River," and concentrated on revising and sending out Old Jules to the best publishing houses in the East. Alfred A. Knopf rejected it, as did Houghton Mifflin and several others, perhaps because of its unusual style and the unattractiveness of its protagonist, and because the geographical setting was considered an agricultural wasteland, hardly worth the effort to settle or farm. It was not an appealing area to feature in a nonfiction book about pioneering. When Dodd, Mead also returned the manuscript, commenting that it was unusually interesting but that the construction and organization would not likely lead to a popular sale, she prophesied that the book would remain in print long after she was dead, provided it was published by then.[29]

Casual acquaintances did not know of Mari's discouragement. Always talkative, she disguised her feelings with sparkling conversation on almost any subject under discussion, her friendly smile and apparent ebullience. But she poured out her bitterness in her writing and to a few close friends. They felt her temper, her impatience and irritation, and knew her capable of occasionally holding a grudge or resentment. At times, though not often, she doubted her ability as a writer. She once remarked that she was so disappointed in *Old Jules* after about a year of writing on it that she would have jumped off the state capitol tower but decided it would not improve the book any.[30] After the rejection by the Atlantic Press, which had held it so long, she was numb with misery for months. Those who had believed her arrogant and egotistical in assuming that she had any ability or anything to say were right, she felt; as they always implied, she had been trying to live above her fellows, to live without working. Even the weather seemed to turn against her; the temperature soared into the nineties and past the hundred-degree mark day after day and the dust storms were so severe the street lights had to be kept on all day.

In the fall of 1933 she gave up. Very thin, malnourished, suffering from migraine, Mari now had spots on her lungs, so she returned to the sandhills and home. Before she left Lincoln, she called in three friends—Mamie Meredith, Marie Cronley, and Helen Mary Hayes—to help her gather up her stories, over seventy of them, carry them to a wash tub in the back yard of the Boston home, and burn them. That, she declared dramatically, was the end of Mari Sandoz as a writer.[31]

At home, she did not feel particularly welcome. Her mother reminded her often of her foolish notion of making a living "without working." She still felt, too, that there was no discounting the antagonism many mothers feel toward the eldest daughter.[32] Her family, more concerned than she knew, actually feared that in her dejection she might attempt suicide. She was too responsible and too much a fatalist for that, but she had to face the fact that it was a time of drouth and depression, jobs were unavailable, and she was thirty-seven and had very little to show for all her high hopes and hard work. She had written prodigiously, more than seventy short stories, uncounted articles and miscellaneous pieces, and two books, but her writing had earned her only $250 in sales to publishers and $75 in prizes. Not much to show for over ten years of hard work and the failure, sadly acknowledged, to attain her early goals of independence and recognition.

In some respects Mari exaggerated her situation, for example, her acquaintances' attitude toward her work. Several staunchly supported her belief in herself. Mamie Meredith kept one copy of the manuscript of *Old Jules,* in whatever revision was current, locked in her desk in Andrews Hall at the university, because Mari feared it might be lost in a fire. She could not afford a safe-deposit box. Eleanor Hinman had ambitious plans for her. Shortly before Mari left Lincoln for the sandhills that fall, Eleanor offered to finance a trip to New York for her so she could visit some publishers and learn their point of view. Mari, fearing that her friend was trying to mold and influence her, something she could not tolerate, said bluntly that she was grateful for the proffered help but would be more grateful if even one person in Lincoln could give her understanding. Eleanor opposed the move to the sandhills and urged her friend to reconsider; she hoped that Mari would instead allow her to pay her living expenses while she went on with her writing:

I can pretty well guess, not only what you are feeling at this moment, but what you will be feeling next spring if you go out "into the sticks," and I'm very anxious for you not to go. The worst of it is, in your case I'm not at all sure that any of this is necessary. I think you are like those storm-blinded travellers who used to be told about, who fall exhausted into the snow-drifts not a rod away from the farmhouse. All this has little to do with pity, but much more with that other tragic emotion, terror.[33]

Even after Mari had returned to the sandhills, Eleanor attempted to get her to return to Lincoln. She sent Mari ten dollars toward her railroad fare and offered her a job as her own assistant. She felt that Lincoln was the place for her until after her book was sold; she worried about her going where no one could understand what she had been through. At this, Mari exploded, expressing the feeling reflected in *Capital City* a few years later:

If I'm tired and disgusted and want to lay down with my face in the sand, please remember that sand is plentiful and the face is after all, mine. Furthermore, I've made no secret of my opinion of Lincoln as the last word in decadent middle class towns, sterile, deadening. Only by a constant isolation of conscious defensiveness did I exist there at all. While the sandhillers are equally antagonistic to the creative mind they at least are not superior or patronizing about it; do not set themselves up as beings of supreme culture. The sandhills have nothing more to give me, true, but neither has Lincoln or perhaps any spot on earth. And at least the sandhills do not pretend that they have. Has it ever occured [sic] to you that any traits you Lincolnites may have found interesting in me are Panhandle survivals forceably conserved by deliberate retreat, rudeness, and "busy" signs.[34]

Much of Mari's bitterness may have come from the cynical view of Lincoln held generally by her literary friends, fostered by their devotion to H. L. Mencken and his contempt for the "booboisie." However, her feeling that some Lincolnites either ignored or condescended to her made her emotion genuine and personal.

She ended by castigating Eleanor for presuming to interfere with her life and pointedly reminded her that her own novel had not yet been written. Eleanor, who had thought Mari intended to give up her writing permanently, was shocked and hurt: "You have all those gifts and qualities which I so deeply desire, and so sadly lack. I cannot believe but what I shall some day see you in that position of distinction in which I have already placed you. I have the greatest faith in your ultimately reaching the place you are resolved to reach; but it drove me nearly frantic to see your resolution apparently turned in this new direction."[35]

Once Mari convinced her friend that she could not be made into anything she was not, she admitted she could not stop writing, even in the sandhills. She built herself a shack, re-modeling an old garage with the use of a meat saw and tapeline. The sixteen-by-eight-foot shack had three rooms and a closet. The interior was finished with pinkish builders' paper with large fly specks all over it and pinkish rough lumber slabs from Pine Ridge. The furniture, too—bookcase and table—and cas-ings were made from the slabs. The outside was shingled with slab ornamentation, "all in audaciously bad carpentry." She had a day bed, some books, and her files, and she worked here by kerosene lamp from seven in the evening until sunup, leaving the shack only for ranch duties. She hurt her mother's feelings by putting the door and windows in the side toward the hill, away from the house, in order to work uninterrupted by her mother's many suggestions of better ways to spend her time. She was, in fact, well into her next book, a novel she called *Slogum House*.[36]

Doggedly Mari kept sending out the *Old Jules* manuscript, to Longman Greens, then to International Publishing, but the rejection slips came with discouraging regularity. She had been angry in Lincoln at editorial notes explaining how her work failed to meet requirements for publication, but now things seemed even worse. The change of address from Lincoln to the unknown sandhills hamlet of Ellsworth resulted in fewer editorial letters; now she received form rejection slips. The actual quality of the work seemed to her to have little to do with its reception. That fall she had one short story accepted, "Musky," based on her experiences with a pet muskrat the first summer she and James stayed alone on the Kinkaid claim, but that was not enough to lighten her discouragement.

Despite the therapeutic value of being close to the land once more, Mari was not happy in the sandhills. When A. E. Sheldon wrote in December that he might have a job for her at the Nebraska State Historical Society, she applied at once and returned to Lincoln in January 1934. Sheldon had obtained some federal money to research and write a book on land practices in Nebraska, one of the many projects to come from President Roosevelt's attempts to create jobs.

Hired under the New Deal relief legislation, Mari was soon one of more than five hundred people on the federal payrolls in Lincoln. Her duties expanded: in addition to helping Sheldon in his research for the new book, she was made director of personnel for the Historical Society as well as associate editor of the *Nebraska History* magazine. She also had charge of some of the manuscript collections, directing the organization, filing, and moving of archival material, as well as binding the newspaper collection. She sometimes had thirty to forty people working under her; she also used the secretarial skills she had learned at the Lincoln Business College in acting as secretary to both Sheldon and A. T. Hill, the business manager and museum director.[37]

Mari tackled her new job with her old enthusiasm and energy. The small but regular salary gave her the independence she needed. Her spirits lifted, and she was full of pep: a friend dropped by her apartment one evening to find her making plum jam, tomato preserves, and pickles all at the same time. And she again shopped the bargain basements of Miller's and Gold's for her favorite fashion in hats. To her, the right hat was like the right title of a book, "the one not just covering the head and the other not just stating the subject but doing something extra."[38]

Meanwhile, the manuscript of *Old Jules* was back in New York. She sent it with a university friend, Tyler "Buck" Buchaneau, now working for a publishing house, who might be able, through personal contact with publishers, to interest them in it. He had no luck, however. Appleton-Century felt that the leading character needed more personalizing and the book was too long, with occasional dull moments. Mari told them she would cut it if necessary, but she doubted that it would improve her attempt to portray a certain period. Then she dramatically ordered her friend to burn the manuscript. When he sensibly returned it instead, he received an explosive accusation that he had betrayed her. In answer to his mystified query as to the manner of betrayal, he received an apologetic reminder that Kafka's literary executor had refused to carry out that author's request to burn all his unpublished works.[39]

The manuscript continued its rounds via the mails until August 1934, when Mari sent it to Caxton Printers, a firm in Caldwell, Idaho, that wanted to publish the book. Caxton asked her to share the publishing costs, since it was a small company and such costs were high. The estimated cost of the first edition of fifteen hundred copies would run $2,500 for publicity, printing, binding, and so forth. Would she be able to contribute $1,125 for her share? Under the circumstances, Mari asked for the return of the manuscript. The publisher pointed out that since he had limited funds and a number of worthwhile manuscripts, he could bring out work sooner if the author was able to help with costs. The merit of *Old Jules* was such, however, that he would still like to offer her a contract and publish the book when conditions permitted. Mari agreed to this arrangement. Neither the editor nor she felt the book had best-seller qualities,

although the editor thought reviews would be good. Mari remarked that her work usually aroused violent discussion and if
that held true in this case the book might do well.

Caxton then sent a reader's assessment of the manuscript
which praised it as an impressive piece of work handled by a
person of unusual literary gifts. But the reader also suggested
revisions. He treated it as fiction throughout his evaluation: "It is
a novel, yet not a novel, rather a pageant of human nature in the
struggle against the untamed forces of wilderness."[40] He felt that
its peculiar hybrid nature gave the work both its power and its
weakness: it was a masterful human drama swamped by its
panoramic details. The scenes between Jules and Mary, especially, indicated the author's superb ability to handle dramatic
material. He noted the occasional awkwardness in style but felt
that with revision the book would be truly great. Mari reluctantly agreed to consider the suggested revisions, but the reader
had talked of fictionalizing scenes she wanted to keep factual,
and other recommended changes would, she felt, make it too
sterile. She began sending it to other publishers once more.[41]

Meanwhile, she continued to experiment with and revise her
Indian material. "The Great Council," following the familiar
pattern, was sent systematically from one publisher to the next,
but editors were not interested in it. In February 1935 she did
place "The Birdman," a short story about a young Indian boy
who finds a buffalo herd for his hungry village, in the *Omaha
World-Herald* Sunday magazine section. This story and occasional newspaper articles were her only Indian writings to be
published for many years.

Once again Mari sent *Old Jules* to D. Appleton-Century. She
told them she was willing to make revisions that would not
emasculate the book, but by now she had received so much
contradictory advice from publishers she was bewildered. When
they returned it, she tried once more to enter the *Atlantic* nonfiction contest. She reminded the editor that in 1932 they had
held the manuscript eight months but had returned it after it
reached the final judging. Since then she had rewritten every
word and substituted the actual names of the characters for the
fictitious ones of the earlier version. Would she be allowed to

enter the present work in the 1935 contest? The editor replied that the book would be eligible, and in April 1935 she sent it in, with the title *Home on the Running Water*. This time it won.

There was drama right to the end. Three days before the deadline the manuscript was dropped in a scrub bucket. The last carbon was in the sandhills, a week away from Lincoln by mail, so, using her penultimate revision, Mari revised and proofread day and night while her friends, Marie Cronley, Helen Mary Hayes, and others, typed separate chapters. The manuscript was completed and assembled about four in the morning, and then Mari typed a "rambling letter" to go with it. She later told a friend that when that letter, with just a few words changed, turned up as the foreword to the book it sounded strange to her, for she did not remember a word she had written.[42] Her memory seems to have failed her here, however, for shortly after her book had been accepted she discussed with Edward Weeks, the *Atlantic* editor, using the letter as the foreword, detailing small changes to be made at the beginning and end, and assuring him she had gotten confirmation from Frank L. Williams, one of her references, of certain details.[43]

The telegram from the Atlantic Press arrived during the work day at the Nebraska State Historical Society. It read:

HAPPY TO ANNOUNCE THAT YOUR MANUSCRIPT WINS ATLANTIC CONTEST STOP PRIZE AWARDED ON CONDITION IT BE EDITED AND REDUCED TO APPROXIMATELY ONE HUNDRED THIRTY FIVE THOUSAND WORDS HOPE YOU CAN COME EAST TO ASSIST WITH EDITING PERSONALLY STOP WISH TO ENTITLE BOOK OLD JULES STOP KEEP THIS NEWS STRICTLY CONFIDENTIAL UNTIL JUNE SEVENTEENTH WHEN ANNOUNCEMENT RELEASED TO NEWS-PAPERS BE PREPARED FOR INTERVIEWS LINCOLN STOP SEND ALL AVAILABLE PHOTOGRAPHS YOURSELF AND JULES ACKNOWLEDGE THIS WIRE HEARTY CONGRATULATIONS—EDWARD WEEKS

The news of Mari's achievement soon reached those working throughout the society, for her voice, normally rather high-pitched and now even more penetrating in her excitement, could be heard telling A. E. Sheldon that she did not believe it, that it could not be true.[44] The shock did not wear off until a few days later, when she received a telephone call from a former university acquaintance, Volta Torrey, a reporter for the *Omaha*

World-Herald. At his words, "Don't you have some news?" she finally realized she had won. Thirty years later she reminded him that his voice on the telephone from the newspaper office gave her the first outside notice that *Old Jules* had won; until then she had not dared to believe it: "It is curious that nothing has ever had the same impact on me as your voice that day. I gave you the information you needed. I sent notice to Mother and then I had to go Van [den Bark]'s place to tell him. He stood leaning on a shovel or a hoe in his back yard, and after a while he began to talk naturally again."[45]

Mari's life would change drastically in many ways. For the first time she would have money and time for research. She would meet many new people, among them Paul Hoffman, the Atlantic editor who "discovered" *Old Jules* on its entry in this second contest and who would play an important role in her career. She would travel. But writing would continue to be her imperative concern.

Old Jules and Mary

Five
Old Jules

The success of *Old Jules*, which was chosen unanimously over 582 other manuscripts in the Atlantic Press nonfiction contest and was named the Book-of-the-Month Club selection for November 1935, confirmed Mari's belief in her work, in its worth both as history and as literature. But her victory carried within it the seeds of further battles—at times full-scale warfare—between the author and her publishers. In her first letter to Edward Weeks, expressing her appreciation for the honor and recognition given her, Mari expressed her confidence that the revisions requested in his telegram could be managed when she came to Boston at the end of the month, since her own editorial work on magazines and newspapers had given her experience as well as a certain detachment. What happened next set a pattern that continued throughout her career as an established writer.

Weeks sent a seven-page, single-spaced letter detailing changes he wished to discuss when she came east. He began by asking for revision of the first fifty pages. He did not think the shooting of a man at her father's side in the Valentine tavern credible as it stood; could she verify it? He wanted more details about Jules's first years in the United States, more on his first marriage, more on his change from a fastidious young man in Europe to the slovenly pioneer he became. He felt Jules must have worked much harder on the fruit orchards than his daughter had indicated: "There are very few allusions to the work he actually performed in cultivating his trees. It is not enough to tell us that his fruit won forty prizes in one year. We should see the sweat and industry that went into this achievement."[1] Mari discovered then that Edward Weeks did not see her work in the same perspective as she, and she began her long battle to retain structure, point of view, and idiom. Later she described the Boston discussions to an interviewer:

The fight over the book lasted ten days. . . . Ten days of nice, peaceful, Boston fighting, the polite kind, which is much worse than the other. They didn't believe that a frontier still existed fifty years ago. But I had heard Old Jules tell the story of that vigilante killing many times. So I pointed out that Boston was probably a nice, orderly place in 1884, but that the facts were that things were different on the Nebraska panhandle.[2]

She was hard put to keep her temper in the struggle for her authorial integrity.

Edward Weeks, in the October 1935 *Book-of-the-Month Club News*, admitted that "the disposition does exist among Easterners to suspect that Westerners occasionally indulge in long words and tall stories. I wanted to make sure that readers the country over would be able to follow her sometimes staccato Western idiom." The editor noted that Mari's appearance was as unusual in Boston as her writing: "I'm not used to seeing pioneers in the flesh and Hollywood's version had not prepared me for this one. Mari Sandoz is not strapping, she is wiry; her strength is not that of muscle but of well-knit bone and nerve." Still painfully thin, with her high staccato midwestern voice, her craggy face, as she herself described it, "all curls and bows," she was noticeably foreign to the East. The *Boston Transcript* spoke of her as slender and vivacious, having the sort of poise that easterners never acquire, vibrating with nervous energy and vitality, thin, wiry, restless, sharp-faced, with shrewd lines about her mouth and eyes. "Mari Sandoz is ruthless, intolerant, sharp in her judgments, suffering fools, or those she considers fools, not at all gladly. She is honest, real, warm-hearted, much loved by her friends, to whom she is generous with possessions, time and energy."[3]

No matter what she wore, her hands gave evidence of the hard work of her youth. As one observer noted, "They were the hands of a farmer—broad, calloused, knobby. When you looked at her hands, you knew Mari Sandoz had worked mighty hard in the fields and the barns."[4] Her behavior, too, gave indication of her childhood environment. The meat she ate must be cooked until leathery; she had seen too many diseased animals in the ranch country to trust that all the bacteria in her food were dead or harmless.

Mari enjoyed the attention, at least at first. When she met a group of eastern critics, she knew she disappointed them because she did not fit their stereotyped image of a frontier woman; she had to show Lewis Gannett of the *New York Herald-Tribune* the broken bone in her hand to prove she really was the daughter of Old Jules and writer of the book. She was stimulated by talk with persons interested in world affairs, who seemed to her not as misled by current hysterias and propaganda as midwesterners, and she was impressed with the easterners involved in writing. She established lasting friendships with several Atlantic Press editors—Stuart Rose, Edward Aswell, and Paul Hoffman, the young man who had first read her manuscript and insisted that Weeks consider it. She encouraged Hoffman's own writing and later followed him as her editor to two publishing houses after he left the Atlantic Press.

Mari did not like Boston much, however. She found the room reseved for her in a women's residence hotel dreadful, a "Rose for Emily" kind of room, she called it.[5] The weather was almost intolerable. Boston in July was hot and even more humid than Lincoln. Mari always suffered in that kind of climate. In 1935 few offices had air conditioning; the editor and author worked in the sweltering heat. Her migraines became so severe she could not stay the two weeks she had planned. When she was reduced to toast, coffee, and aspirin, she cancelled plans even to see old Nebraska friends and caught the next plane back to Lincoln. Her migraines plagued her with particular severity throughout the next two years.

Not all of the editing problems, especially the difficulties caused by the difference in idiom, were solved during this stay in the East. Evidently thinking they were, however, Mari wrote Weeks that she appreciated his fine attitude toward "our language out here," that she always used a dictionary religiously outside her own field, but that she, as a specialist in her own area, certainly should not need it there. Though Weeks thought her manuscript was remarkably clean and vigorous, he found flaws in it. From Lincoln, Mari sent detailed corrections, proper spellings for Indian names and place names and the reasons for them, and the proper pronunciation or colloquial meanings for other terms. Soon she felt the manuscript was being cut to the point that it was no longer coherent. When she saw the proofs, she protested the changes, such as the substitution of *plough* for *plow* and *centre* for *center*, proper spellings for a scholarly work but incongruous in her Old Jules story. She also complained that some incidents had been cut without her approval. By the middle of August, thoroughly irritated, she wrote the editor that one sentence he had questioned was self-explanatory and that he was vastly underestimating the intelligence of the average reader, and she insisted that he not put in another "damned footnote." He replied, "Peace, peace, troubled spirit! The fourth version of that [Kinkaid] sentence gave it the lucidness I was after. It may always have been clear, but the presence of fifty-three subordinate clauses, impinging one upon another, was more of a mouthful than any lover of good English could easily swallow."[6] The revisions requested by the editor, together with the many discussions of the meaning of her language, aggravated Mari to the point where, she often declared, she could not ever read the book in print.[7]

Unquestionably, she wrote awkwardly or obscurely at times. The influence of her first language, German Swiss, sometimes twisted her sentences into Teutonic constructions. Her early affinity for Joseph Conrad showed up in occasional convolutions of language, those "impinging clauses" that Edward Weeks found so difficult. An entirely different influence, although one certainly as strong, was that of Louise Pound, who had encouraged her to believe in the rightness of her sandhills colloquialisms.[8] Mari was adamant about retaining her idiom. Furthermore, because of the very nature of her meticulous revising, her sentences were, in a sense, hand-crafted, each word polished and shaped to fit. When someone tampered with her prose, she reacted as a poet would, resentful that anyone would dare interfere with the syntax, the rhythm, or the meaning. She considered English a living, growing language, and she tried to use it as a dynamic instrument. "The creative writer gives [words] special meanings by unusual usages and arrangements," she once noted.[9] This was especially true, she felt, for those who attempted to use rhythmic prose for special connotations or emotional impact, a usage that meant placement of words by ear as well as eye.

The battles that began with the first letter from the Atlantic Press and continued throughout the years with most of her publishers—eventually she had eleven—only pointed up the sharp philosophical and cultural differences between East and West. Mari accused the eastern publishers of crass provincialism and bland disinterest in anything that happened in the vast middle of the country; easterners often frankly saw little of interest in the hinterlands or viewed the inhabitants as quaint. Thus, whether Mari was defending her writing or charging her publisher with lack of marketing aggressiveness, as she did for almost all her books, she was actually saying that easterners did not care enough about the rest of the country to make the effort to understand it. From the time of her early disenchantment with the Atlantic Press and its publisher, Little, Brown, she was never happy with her relationship with them, although they published her next two books.

A major problem Mari had struggled with was classification of *Old Jules*; was it biography or fiction? Her use of fictional techniques gave some readers pause. Although she offered affidavits verifying events, the eastern publishers often seemed unconvinced that the portrayal of Old Jules, in particular, was true to life. They were not sure but that she was combining fact and fiction. And if so, which was which?

Shortly after the completion of the first version of *Old Jules* Mari had written Dodd, Mead that her aim was to show some reason, or some pattern, which would make the book philosophically as well as historically true, but she resolved the problem of genre only in the last revision. In her efforts to sell the manuscript she tried every variation she thought would make it attractive. In all the versions the incidents were based on fact, but sometimes she created imaginary towns, distorted distances, and changed the names of the people. In 1930 she called it fictionalized biography; in 1931 she referred to it both as fictionalized history and as biography.[10]

In the 1932 version Mari sent to the first Atlantic Press contest she entered, she used fictitious names for the most part: outside of her family and relatives she had used no real names except for such well-known characters as Theodore Roosevelt; the governor of Nebraska; Doc Middleton, the horse thief; and her father's friend Charles Nippel. She had preserved the actual names of the towns in this version, because Frank L. Williams, who she claimed was the one person in Lincoln to read the entire manuscript, had advised her that authentic localization would be a good idea. A year later she sent the manuscript to another publisher, completely rewritten twice since it had been returned from the Atlantic Press. In this 1933 version she also used fictitious names except for her immediate family. She had changed people's characteristics so that no one in their community would recognize them. She had again distorted distances to disguise the background. Major incidents, speech, food, clothing, and attitudes of the time were as authentic as she could make them, however; her ambition was to give a true picture of life in a late frontier community.[11]

In later years, as an established writer, Mari did not seem to worry about the question of mode; she spent little time categorizing her nonfiction. She seldom wrote or talked much about the problems of the biographer, although she was continuously defining the purpose and methods of a historian. She maintained that a book can be anything an author wants it to be if he can get away with it long enough for the reader to get through it.[12]

Throughout her career Mari was inclined to speak of her biographies as novels, although she also insisted they were nonfiction. The fact that she used fictional techniques in writing nonfiction had some influence on her understanding of mode. Speaking to an audience in 1959, she exhibited this lack of concern, referring to *Old Jules* as both a novel and nonfiction:

"The chronicle novel uses a portière idea. The chronicle novel starts that way because you have a whole lot of people to keep up with, . . . many, many members of a family. But you work out a little design . . . your business is to make some sort of pattern. This is the kind of writing you find in all of the Galsworthy novels. They're family chronicles."[13] She pointed out that the family chronicle, tending to be slow-moving, almost glacial, works nicely for biographies, and "for biographies of a region in the nonfiction field." She apparently saw no need for a distinction of form in this case between fiction and nonfiction.

She did, however, see a difference between the two genres in the points of view the author used. The omniscient approach was only for novels: in that case the author could go into the mind of anyone. For nonfiction, the perspective was external, as in a play. Here the author set his reader down "in a good seat at the foot of the stage"; all he would know is what he could see and hear and surmise. He would not see into anyone's minds. This, she affirmed, was a good approach to nonfiction, because one does not know what people think. Her concern here was with fidelity to historical accuracy. She agreed with the view her friend Wallace Stegner posits in *The Sound of Mountain Water*, that mode is not the determining factor in the validity of a biographical account. Stegner remarks that falseness in such writing "derives from inadequate or inaccurate information, faulty research, neglected sources, bias, bad judgement, misleading implication, and these afflict the expository among us about as often as they afflict the narrative."[14] Mari agreed that one can dramatize historical events but must not invent them. She was adamant that truth is essential to nonfiction, and that the writer must know the difference between reality and his own imagination.

On publication of *Old Jules* the critics were no more concerned with definitions of genre than was the author. Her long battle to retain the uniqueness of subject matter, form, and style brought overwhelmingly favorable response. Accolades came from *Life*, *Yale Review*, and the *New York Times*, among others. Stephen Vincent Benét used the entire front page of the book section in the *New York Herald-Tribune* for his comments. Several critics thought the book should receive the Pulitzer Prize. Reviewers were startled by Mari's subject matter, the way she portrayed both her father and the frontier, and her style. One remarked that her book made him aware of the yet untapped layers and layers of historical soil of our own American heritage. "She writes with the detachment of an impartial observer," said another one, "with no perceptible tug of prejudice at all."[15] A few pointed out that the book was really a tragedy because Jules had been wrong about the country's suitability for farming: "All the time the cattlemen were right and old Jules was wrong. It is a tragedy of hardened, tortured men and women giving their lives to alien soil over which the winds and droughts carry a curse."[16]

The *New York Sun* brought up a point seconded by many. The book was magnificently written, but with a frankness of expression so uninhibited that many readers would question its good taste: "Racy of the soil, *Old Jules* is also racy with the coarse and uncontrolled lusts of men who have reverted to the primitive. The book is strong meat; not merely that, but strong meat with a decidedly gamy flavor."[17] Bernard DeVoto went to the heart of the matter:

I am afraid for this book. The prize award will get it publicity and flattery, but how well will it be understood? It is a magnificent job and Miss Sandoz has come close to making it, as she said she wanted to, the biography not only of her father but of the upper Niobrara country itself. That is just the trouble. It is achingly, glaringly necessary to get the High Plains written about and understood, to force a realization of them and their place in our culture and our problems on the national mind. But Miss Sandoz is a native and a literary artist and, I suspect, disqualified on both counts. Her accents and rhythms, her assumptions, even her vocabulary, are alien.[18]

DeVoto was right about the differences between East and West, but *Old Jules* itself held such interest and drew so much attention as the Atlantic prize winner and Book-of-the-Month Club selection that urban and eastern readers evidently overcame the problems.

On publication of *Old Jules*, Jacques Chambrun and Harold Ober, both well-known literary agents, wished to represent Mari. Since she already had a contract for the book, she accepted

Chambrun for her short stories and Ober for subsidiary rights. The film industry was interested, too. Irving Thalberg of MGM took an option on *Old Jules* for twenty-five hundred dollars, and several major stars were suggested for the leading role: Paul Muni, Wallace Beery, and Emil Janssen from Sweden.

At home in Nebraska, the book was both praised and condemned. Mari's Lincoln acquaintances were astounded. While everyone knew she wrote, few had any idea of either the scope or the mode of her work. Dorothy Thomas, who had known her for years and was a fellow member of Quill, recalls, "We had first in common that we were both unpublished writers. I would listen, hours, while Mari, then Marie Macumber, read aloud stories," but she never heard Mari speak of her plans for larger works.[19] Strangely secretive about this aspect of her writing until she won the award, she did not confide even in Melvin Van den Bark that she had switched from fiction to nonfiction. She was not sure he would approve the change.

That fall of 1935 the Nebraska State Historical Society honored the Sandoz family at their annual meeting and Mari gave the dinner address. "Biggest crowd we ever had," said one of the directors. Her success also brought attention from other friends in Lincoln, who did what they could to help her get her bachelor's degree from the university, but in this they were not successful. With more than three and a half years' credit, she had almost enough hours for a degree but lacked the necessary high school credits, and her college coursework did not include the required subjects for any specific recognized program.[20] She wanted the recognition of a diploma. In 1934 she had offered her written work to the office of the registrar as evidence of her fitness for a degree, but it had not been accepted. That the university did not grant the degree rankled at times and added to her dissatisfaction with some departments of the university, with Lincoln, and with bureaucracy in general.

Most newspapers in the region expressed pleasure that a native Nebraskan had achieved national success and praised both the author and her work. The *Nebraska State Sunday Journal-Star* proclaimed, "Mari Sandoz crashed the headlines and the critics labored over her *Old Jules.* It is so strange, so strong and virile, that some keen critics have wondered if the nonfiction label lied. Nebraskans know it did not."[21]

People in western Nebraska reacted with mixed emotions. Although editors were enthusiastic about a work that brought attention to their region, other residents were less happy. Some resented her portraits of them or their families. Others, according to the author, resented being left out of the book. Some protested that Jules could not be considered a typical pioneer or that he simply could not have been a real person. But in the main, those who knew Jules and the history of the region agreed that the book did not exaggerate. The Hartington News ventured: "Some people will read it and be shocked by its frankness. Others will look at it and remark: 'Why, the dirty old stinker!' Still others will know at once that Old Jules is the neighbor they knew and that Mari has done the job her father wanted her to do."[22]

Along with admiration came considerable criticism from those throughout the state who disagreed with or questioned her picture of the sandhills, but the most common complaint concerned her brutal frankness in revealing her father's character. On the other hand, some readers sympathized with Mari for having to live under such difficult conditions. She did not want pity, for she felt that few men were given either such courage or such self-love as Old Jules. Although it appeared that the women and children of his family had been sacrificed to his ego, they had actually been privileged to "look upon the lightning." It was only rarely, she felt, that a unique man gave the rest of the world a glimpse of the life denied the ordinary person.[23]

The author's ability to detach herself from her early life allowed her to write without undue emotion of her father's ruthlessness. At the time she was researching and writing the book, her friends noted her means of objectifying the father-daughter relationship. Mari often called her father "the old man" or "Old Jules," but she did not feel it particularly disrespectful, since he was an old man and everyone called him Old Jules or worse. She seemed able to view Jules as a dual personality. She would speak of him historically in an unemotional way but immediately afterward refer to him as Papa when telling an anecdote about him. In her correspondence and notes she referred to him as Father and Papa, as did others in the family, but when he became the subject of her writing she could place him outside of family ties by calling him Old Jules.[24] None of the other children referred to him by a nickname, except for an occasional "Dada" when he was out of earshot.

When charged with forming a distorted picture of her father or the country, Mari invariably replied that every incident could be authenticated.[25] Once she had done her very thorough research and made up her mind about something, she saw no reason to change it. A resident of Knox County, where Jules had first homesteaded, for instance, discovered in 1936 two 1883 affidavits for marriage licenses for Jules A. Sandoz. One listed his age as twenty-three, the other as twenty-five, and each named a different woman as potential spouse, one listing Estelle (Stella) Thompson and the other a Mlle Balmer. Mari had not been aware of the second application with its discrepancies in age and other details, but the situation was perfectly in keeping with the character of Old Jules as she knew it and tried to picture it. She reminded her correspondent that Jules was never certain of his age or that of any of his children, so the age discrepancy was not surprising, and there was no evidence that Mlle Balmer was more to him than just one of the many settlers he wrote to in an effort to bring them to his new settlements. She did admit, however, that he always seemed to be in need of a wife and probably "had hopes."[26]

When Elmer Sturgeon, one of the early settlers appearing in many episodes of the book, wrote her shortly after its publication, recalling some details of the well episode that varied from her version, she was sharp in her own defense of both her methods and her interpretation. Although the old neighbor's letter was cordial, Mari reacted sharply to the implied criticism of her information, recalling that she had tried to interview him in 1930 and 1931 but that he had not been at home, and that she had sent him a three-page questionnaire which he had not returned. Explaining how she had arrived at her understanding of the situation, she pointed out that she had investigated endless sources: letters, interviews, medical records at Fort Robinson,

Dr. Walter Reed's account as he got it from the soldiers, the account Jules Aubert sent to Switzerland, Old Jules's letters, and a goodly bundle of a Mr. Matthew's badly spelled but authentic letters. She was sorry she had not known some of the details he had included, for they were truly typical of her father. Mr. Sturgeon also contended that Jules had not filed on the Flats until after his own group had filed their claims in June 1884. Here, too, she disagreed. Although no two stories of the dozens she had on this subject bore any resemblance to each other, she had considered what she thought to be the weightiest historical evidence, the letters and documents of the time, and again listed sources. There was a letter written by Rosalie, Jules's sweetheart back in Switzerland, acknowledging one he had sent her from Mirage Flats on 28 April 1884; another from his friend Charles Nippel at Verdigre, dated early May 1884, responding to Jules's enthusiastic report of the Flats; and others.[27]

Characteristically, in both cases Mari refused to change her mind or her story, trusting to her prodigious research and study. At some point before she began to write a book, she would begin to formulate the character of her people according to her source material. Once she had determined its validity, other views could not shake her. Her conclusions appear to have been remarkably accurate in the light of later historical research.[28]

She did not, however, consider her writing flawless; she never felt that any of her works matched her own original expectations and apparently could not bear to read them once they were in print. She admitted that the finished product never lived up to her first image of it, although she admired the cover design and frontispiece of *Old Jules*.[29]

Why was this prize-winning book so often rejected and why was it ultimately so well received? Undoubtedly a very large problem the author had to overcome was that of locale. The area she wrote of was practically unknown to the East—the sandhills of Nebraska, a relatively small, isolated, sparsely populated, marginal farm area. The scenery is not spectacular or breathtaking; the people were mostly ranchers and farmers; the towns were small, dusty, unremarkable. A region that "for years had been looked upon as the Creator's waste material dumping place," according to one Nebraska newspaperman,[30] the land, hard hit by the long drouth of the thirties, was worth almost nothing at the time the book was published. Attempts to interest publishers in such a remote and unglamorous area were almost always futile. Vardis Fisher, who encountered similar frustrations in getting published, wrote scathingly of what he considered a major problem for serious western writers: "To bury most of the serious writing in the West by trying to discredit it, not with knowledge, of which they have too little, but with adolescent wit or malicious distortion, has been the objective of the Establishment's critics as far back as I have looked at the record."[31] This provincialism of easterners who failed to see beyond the popular streotype of the American West, this East-West dichotomy, would affect Mari Sandoz's relations with her editors and publishers throughout her career.

There were other reasons for the book's fourteen rejections as it went from one publisher to another. The anecdotal, plotless shape was criticized often. In its final revision, this structure works well, but the "beads on a string" book is difficult to manage well. As Kathleen Walton points out, the strength of the book is the author's ability as a storyteller; its weakness is its structure.[32] Her language, too, as the critics noted even after publication, sometimes proved difficult. In her zeal to employ sandhills terms, she sometimes took too much for granted in assuming her readers would ferret out her meanings. In addition, her book included shockingly frank language for the time. Mari made no effort to supply euphemisms in the dialogue. When her characters swore, she included the swear words. When they talked of subjects usually avoided in books of that period, she did not omit them. The biggest hurdle was her main character, Jules himself. He was a strange protagonist—a dirty old man, often mean, cruel, vindictive. Publishers did not believe their readers would be interested in someone like that.

In spite of all these strikes against it, the judges for the Atlantic Press praised *Old Jules* unanimously when they awarded it the first prize, and their judgment proved accurate. But they were not judging the early versions. Although none of the early manuscripts are extant, it is reasonable to suppose that some of the early criticisms were valid and that Mari attempted to rework the material accordingly. She always revised her work extensively, and with good reason. As she remarked, none of her own writing students ever wrote as bad a first copy as she did. Her unpublished works are uneven in almost every aspect: plot line, structure, language, characterization, believability, even grammar. Some of these faults undoubtedly existed in the early versions of *Old Jules*. Mari's sister Flora, who read the 1932 manuscript rejected in the first Atlantic Press contest, recalled that the final book was much superior, much more mature in outlook, with less sense of accusation. Edward Weeks also pointed out to Mari that the 1935 version was markedly better than the one he had seen three years earlier.[33]

The long, long stretch of writing and rewriting was onerous, yet it had tremendous therapeutic value. By the time the final manuscript was accepted, the author had achieved the necessary objectivity. Her early years of long apprenticeship allowed her to write out the bitterness and frustration she felt, to come to terms with her relationship with both her mother and her father and to rid her work of the self-pity of such early stories as "Dumb Cattle" and "Murky River." She now had the aesthetic distance, perhaps the most remarkable feature of the work, to present both the good and the bad in her father, her family, and her region. It is the portrait of her father, objected to by so many publishers, that is the strength of the book. His relationship to his region and the effect each had on the other were recognized by readers as Mari had hoped; but it was Jules himself who made the book a success, as she later learned when she wrote of others in her region whom the public did not find so colorful. Without her dispassionate portrait of Jules, the book, no matter how well written otherwise, would not have become the classic it is. There is no other book in American literature quite like it.

Six
Two Thematic Novels

With the publication of *Old Jules* imminent, Mari resigned her job at the Nebraska State Historical Society on 1 September 1935. She had enjoyed her work at the society. She was busy right up to the end, helping her coworkers move from the ninth floor of the state capitol tower to their new location on the first floor, and she continued her close association with them for many years. But now the career she had sought for so long took all her attention. There were suddenly luncheons, teas, and other functions in her honor; newspaper and magazine interviews; and requests for articles and lectures. Her second trip east, two weeks in October and November, went much better than the first. The weather was comfortable and she took pleasure in seeing a Van Gogh show as well as in meeting new people interested in writing and publishing.[1]

Soon after her return, the *Lincoln Star* noted that the "Busy" sign was again on her door at the J Street apartment, "the cell where she cloistered herself for years turning out *Old Jules*."[2] She was back at work on *Slogum House*, the novel started during her 1933 trip home to the sandhills. For the setting of the story, a grim one, she used an imaginary area, two fictitious counties and an oxbow on the Niobrara River in northwestern Nebraska. Her main character, Gulla Slogum, is a ruthless, will-to-power woman who extends her power through the members of her family until she controls the entire region. On the surface, the story is one of violence and mystery in the struggle for land in a small portion of the West, but Mari intended it to be an allegorical study of a domineering nation using force to overcome opposition.

The idea had come from a number of sources: from her shock as a child at seeing people live entirely and deliberately off their own kind, and from John Hicks's course in frontier history. She had long criticized the power of the eastern industrialists and bankers in America. Her reading of the European novelists Franz Kafka, Thomas Mann, André Malraux, and Jules Romain influenced her, together with a few, a very few, American writers she felt worthwhile, such as Willa Cather and Theodore Dreiser. But the book that influenced her most was Adolf Hitler's *Mein Kampf*. She had watched him gain power in the early 1930s, and now he was rearming Germany while Italy's Mussolini was invading Ethiopia unopposed by the civilized world. She thought all too many Americans were attracted to the fascist ideas of those two demagogues, and she feared that Hitler would one day invade the United States. She wanted to demonstrate the evil of greed, to her the worst of all sins, and to study the effects of individual megalomania, which fascinated her in the years of the great dictators, Hitler, Mussolini, and Stalin.[3]

Never satisfied to work on one idea at a time, Mari outlined a Polish novel for the Atlantic Press. She had been interested in this ethnic group since her childhood, when a Polish family had lived across the river on the Niobrara, and had four Polish stories in her collection. Although she never developed the novel further, her interest in these people can be found throughout her writing; in the Polish wedding chapter in *Old Jules*; a short story, "River Polak," later published in the *Atlantic*; a short tale, "The Daughter"; and the Polish girl in *Capital City*.

The symbolism Mari saw in the state capitol tower, which was to be the predominant image for her at all times when she lived in Lincoln, was also the basis for a short story, "Mist and the Tall White Tower," published in 1936 in *Story*. To her friend Paul Hoffman she described the tall white tower with its golden dome and its band of blue thunderbirds, concluding sardonically, "The sower treads his stationary way, casting his futile seed upon the dying earth."[4] She admitted that was a false note, but it fitted the mood of the story, in which the state capitol itself can do nothing to alleviate the problems of the people it serves. All of the symbols honoring the pioneers and the carved words promising equality before the law prove to be meaningless for her young hero. The story illustrates in fine detail the author's concern for the farmers who had earned their land, working against incredible odds, only to lose it to the foreclosures that occurred in appalling numbers during the twenties and thirties.

Her Indian material continued to hold her interest, too. After her first trip in 1930 with Eleanor Hinman, Mari had returned to the reservations in 1931 and 1932 to continue her research on the Sioux and Cheyennes and had written several articles about them. One long feature story in the *Lincoln Journal and Star* in 1931 was based on her 1930 trip, and since 1932 she had been sending out to publishers various accounts, both factual and fictionalized, of the great Indian council of 1875 at which the United States tried to persuade the Sioux to give up the Black Hills. In 1934 she was working on two Indian narratives, and in 1935 she again sent out "The Great Council" several times, but it was repeatedly rejected.[5] Lincoln newspapers reported that year that she had several notebooks of information on the Oglala Sioux and planned research in the Indian country as the probable basis for her next book. But she feared that writing two works of nonfiction in succession would stereotype her and might restrict her field of endeavor.[6] Since she believed authors should vary their style according to genre—biography, fiction, or belles lettres—she chose to publish her allegorical novel first.

One aspect of Mari's life did not change much. Used to poverty, she continued to be thrifty. She paid off her outstanding notes quickly and had money she could lend to friends, but she told one of the many strangers who asked for money that she owned neither a radio nor a car and she still made over her own clothes.[7] She continued to live in the fifteen-dollar-a-month apartment at 1226 J Street.

In spite of the "Busy" sign, Mari still had time for her friends among the creative people of Lincoln. Helen Mary Hayes from the *Journal* was a particular friend. Perhaps it was she who introduced Mari to the world of modern art, a major interest they shared all their lives. Mari also counted among her friends

Louise Austen, Leonard Thiessen, Dwight Kirsch, Weldon Kees, and other artists. As for her writer friends, she read their manuscripts with infinite patience, encouraging them and sometimes lending them money. Others, too, connected with the arts, journalism, and academia claimed her friendship. Although some found her aloof, others saw her as gregarious when time permitted and she alluded to her apartment as the town hangout. Some found her a good confidante, though she herself thought it strange since she seldom offered sympathy or pity. She heard so many intimate revelations that she called her favorite booth in the Cornhusker Hotel coffee shop "agony corner."[8]

Mari had her share of romance as well. Responding to a magazine article entitled "Sex in Biography," she argued that while she did not agree with Freud that sex was everything, still she believed there never was a man or woman worth anything who had not been affected in some way by sex.[9] Several men proposed marriage and people speculated about her private life, circulating rumors that connected her with one man or another. Nevertheless, she preferred her career. She told one suitor she detested anything domestic.[10] She recognized that she could not divide her interests, and writing was more important to her than marriage.

Inundated with letters from readers of *Old Jules* and concerned about new social pressures because of its publication, Mari had a severe recurrence of migraines. She was also disappointed because MGM dropped the option on the book when Irving Thalberg became ill and died, although she heard that David O. Selznick was still considering it.

Her new affluence allowed Mari to escape from Lincoln's heat that summer of 1936, to the cool, high mountains of Estes Park, Colorado, to finish *Slogum House*, which had occupied her winter and early summer. She sent it off to the Atlantic Press in August, hoping now to begin her long-postponed Indian book. Instead, angry letters were soon flying back and forth between the author and Edward Weeks. This time Mari was not about to allow any major changes in her work, any elimination of her westernisms: she would guard them as her mother used to guard the family dinner against premature reachings, "with a knife handle against the knuckles."[11] When Weeks spoke of the potential eastern market for the book, she replied that she did not care about the whole raft of readers, or critics either. As to specific points Weeks wanted clarified, she recognized that *Slogum House* still had weak points, and she was willing to rewrite to make clear to her readers that both the framework and foundation of the book were based on the contrast of eastern and frontier civilizations, but she wanted freedom to do it her way. When Weeks asked her to come to Boston to discuss it in person, she refused. "This time there would be nothing to keep me from throwing you a kiss and departing in my highest manner when my Old Julesian temper got to building."[12] She refused to allow *Slogum House* to be serialized or cut in any way, even if it meant the book would bring in more money.

Still angry about editorial suggestions when the manuscript was returned to her in October, Mari was not sure she would ever send it back. She was planning a trip to Europe and she might just forget *Slogum House* for a while. Although it might not be a great novel, she wanted it to be as significant as she could make it. She was anxious, too, to get to other writing. There were many ideas she wanted to carry out, and since the success of *Old Jules* she was showered with requests she would like to fulfill. *Country Gentleman* published her article about her mother, "The New Frontier Woman," in September 1936, and Bernard DeVoto, a fellow westerner sympathetic to her ideas, insisted that she must have something available for *Saturday Review of Literature*. The *Saturday Evening Post* was also interested in her work, as were several other periodicals.

Mari wanted to work with her Indian material; since 1930 she had been interested in the Oglala Sioux chief Man Afraid of His Horse, and she had also been collecting notes on the Cheyennes. Now she decided, after much consideration, to delay the Man Afraid book, since both Eleanor Hinman and A. E. Sheldon were still working on their biographies of Crazy Horse and Red Cloud, men of the same tribe and contemporaries of her subject.[13] Although she was sure neither would finish, she felt ethically bound to give them a little more time. Furthermore, she thought she could handle the Indian psychology of the Cheyenne story more easily than the Sioux biography, since the Young Man Afraid story would deal with troubles within the tribe, whereas the Cheyenne conflict was between the Indians and whites.

Definitely committed to the Cheyenne book now, Mari planned her archival research and interviews for "Flight to the North"—the original title. It would describe "the tragic, epic escape of the disarmed and dismounted Cheyennes" under Little Wolf and Dull Knife in the winter of 1878 from Indian Territory toward Montana, pursued by "the whole frontier and the United States army," aided by personnel, equipment, and communication assistance from frontier forts, the transcontinental railroads and telegraph.[14] She was already familiar with the general events of the story from her research at the Nebraska State Historical Society and her interviews on the reservations, and she recalled the stories told her as a child by Old Cheyenne Woman and the other survivors of the Cheyenne massacres and battles. She was only postponing the Sioux biography, however; she had spent too much time collecting material to drop it.

Mari also had at least five good nonfiction books in mind to write about the plains; for the first time she mentioned her Great Plains series by name.[15] But her ideas were not yet crystallized and she would change her mind several times about which books to include. One problem that worried her, foreshadowing later difficulties, was that of plagiarism. She warned her secretary (she was now affluent enough to have her manuscripts typed) to be very careful not to let any material get out of her hands. Someone might copy a story and try to market it. Until a story was published, she feared, the writer had no protection from a plagiarist. An editor had written her that someone was sending around a story she had thrown away, some garbage man or his daughter, she supposed.[16]

Mari put off her plans for the European trip that fall and returned to revising *Slogum House*, a task not made any easier by a severe attack of jaundice.[17] The battles with her editors and publishers lasted throughout the winter and into the spring and summer of 1937. During the verbal skirmishes with Edward Weeks, even Alfred McIntyre, president of Little, Brown, became involved. Mari was angry not only because of their criticism of her colloquialisms, unjustified in her eyes because her terms expressed her meaning better than the formal language of scholars, but also because they disagreed with her depiction of the West as a ravished colonial region in the period of which she was writing. She charged that the editors did not object to her portrayal of her characters as strange and grotesque, but refused to agree that they were so because of the treatment of their region by the East. She suggested irritably that the Atlantic Press should keep to writers "whose meat is not 'strong' with the natural flavor of my bitter prairie sage," and announced that she had no intention of deodorizing her work.[18] McIntyre attempted to placate her, assuring her that the book was indeed suitable for their list and promising that the editorial work done on *Old Jules* which had so annoyed her would not occur again. The manuscript she sent in would be considered final except for routine copy editing.

As with *Old Jules*, much of the trouble stemmed from her use of language. Although *Slogum House* was fiction, Mari had researched the speech patterns of people in Ohio in the 1880s and 1890s as well as the language of the sandhills. She knew the use of colloquialisms in *Old Jules* had been successful; a woman who had homesteaded and taught in an area of northwestern Nebraska populated by Germans, French, and Bohemians had even written to her, "How much an Easterner or a Twentieth Century Westerner misses in your pioneer Western vocabulary. What an assembling of choice bits of speech which I have not heard for years."[19] The author won the battle for *Slogum House;* Weeks reported that while the spelling and punctuation would be in accord with Atlantic Press usage, the text would follow her original without deviation. He went through each sheet of proofs himself to be sure the colloquialisms had not been tampered with. He admitted that he understood why she was prepared to fight for their retention, "for the truth is that the idiom, however it may differ from more formal syntax, is the very breath of the book."[20] Mari replied graciously, thanking him for his tolerant attitude toward the idiosyncrasies of her style and approach.

There were irritations that did not have to do with editing alone, however. *Old Jules* had been running in a German magazine, *Atlantis Verlag*, beginning in January 1937, but Mari discovered it by chance some months later and was not notified by her publishers until she wrote them about it, observing ironically that she was "only the author." When Harold Ober, attempting to place the book with English publishers at her request, succeeded in signing a contract with Chapman and Hall, she remarked it was too bad Little, Brown had let so much time go by without making the sale, that had Ober had the commission earlier he could have sold it much sooner. Although Ober pointed out that Little, Brown had offered it to fourteen English companies, all of whom rejected it, her dissatisfaction with the publishers continued. When Paul Hoffman left the company in 1937, Mari was delighted he had escaped the Atlantic Press and Boston—the people, not the city—and she cursed her western sense of obligation that held her to them.[21]

Old Jules was chosen as the *Evening Standard* Selection of the Month, the English equivalent of the Book-of-the-Month Club, assuring its success there. English reviewers were impressed. The *Evening Standard* remarked that it "knocked the stuffing out of the covered wagon sentimental epic: strong men and comely virtuous women, the one with a banjo and the other with a baby on the knee." The *London Observer* noted the author's candor about her father, "as impersonal as the weather, and sometimes as devastating."[22] All the reviewers observed with interest the struggles of the pioneers with the weather.

The revision of *Slogum House* was only one of the affairs concerning Mari in 1937. Always interested in politics and herself a liberal, she was a close observer during the opening week of that year's session of the Nebraska state legislature, meeting in January for the first time as a unicameral, nonpartisan body. Mari's friend, Nebraska's liberal independent senator George W. Norris, who had worked actively since 1932 for reform of the old bipartisan, bicameral legislature, was home from Washington to address the opening session. And after fourteen years in the Boston home on J Street, Mari moved to a new apartment building, the Shurtleff Arms at Seventeenth and H streets, even closer to the capitol—one block east of it. Her windows overlooked its eastern façade. The apartment was really too grand for her, she thought, but she had much more room for her writing materials. She was still within walking distance of the Cornhusker Hotel and her favorite booth in the coffee shop.

That spring Mari gave two speeches, "Stay Home, Young Writer," to Chi Delta Phi, honorary women writers' society, and "Nebraska's Place in the New Literature" to the Nebraska Writers Guild. In the two talks she outlined the advantages and disadvantages of the writer's craft. In the first speech she called attention to the state's rich resources for writers. Nebraska had material great enough for a Tolstoi, Balzac, or Hardy. "No matter where you may come from in Nebraska there is always someone near you who has seen the Indians moved out, and the settlers rush in." She stated the theme that became the *raison d'être* for her Great Plains series: "Here, within one lifetime, we have assembled the conflicts of nationalities and races from all over the world, from the first settlers who came in by way of Bering Straits to the last Mexican, perhaps smuggled in only last night . . . society from the stone age to the present, one whose processes are not lost in antiquity." She stressed her interest in the farmer—"For me the most important themes of Nebraska will always be those of the farmer and his dispossession"—and touched on the idea of writing about the capital city: "And then there is Lincoln. If I could choose my talent, I should want to be a modern Aristophanes and do a biting satire of our city called the *Light on the Tower.*" She urged young writers to stay in the state, for it was not good for a writer to wander too far from the region with which he was emotionally identified.[23]

In her second speech Mari reiterated her belief that Nebraska could fulfill a writer's need for subject matter, but, ironically, this speech foreshadowed the dilemma she would soon face. She felt Nebraska was exceptionally unkind to its artists, often treating them as moral reprobates or assuming that because they did not work at conventional jobs they were lazy. "Never will they credit any Nebraska writer who happens to be critical of the contemporary scene with anything better than mere personal disgruntlement."[24]

Mari was also engrossed in her Cheyenne research much of

the year. She already had a good deal of information, but there were still many holes to fill. When Edward Weeks asked her in March 1937 if her book would be ready for late fall publication, she told him it would take another year, possibly two, for research. A second summer at Estes Park alleviated her struggle with the Lincoln humidity she hated so. From Estes she went to the Pine Ridge Reservation and on to Lame Deer, Montana, for interviews. That fall she went on the first real vacation of her life, to New Mexico for two weeks. She and friends from Lincoln, Helen Bixby and Peg and Bob Ferguson, toured the pueblos and spent time with old friends now living in Taos and Sante Fe. She visited the writers' colonies in both communities but was not attracted to their way of life.[25]

Slogum House came out in November 1937 and drew mixed notices from the critics. Several observed, as the author had hoped, that the book showed her tremendous literary power, proving that she was not a one-book author. Howard Mumford Jones, writing one of the more favorable reviews, which appeared in the *Saturday Review of Literature*, called it a powerful, somber novel, its opening chapter one of the most graphic in recent fiction and Gulla the best character depiction since Balzac. "Gulla looms out of the book like a malevolent spirit. The selfish cunning of insatiable desire has seldom been more sweepingly given in fiction." The book was, as Mari predicted, controversial. One friend described it as "viewed as a work of genius by one school of thought and carried gingerly to the ashcan by paler academic souls."[26]

In Nebraska the latter reaction was the most common. The strong language and violent action caused a furor. Dan Butler, mayor of Omaha, banned the book as "rotten" (although he admitted he had not read it);[27] it was also banned in McCook, in the western part of the state, and many libraries kept it on the special reserve shelf along with books about sex and other forbidden topics. In the sandhills, the book suffered the fate of so many novels based on a recognizable locale. Those who thought they recognized the actual prototypes for the book's characters were angry, and those who were sure the characters were entirely fictitious were angry. The *Hay Springs News* stated that the author might just as well have used the real name for the roadhouse "because most readers of the book know or have known each character in life." John Peters, one of the settlers who had appeared in *Old Jules*, argued from the other point of view: "In the 45 years I have lived in Sheridan County, I can truthfully say there never existed a family that was anything like the people in *Slogum House*." Elmer Sturgeon, also an old pioneer in *Old Jules*, stated the general sense of concern: "It would not be fair to place all in the class she principally portrays in *Slogum House*."[28]

In spite of her warning about Nebraska's treatment of writers in her speeches earlier that year, Mari was surprised and hurt by the animosity. She felt she had not exaggerated the truth, and no one recognized the allegory—the attempt at social criticism through the graphic, the concrete, the realistic. She insisted that the setting and characters were imaginary, but some readers, especially in the sandhills, did not agree. Her mail, however, corroborated her remarks in one particular: Gulla, at least, seemed to be a universal figure. People all over North America wrote that they knew Mari had been in their community, for there could be only one person like Gulla, and she lived in their vicinity.

A great deal of criticism came from Lincoln citizens, too, more than Mari had anticipated. After the publication of *Old Jules*, some readers had castigated her as an undutiful daughter, but she had shrugged it off. Now, however, strangers came up to her on the street and spoke disparagingly of her writing. She began to receive hate mail and finally reported to the police that she was being threatened.[29]

In January and February of 1938 Mari escaped the local critics by going to Washington, D.C., to delve into the government archives. As she discovered material pertinent to her Indian books, she thoroughly enjoyed her investigations, which often bordered on detective work. The archives at that time were housed casually in several buildings, including old garages, warehouses, and lofts. The records she sought were sometimes still in bundles of three-inch tubes, tied with mule twine, just as they had arrived from the western army posts in the 1800s and never opened by the records office in Washington. At times she came upon papers and reports that later disappeared from the public records when the archives were moved to a new building a few years later.[30] The information she gathered was sometimes contradictory, but she found much no contemporary historian had seen or was aware of. Deep into her research for *Flight* that winter, she was also alert for material useful to the Nebraska State Historical Society. She told A. E. Sheldon about maps and blueprints that might be helpful for his Red Cloud book and at his request duplicated them for the society.

Typically, Mari was writing or thinking about several manuscripts simultaneously. Returning to Lincoln, she broke the monotony of serious work by spending three months, wasting it she declared, on a novelette.[31] It was probably "The Girl in the Humbert," which she later sold to the *Saturday Evening Post*. She wrote it to relieve the tension of her serious research and writing, as well as for money. The reworking of an earlier, unsuccessful story, it was a pot boiler, and she was not proud of it.[32] Then, once more returning to her Cheyenne research, she visited several midwestern historical societies. The Cheyenne story was shaping up to be magnificent; she hoped she could master it.

In June 1938, *Old Jules* was dramatized as a pageant for the fiftieth anniversary celebration of Alliance, forty miles from Mirage Flats. Mari, always interested in local opinion of her work, was delighted that the town chose *Old Jules* and attended the performance. Now she could point out that her book was indeed accurate; many of the characters still living attended the performance and could vouch for its truth. As she wrote one doubter:

About the authenticity of *Old Jules:* no one in our regions would question it. In fact the town of Alliance made a play of the story for their anniversary and the rehearsals were always full of people who came to see that the story was put on as the book had it, and they were qualified to speak, for they were the characters in the book. I made up nothing but the dialogue and even that I either heard or had it told to me so many times.[33]

One of the high points of Mari's life, this event was a combination family reunion and old-home week, and she the star of the affair. She had another reason to cherish the occasion, for her mother, who was ill, was able to be there and received much of the attention. Mary died that fall. Although there had been conflicts, Mari valued her mother and tried hard in many ways to please her.

Because her mother's death necessitated financing the Sandoz ranch to keep it in the family and because she wanted to help her brother Jule enlarge his own ranch, Mari attempted negotiations with Hollywood to film either *Old Jules* or *Slogum House*, but despite several promising nibbles, neither was taken up.[34] *Slogum House* had too many scenes in it that Hollywood was not yet ready to put on film, and both books had a leading character difficult to cast.

Wider recognition as a writer and historian was beginning to come to Mari, however. The University of Iowa invited her to be one of the speakers at their creative writers' workshop the following summer. The list of other writers invited included John Frederick, Archibald MacLeish, John Steinbeck, Ruth Suckow, Wallace Stegner, Donald Davidson, and Josephine Johnson. Mari had long been interested in Iowa's creative writing experiment and had hoped earlier to be able to finance a year there, but she had not been able to manage it. Her short story instructor, Melvin Van den Bark, had studied there.

Mari pointed out that her approach to writing might not be a very good one, since she worked by the most grueling method imaginable. Because her verbatim memory was poor, she constantly jotted down bits and scraps of dialogue, events, and ideas and stuffed them into shopping bags, hooked by one handle so that they hung open for easy filling. When she was ready to do her plotting, she would sort and assemble all the hodgepodge, usually chronologically. From these bits would come her first draft, handwritten on long sheets of yellow paper clipped to a writing board and looking like squares of a crazy quilt clipped together in one corner. A most important element of her writing was her revising. Some authors could revise in their minds, like Galsworthy, who might write only half a dozen lines a day after mulling them over and over, but her method was a torturous rewriting after rewriting. She composed in longhand, slowly and painfully, revising her work repeatedly, then typed the manuscript. She wrote in longhand first because she was concerned for the rhythm of her prose and found it easier to get the pattern into the prose that way. When she began her first draft, she would buy ten reams of paper, knowing that it would not be enough. The first drafts were done very rapidly; often she would not even complete words or sentences. She was after movement and characterization and felt they came best when she worked rapidly. After the first rough draft was completed, she would cut the book into sections or chapters. Then she would interline, write on the back, cut and paste until the book began to feel as if it were whole, a process that recalls the mother bear in the old Indian myths who licks her cub until he assumes the shape she wants.

One should not aim for the polished paragraph too soon, Mari believed; she would revise until she got the whole picture of what she wanted to do. Then she could go back. Her first drafts were very bad. She reported that she sometimes revised a page "fifty or sixty times."[35] This may be an exaggeration, but one friend saw her rework a short article for the *Lincoln Journal and Star*, "I Remember Lincoln," eighteen times.[36] Although many revisions of her books were destroyed, her papers contain ample evidence of her method.

In revising Mari aimed for a tighter plot structure, intensification of language and action, and a more subtle theme. The last revisions were for sentence rhythm and the elimination of unpleasant repetitions of sound. She would work for days with bits here and there in the conviction that a book could not be denied, once it was out. A child could be disowned, but not a book. She was fond of that analogy, and it aptly explains her intensity toward her work. Once her book was published, whatever was good or bad about it would be credited to her: it was her reputation, no matter how many publishers' revisions and emendations had come between her original manuscript and the final version.

At this time an offer came Mari wanted very much to accept. She was asked to write the story of Robert Henry Cozad, who became famous as Robert Henri, painter and teacher of the Ashcan school. His father, a gambler and visionary, had founded the town of Cozad, Nebraska, and then had disappeared with his family after killing a man. Much of the story had never come out and modern-day residents of the community had little knowledge of the events. The offer flattered her, because a member of the Cozad family would not allow anyone to work on the material whose integrity and artistic skill he did not trust. But the project would have to wait; Mari told him it would be at least 1942 before she could work on it. She had the Cheyenne book ahead of her and others in the planning stage.[37]

The Cheyenne research had to be put aside the fall of 1938 because of her mother's illness and death, and Mari could see that she would not be ready to write the book that winter. Instead she turned to a theme she had been contemplating for some time, that of a midwestern city whose existence depended almost entirely on government payrolls. At first she called the work "State Capital" and intended to write it as a satirical play, but soon decided she could best utilize the material in a novel, and that she could handle allegory better than satire.[38] The setting was to be contemporary, the time period short, from the state fair in early September to election time in November. She had no one capital city in mind, but wanted to reveal what she saw as a trend in the capital cities of the Middle West, towns that produced little, that had little commerce, but lived off the state capitol and the adjacent university—parasites, just as Washington, D.C., seemed to her the archparasite. In preparation Mari subscribed to newspapers from ten capital cities between the Mississippi and the Rockies, from Bismarck to Oklahoma City; wrote to the chambers of commerce at Pierre, Des Moines, Jefferson City, and elsewhere for pertinent information; visited each of the ten state capitals; then organized her index cards; drew a map of the mythical state of Kanewa—obviously an acronym for Kansas, Nebraska, Iowa—and set to work briskly on the new novel.

To this new work she brought much experience. She knew many people in state government, often through her earlier work at the Nebraska State Historical Society. Nebraska supreme court justice Bayard H. Paine published several articles in *Nebraska*

History and he and Mari corresponded on many matters of mutual historical interest. Nebraska governors were always ex officio members of the society board and state senators were often concerned with the society's work. Moreover, as a historian, Mari was always alert to the workings of government. Even her childhood experiences contributed to this, as she commented: "The underpriviliged child, if he becomes a writer, is interested in social justice and in the destruction of discrimination between economic levels, between nationalist levels, between color levels, and so on. This is the kind of conflict on which he will do his best writing."[39]

Mari was sharply aware of deficiencies in state government. Nineteen thirty-eight was still a depression year. Always sympathetic to the underdog, she was distressed about the plight of the workers and farmers. She remembered the milk riots organized by Iowa farmers, and she had been in Lincoln in 1933 when the desperate farmers had marched silently, over four thousand of them, on the state capitol to demand assistance. Most had not been given relief; many had lost their farms. There had been thousands of foreclosures in the Middle West. Now, in 1938, after so many farms had been lost, the Nebraska state legislature declared a moratorium on farm mortgages—an event her *Slogum House* had anticipated—but the state supreme court declared it unconstitutional. Mari wrote Edward Weeks that she had been deluged with calls, telegrams, and night letters, although she had no authority to do anything about the ruling. (Whether she did indeed receive such a deluge of mail and calls is a moot point; she tended to exaggerate her statistics when they related to her own life—to "throw in another bear" to impress her hearers, as the teller of tall tales expressed it in one of her books.)

Mari's disenchantment with Lincoln and her disillusionment with descendants of midwestern pioneers were of long standing, like her interest in politics. John Hicks's history class, with its emphasis on the Populist point of view, had helped to shape her view of the midwestern capital city as a parasite, although she had been disturbed even earlier about its role. A capital city influenced the thought and culture of its region, and she felt that certain attitudes and fears developing in such a city exploited that area of influence. As early as 1933 she had described Lincoln in that scathing letter to Eleanor Hinman as "the last word in decadent middle class towns, sterile and deadening." Furthermore, her own liberal political views in a city essentially conservative had created problems for her more than once. Her outspoken views had irritated some of her co-workers and board members of the Nebraska State Historical Society.

Mari seemed on occasion to mourn for past times and other places. She spoke of the advantages of the country or small town over the city. Life could be as full and rich in an outstate county as in the capital city, and certainly it was more genuine. The pioneers had belonged to a great generation of midwestern insurgents who could not be bought or frightened from their vision, but she felt that generation was almost gone, leaving no spiritual descendants. It seemed to her that the great tradition of midwestern liberalism—the agricultural liberalism of the Bryans, the LaFollettes, the Norrises—was doomed. She worried, too, that Nebraska was rapidly being taken over by absentee landlords. She was glad her father was dead and did not have to see his once prosperous region under the auctioneer's hammer, the local bankers benefiting from the forced sales, the state government helping the farmers little if at all. Surely a state that was willing to try something as new as a unicameral legislature, that could build a state capitol building of such beauty, and that had been the home of men like Bryan and Norris should be able to do more for its citizens. Although she admired the initiative that was giving farmer cooperatives a fair start in Nebraska and saw movement toward farmer-labor collaboration (an idea she had promoted for many years), her feeling about state government was that it must be tolerated, something like a club foot, not desirable, but not conveniently remediable.[40]

Mari was not a pessimist; she was, perhaps more than she realized, an idealist. She believed that although there were ills, people, once aware of them, could cure them, but she did not approve of some of the cures offered. Many writers, discouraged by the government's failure to solve the country's problems, became communists, but the extreme left never attracted Mari. She read the proletarian novels of the 1920s and '30s (some of her ideas in *Capital City* may have come from them), but she believed as strongly as her father in democracy. She had too much knowledge of the methods of the European dictators, too great a dislike for them, to believe their ways could solve the problems of the United States. More than the communists, however, she disliked and feared the rightist groups, patterned on the fascists of Europe, who called themselves Black Shirts, Silver Shirts, or Tan Shirts. Operating in various cities in the Middle West, they marched, wore uniforms, and acted as vigilantes. Mari abhorred their narrowness, fanaticism, and bigotry, and she feared their popular attraction.[41]

Because she could attack so many political problems, she enjoyed writing her protest novel, *Capital City*, more than many of her other books. Written between the fall of 1938 and August 1939, it was completed much faster than most of the others. Not that Mari deviated from her usual method of preliminary organization and subsequent revision. Always methodical, she organized her working environment carefully. Her top-floor apartment was dominated by a table, extended with leaves as far as it would go, holding a typewriter and stacks of papers, a separate stack for each character, who was individually written up practically from birth until she was through with him in the book.[42]

Each of the characters was to represent an aspect of the city in her "microcosmic study of the macrocosm of this world" that Mari hoped would recall Zola's *Germinal*.[43] In her view, man as a true individual had not existed since the time he found out that "with two or three other fellows from along down the cave wall, he had a better chance of killing the cave bear than he had by himself." From then on, he had started to lose his individuality. She had another analogy, too, from her college laboratory experiments on protozoa. She knew that protozoa tend to congregate in an optimum of light, warmth, and food and to stay together for protection from cold or an enemy. She saw similar patterns in human society, and she wanted to make society itself the protagonist. Before she began writing she determined her theme statement, her main characters and their dominant traits, the locale, and the situation or conflict. She wanted to experiment with an approach in which the main character was the city itself; the people were not to be individuals, but rather units in society.[44]

Using material from current newspapers on racist, antidemocratic individuals and groups, she fictionalized the various flukes and forces that led to a coup at election time by a shrewd rabble-rouser supported by a group of fascist "Silver Shirts." Although some characters are sympathetically presented, Mari did not intend her readers to find them attractive. They were "parasites, created by their environment, deprived of the power of positive action until it is too late."[45] She disclaimed any attempt to model them after actual persons: real individuals, according to her, were far more complex. She had to make all her characters fit the theme. She spoke of two of her characters as representing not two people, but two aspects of the artist in decaying society.[46]

The setting for the novel, the city of Franklin and the state of Kanewa, was also wholly a place of her mind, broadly general to the trans-Mississippi region, she insisted. The population and place names were to represent the world; the economy was primarily agrarian; the capital city ruled the area but did not produce. All the prototype cities, she asserted, had some state institutions, but none precisely those of Franklin. All had state fairs, but none a coronation, although in Nebraska, Omaha had its Ak-Sar-Ben and in Missouri, St. Louis had its Veiled Prophet Ball. In comparing the clippings from the various state capitals, she found them so similar she had to label them or she would not have been able to identify the locale of the items. Clippings from nearby commercial centers, on the other hand, showed a tremendous contrast, not only to the capitals but to each other.

Capital City was due at the publisher's in July 1939, but Mari, as always frantically finishing up details, was late again; she sent it in early August. Within days, appalled by her own bad writing, she asked to have the first three chapters returned for revision. Edward Weeks agreed that the chapters needed revising but seemed more concerned that she consult a Nebraska

lawyer about the possibility of libel.[47] Denying that any characters other than the few with well-known names like Norris or
Bryan were based on any one person, the author sent Weeks a
large group of clippings from the newspapers she had subscribed to, to support her contention that both the people and the
incidents in the novel were composites and assured him that she
did not use any of her material without some modifications.

The Atlantic Press accepted the manuscript with little enthusiasm, and Mari did not hesitate to criticize their lack of
interest. She wrote Jacques Chambrun, her agent, that she and
her publishers were equally bored with each other. Later she
complained to Chambrun about their sloppy job on the book;
part of the manuscript had been lost and the Atlantic Press had
not even realized it. She told him that before her Indian books
were written, she wanted out of the contract that gave them an
option on her next two books.

Capital City, published in November 1939, sold poorly. Mari
had remarked during the writing that the book was unlike anything she had ever seen; it had grown so convincing to her she
could hardly believe it was not the story of a real community; it
held even more actuality for her than *Old Jules*. The reading
public did not agree with her. Most of the reviews were, at best,
lukewarm. The *Nation* commented favorably on 16 December
1939, calling the book a substantial, sharp-visioned assault on
the fascist and near-fascist forces in America, but others felt it
suffered from the lack of a vital central character. B. E. Bettinger,
in the *New Republic* for 13 December 1939, remarked that "un-
alloyed spiritual earnestness is as hard to live with and for as
wickedness."

Mari never admitted that *Capital City* was less than a good
book, although she acknowledged that her choice of a city,
rather than an individual or a family, as a protagonist, caused
problems. She saw her two thematic novels, *Slogum House* and
Capital City, as companion books, intended to be read together,
to show what could happen if demagogues or the fascist state
gained control. *Capital City* could be the most important book of
the decade, she told a friend, "if it were read. But it won't be."[48]
Nevertheless, the book is an interesting experiment in writing,

and its allegorical aspects merit consideration. It is worthwhile reading today, after the fact of World War II, because of certain parallels one can see with actual events. But it is not a successful novel.

Capital City may not have caused much of a ripple nationwide, but it caused a considerable stir in Lincoln. Mari thought that Lincolnites would assume she was writing about their city in particular; it had been her home for some years. Moreover, she believed that few Lincolnites could conceive of any other capital city as being as important as theirs. She thought, however, that after reading the book they would be apt to be angry because they could not recognize incidents or individuals, since these were her inventions. Her friend Helen Mary Hayes, reviewing the book for the *Lincoln Evening Journal*, was more nearly correct when she prophesied, "Here are many men and women who will be recognized, rightly or wrongly, by many readers. Here is even a great deal of Mari Sandoz herself. It is a pity that the book is so much a *roman à clef*, for many readers will rush thru it, bent on identifying this one and that, and perhaps miss much of the point."[49] Her reaction is not surprising, for the foreword says: "Here, in the region that required far over a hundred years to settle, all the nations of the earth contributing, I have placed my state of Kanewa, with the high white tower of its capitol." Few places other than Lincoln had a state capitol building with a tower that fit that description.

Many Lincoln residents who read the book bitterly resented it, refusing to believe the author's assertion that it was an allegory and that the people in it were not based on those in Nebraska's capital city. One friend criticized both the subject matter and her approach to it. He suggested *Old Jules* had been a success because she knew what she was writing about. Now she had wandered off into fields of sociology and economics, in which her ideas were sketchy and vague. He referred to the Lincoln setting: "Also you did a little too much digging in manure piles," and concluded with another reference to Lincoln: "You must not go wandering afield in the direction of the sewage disposal plant."[50]

Mari reported to friends that she was harassed to the point

that it became more than annoying; it was sometimes frightening. Prominent people snubbed her. She was hissed at on the street and even, she claimed, spit upon on occasion. Newspapers reported that she was receiving obscene letters and threatening messages over the phone. Once she returned to her apartment to find her files rifled.[51] Some of her friends, knowing her flair for the dramatic, thought she was exaggerating. Yet others accepted her word, escorted her home, and checked regularly on her safety.[52] Her remark in her 1937 speeches to the Nebraska Writers Guild and Chi Delta Phi that Nebraska was unkind to its writers had come true for her.

Seven
Denver

Mari Sandoz suffered mixed fortunes that winter of 1939/40. She now had three books to her credit, and both *Old Jules* and *Slogum House* had European publishers; she also had placed several short stories and articles. But neither *Slogum House* nor *Capital City* sold as well as she had hoped, and she was facing hostility to both novels in Lincoln.[1] Then came an unexpected blow, an event more devastating than any other in her active career. She never overcame her resentment of the incident, yet it led directly to the writing of possibly her finest book, *Crazy Horse*. She learned that winter that the novelist Howard Fast was planning a book using the Cheyenne Indian story she had been researching for so long. His book would be ready for publication long before she could finish hers. A clipping Helen Blish sent her from the 10 December 1939 *New York Times* announced that Simon and Schuster had commissioned Howard Fast to fly to Oklahoma for research; his book was to be ready the following spring.[2]

Mari was furious: she considered it unethical to appropriate another writer's field of interest. She had begun her research long ago, and it was well known in eastern publishing circles that in 1936 she had started serious work on the double biography of the Cheyenne chiefs Dull Knife and Little Wolf, leaders in the trek of the Cheyennes from Indian Territory to Montana in 1878 and 1879. Her investigation had been postponed during her mother's illness, but she had hoped to finish by 1942. Protesting to her publishers, Atlantic, she questioned how Fast could do the research and writing in such a short time, when it had taken her years, even with her background in Indian and frontier history, to gather the necessary information.

Edward Weeks wrote Simon and Schuster for an explanation, but Max Schuster denied any conflict between the two books. Simon and Schuster's editor, Quincy Howe, outlined the intended content of Fast's novel: "The great migration and battle that the Cheyenne Indians fought against the United States Government in the late 1870's, after they had been marched off to the Indian Reservation, and then broke away to their original hunting grounds in Colorado. His book is to be of this particular episode." Fast had promised them the manuscript by May. Weeks passed this information on to Mari and suggested, "Since you know the domain so well and have been giving thought to it ever since your trip to Washington, why not get your own scalping knife out and beat him to it?"[3]

Mari recognized the two books would indeed deal with the same episode. She considered the possibility of serializing her story to beat Fast into print, since she planned to use the Indian point of view in her narrative and all her notes were taken with that in mind, but finally decided instead to put her manuscript away until Fast's book was "in the garbage dumps," at least ten years in the future. She did not feel she could rush her book into publication, and she had lost confidence in the Atlantic Press's ability to handle her work successfully under these conditions. She wanted out of her contract with them.[4]

At this point Eleanor Hinman, whose admiration for Mari's ablity had never wavered, offered her friend the use of her Crazy Horse material. Eleanor had suggested it once before, in 1938, so impressed had she been with *Slogum House*, but Mari refused it then. Eleanor's "preemption" of the material could perhaps be challenged on the basis of the length of time she had had it: almost ten years had elapsed since the trip to the reservations. She had delayed her writing in part because of lack of time and money for research in government archives in Washington, but Mari was uneasy; she feared that her friend would regret giving up the story that had absorbed her for so long. When Eleanor reaffirmed her offer, Mari turned from her Cheyenne material to that of the Oglala Sioux chief.[5] Mari later acknowledged her friend's generosity, dedicating the book "to Eleanor Hinman, who spent many faithful months on a biography of Crazy Horse and then graciously volunteered to relinquish her prior claim to me."

Long before she knew she would write the biography, Mari was drawn to Crazy Horse as a hero. He attracted her because of his ability as a leader, his personal qualities, and his tragic death, but, more important, she saw him as representing more than just one individual. Even though he lived in the nineteenth century on the plains and was an Indian war chief, his life had in it all the archetypal elements of a classical hero. He was exceptional in both appearance and actions: he had dreams and visions; he was called on for unusual sacrifice; he led his people well; and he was betrayed and killed. In addition, Mari wanted to portray "the processes utilized to defame, expropriate, and destroy a minority and its whole way of life."[6] Her minority, the Oglala Sioux, had something the Anglo-American majority wanted— the Black Hills with their precious metals—and suffered the lot of minorities anywhere in the world.

She had an additional emotional tie with Crazy Horse; she identified him with her own land. She was convinced that he had taken part in an incident on the spot where the Sandoz homestead was later located. The funeral scaffold of Conquering Bear, a Sioux peace chief, had been placed not far from Indian Hill. The chief, mortally wounded in the Grattan affair at Fort Laramie in 1854, was brought by his people to the Niobrara River, where he died. Mari, in her imagination, saw the part young Crazy Horse (known in his youth as Curly) would have played in this incident, his reaction and his emotions. As she wrote in her introduction:

Down there, about where our old Dyehouse cherry tree grew, they had built the death scaffold of Conquering Bear, their peace chief killed by the whites. And later I knew that if this was not the exact spot, it would not have been far from there, and that our gravel-topped Indian hill must be very much like the one to which young Curly fled for fasting and guidance in the confusion of his heart over this shooting by those who called themselves the white brothers of the Indian. Certain it was that the young Oglala had often walked this favorite camping ground of his people.

In March, after a short visit to the pueblos and cliff dwellings of New Mexico, Mari went to Washington, D.C., once more searching the archives for material both on the Cheyennes and the Oglala Sioux, now concentrating primarily on the Sioux.[7] When she returned to Lincoln, it was only to pack, put things in storage, and move to Denver. She maintained publicly that the crank calls and threats were not the cause of her move and that she wanted to do research in the Denver City Library Western Collections and the Colorado Historical Society.[8] Privately, however, she admitted the hostility in Lincoln caused by *Capital City* was sometimes frightening. The year 1940 was a time of inflamed emotions, and she had angered some readers with her political views on both local and national issues. She continued to be liberal in her politics, seeing much more good in President Roosevelt than did many of her fellow townsmen. Lincoln was strongly isolationist, its politics conservative. Many midwesterners tried desperately to believe the United States could keep out of war, that Europe's problems were not theirs. But while Mari was at heart a pacifist, she was also outspokenly antifascist.

She feared Hitler and predicted that the United States would soon be involved in the war. She seriously believed that Germany could win the war, that France and England would capitulate. She bet her friends Peg and Bob Ferguson and Helen Bixby that the Nazis would be in England by 15 July 1940. Although she was only too happy to pay the one-dollar bet when she lost, she warned another friend to "make hay fast, for the Nazis are coming faster. They'll be in Canada by fall, and in Mexico, I suspect."[9] The conclusion of *Capital City*, depicting a fascist, complete with troops, becoming governor of Kanewa through an election fluke, angered those Lincolnites who took her seriously.[10] They thought her a Cassandra.

The move to Denver began a whole new life for Mari. She found a modest apartment on "the hill," almost the only elevation in the city lying on the plain at the edge of the mountains.

She was four blocks from the state capitol, eight from the city library, and close to the civic center that lay between. Hers was one of a group of buildings named for authors, the Robert Browning, on the corner of Tenth and Sherman. Next door was the Carlyle; across the street was the Mark Twain. She had first contemplated a residence across from the spacious home of the Guggenheims, but characteristically chose the Browning because the rent was cheaper and the building was within walking distance of the library and the historical society.

The apartment had a bedroom, a Murphy bed in the living room, and a combination kitchen and breakfast nook. The latter, rather than her bedroom, would serve for her files this time. She announced to her friends that she had ample sleeping space for their visits, but there would be no cooking foolishness since the kitchen was one big filing cabinet. She was only two blocks from one cafe and four blocks from the Golden Lantern, which had very good food if one felt affluent. Her windows gave her a view of the mountains to the west when she was home long enough to enjoy it, but she was usually doing research during the day.[11]

Although the apartment served more as an office than as a home, Mari made one gesture toward decorating it, buying an oil painting, a still life, from her friend Leonard Thiessen. To the artist she wrote, "Its loaf of bread, its oilcloth bag and the daily paper, I think, is the soundness of the people they symbolize—the common folk of the world, the people who not only do the daily work of the world but from whom have always risen those who create the things of permanence, the beautiful, the noble and the wise. As revolution against all these things spreads, it is good to have at least their symbol before our eyes as long as we can."[12]

Denver itself was exhilarating. The climate, high and dry, suited Mari. There were universities and colleges nearby, and interest in all the fine arts. The playwright Fred Ballard reminded her that the summer stock company at Elitch's Gardens was one of the best in the country. Larger than Lincoln and far more cosmopolitan, Denver had foreign consulates and military installations expanding rapidly as the European situation became more ominous. As a government center, Denver offered sophistication and intrigues. She found here, as she had in Lincoln, political chicanery to keep her eye on, this time in city rather than state government. Even so, there was an easiness, a casualness, about the city that she liked.

Immediately accepted by the Colorado writing community, Mari was soon involved in a busier social life than she had led before. Her status as an author of three published books made her someone of interest, someone with knowledge to offer. She was self-possessed, self-assured; people found her personality and her appearance attractive. William F. Johns, president of the Colorado Authors guild, calling at her apartment to ask if she would speak at one of their meetings, was quite enchanted when she greeted him. She was drying her just washed long red hair and he found her appearance dramatic. By now she had determined her dress style and wore the browns, tans, rusts, and yellows that characterized her wardrobe the rest of her life. She did not dress in any particular current style, but chose tailored suits, skirts and blouses, or occasionally a tailored dress in colors that enhanced her skin tone and red hair.[13]

Mari was welcomed as an addition to the cultural community of artists and painters, authors and publishers, and patrons of the arts. Thomas Hornsby Ferril, the poet, essayist, and columnist, and his wife, Hellie, owner of the *Rocky Mountain Herald*, were friends she saw frequently. She also met Mary Chase, who later wrote the hit play *Harvey*; Ruth Beebe Hill, later the author of the best-selling novel *Hanta Yo*; Alan Swallow, then a professor at Denver University, later an outstanding western publisher; and Allen T. True, the artist who painted the murals in the Colorado state capitol rotunda and also illustrated the 1925 edition of John G. Neihardt's *Song of the Indian Wars*. Many members of Denver's old families were interested in the arts or were practicing artists themselves. In addition, William McCloud Rain, Courtney Riley Cooper, and Joseph Emerson Smith were writing in Denver at that time.

Both men and women enjoyed Mari's company, and she had several escorts among the diplomats and military men. One in particular, for whom she cared a good deal, was assigned overseas early in the war. She knew, intuitively, long before being notified, that he had been killed.

Denver's proximity to the University of Colorado at Boulder, only thirty-five miles away, made it a natural stop for visiting lecturers. Often there were parties after the lectures, or a small group would meet for drinks and conversation. At one such gathering she met Carl Sandburg, at another May Sarton. When her friend John G. Neihardt, whom she had known in Lincoln, spoke in October, the two talked of Crazy Horse.

Mari had long admired Neihardt. A friend later recalled that when she was preparing herself psychologically to write she often read his work for inspiration and mood.[14] She considered his *Black Elk Speaks*, published in 1932, one of the most authentic and valuable sources on Plains Indians and admired Neihardt's poet's hand in the style as well. She recognized that it was a consciously conceived literary work, that Neihardt functions as the voice of Black Elk, a younger relative of Crazy Horse. Even though Black Elk narrates his own experiences as an Oglala Sioux holy man during the last quarter of the nineteenth century, Neihardt does not make any pretense of translating the Indian's speech exactly. Calling his work a "transformation," he attempts to recreate in English the mood and manner of the old man's narration, using imagery and figures of speech identified with the speaker, in a style both graceful and artistic.

Many symbols, images, and metaphors, as well as Indian phrases, terms, and speech patterns in *Black Elk Speaks* later appeared in *Crazy Horse*. Black Elk's black road (the symbol for hardship and despair) is Crazy Horse's road of darkness. Black Elk refers to Crazy Horse as queer. Mari changes the adjective to *strange* man of the Oglalas. She follows Black Elk with more exactness in other instances: Black Elk signifies his readiness to go to war by "getting ready to tie up his horse's tail"; Crazy Horse, too, signifies his readiness to fight with this phrase. Both books refer to General Custer as Pahuska, Long Hair, and to General Crook as Gray Fox. Both speak of whites who have made little islands for the Indians, meaning that the white people have swarmed into the Indian country and forced the Indians into smaller and smaller areas. Names of months, place names, and sometimes events by which time was counted were also similar. Mari, though familiar with these terms from other sources, relied on Neihardt's book for several incidents in her own, especially on Neihardt's description of Crazy Horse's actions as he sought spiritual help during the difficult winters before his surrender to the whites.

Since the authors wrote differently and the Crazy Horse material in Neihardt's work constitutes only a small segment of the whole, *Crazy Horse* in no way duplicates his work. Nevertheless, the two writers were permeated with the Indian world-view and wrote of the same time and the same people. The affinity between them went deeper than that: both were strongly affected by Crazy Horse's spiritual quality, his mysticism, for, as Neihardt said, he was "a god-intoxicated man." Both saw him as a mythic hero and construed the events of his life in that light.

Mari's interest in poetry led to her friendship with Lenore Fitzell, a poet and president of the Colorado Poetry League, and through her with Caroline Bancroft, who became one of Mari's closest friends for the remainder of her life. Caroline Bancroft and Mari had many mutual interests. The daughter of a Colorado mining engineer and granddaughter of early pioneers, Caroline served as book editor on the *Denver Post* for several years. She was interested in mining history and had for some time been involved in restoration work on the old town of Central City and in obtaining oral histories of the mining camps in the state. Through her work with miners, she became something of an authority on Cornish folklore. Mari, too, had been interested in folklore since her college courses under Louise Pound: Caroline, on meeting Louise Pound, admired her great intellect and observed her influence on Mari.

Caroline and Mari shared many less serious interests as well. Both were avid horsewomen; both enjoyed parties, artists, and the arts. Caroline recognized, however, that Mari was secretive, restricting discussion with each friend to the area of his interest. She would talk fiction with novelists, poetry with poets, and social events with those interested in society. Although Caroline had more common ties with Mari than other acquaintances in

Denver, there were areas she could not reach. Caroline often joked about her own age, but Mari never revealed hers, although she hinted that she was a bit older. Never did she admit to her mariage, although she sometimes intimated that she had been blighted for romance because of an early experience and implied she was late in starting everything in her life because of her father.

The two women were both interested in world affairs. They suposed they were in the minority in Denver in believing that the United States must support the Allies in Europe. In spite of the expanding military installations in the area and the increased activity at the foreign consulates, many people in Denver, like those in Lincoln (and much of the rest of the country) were not yet willing to see the European war as their concern. At one luncheon, Mari reported, she was "surrounded by violent tory and fascist outbursts—the sort of thing I was exposed to in Lincoln every day."[15] Both women worked on a volunteer basis for the FBI. In addition, Mari often helped with publicity and propaganda for Citizens for Victory, the William Allen White Committee, and other organizations dedicated to assisting the Allies in Europe, but her activities were managed so quietly that few in Denver knew about them. Hints of her work for the government appear in later correspondence, but it is never fully described. It was to some extent dangerous, exciting, and she hoped, of value to the war effort. At any rate, she stated that it provoked threats several times by fascist groups.

Mari was determined that Caroline and Lenore had writing ability, and she needled, pushed, and nagged them into writing, just as she had always done with prospective writers. Like her earlier Lincoln friends, both women sensed Mari's motherly instinct toward potential writers, an affection and concern thwarted in her feelings toward her own relatives and because she had no children of her own. But her friends professed not to have the great fire of ambition required of a writer; other things came first with them.[16]

While in Denver, Mari formed another friendship that gave her pleasure for many years. Lenore took her on a drive beyond Boulder to visit the Lynn Van Vleets at their mountain ranch.

The visit, intended to last a few hours, extended to three days, and Mari became a frequent and favorite visitor there. Van Vleet bred Arabian horses and kept them at the ranch, the Lazy VV, in the summer. His free horse shows often attracted up to 2,000 or more visitors. He also collected celebrities, famous or exotic, from Metropolitan Opera stars appearing in nearby Central City to royalty from Europe or Africa, inviting them to stay in his guest house or lodge for a weekend, a week, or perhaps the entire summer season, to ride his horses and to enjoy the beautiful scenery.

Mari, in spite of her protestations of being a democratic liberal, was sometimes impressed by the glamorous guests at the ranch. Her old feeling of inferiority because of her family background, her early sense of being an outcast from her family and community, sometimes gave her a sense of awe when consorting with princes, sheiks, archdukes, and archduchesses. But she could hold her own with the other creative people. When the novelist Ben Ames Williams visited at the ranch one summer, he and she would sometimes entertain the guests with their psychic talents. When the playwright Mary Chase and her two sons were guests for a week, Mari engineered an elaborate hunt for buried gold, based on "a legend told her by the Indians," complete with maps of a hidden mine and solemn legal agreements to share the treasure. They spent days hunting the area, ending the search in an ancient abandoned mining town.

There were long daily trail rides on the powerful Arabians, each guest having a favorite mount, and Mari shared her special knowledge of nature lore. She would point out the wildflowers, naming each one. Her friends loved hearing her; she had a sparkling way of giving information. She was the first to recognize that camomile was growing on the ranch, explaining its use for camomile tea, and pointed out the many other plants used in folk medicine. When one of her friends remarked on her knowledge of herbs and plants, she laughed and said that it was to be expected: there were great chemists and pharmacists in the Swiss branch of the Sandoz family.

Her cabin mate most of the summers was Lenore Fitzell. She found Mari a gentle and generous person, but not one to talk of herself ever. If they had not shared living quarters, Lenore would never have known about the migraines. The two, both redheads, enjoyed being taken for sisters. They shared such homely domestic tasks as helping one another mark hems in skirts. Mari continued to urge Lenore to spend less time playing bridge and more time writing her fine poetry, but they did not talk of Mari's books, nor did Lenore see her writing often during those visits to the ranch. What counted most with Mari, her friend thought, was honesty, one's ability to do something creative, and an appreciation of nature.

Mari returned to the ranch summer after summer until it was sold in 1951. Several of the guests she met there, including European royalty, remained her friends, visiting her later when she lived in the East. The setting and people of the Lazy VV provided material for a number of stories as well as a short novel, none published during her lifetime.

In Denver she formed a late night "kaffeeklatsch" friendship with a young couple. When living at the Shurtleff Arms in Lincoln, Mari had often gone across the street in late evenings to visit with Bob and Peggy Ferguson. In Denver, her friends were Ruth Beebe Hill, whom she met in a Denver bookstore, and her husband, Burroughs, a biochemist then with Denver General Hospital. Mari would drop in at their apartment around ten or eleven at night, after her writing for the day. The three would drink huge quantities of coffee and talk volubly on any of a multitude of subjects until three or four in the morning. Often, around four, they would scramble nine to a dozen eggs and eat a complete breakfast before Mari left. Sometimes the Hills would visit Mari, and she and Burroughs, who was knowledgeable in western literature, would examine together the large Crazy Horse map, six by nine feet, on her wall.[17] Ruth, from Ohio, did not recognize the place names, but her husband suggested that she sometime write about this area in the period before Crazy Horse lived. Mari, too, encourage her to write about the subject. When Ruth thought that she might write instead of another researcher's work in Africa, Mari asked, "Why not do the research and write of something that is your own?" Eventually she did just that in *Hanta Yo*. Ruth Beebe Hill credited Mari Sandoz with being one of the two most influential people in her life, adding "She made me *think*. She still influences me."

Suddenly Mari found herself giving many public lectures. The woman who shortly before often refused public appearances because she thought she was a poor speaker now addressed large crowds on a diversity of subjects: forestation, irrigation, and conservation, as well as writing. Her friends often remarked on her endless energy, undoubtedly due in part to her success in controlling her migraines. At last she had found a medication that kept the pain and length of the headaches at a minimum. Long subject to as many as two or three violent attacks a week, she now sometimes went as long as a month without a serious headache. Once she found the particular treatment that worked for her (a drug manufactured, incidentally, by the Sandoz Chemical Company, owned by a distant relative), she could check to some extent the excruciating pain she had had as long as she could remember. This was one of the finest summers of her life. She felt well, she had escaped permanently from Lincoln, and in Denver she found no debilitating heat, no humidity, and no petty fusses.[18]

Mari did not forget her primary purpose in coming to Denver—to research and write *Crazy Horse*. Along with her immense energy, her friends recognized and admired the self-discipline of her writing. After an evening out, she would leave the car, stride to her apartment with her springy, energetic walk, and spend several hours writing before she went to bed. On other occasions, she and Caroline Bancroft, another "night person," might talk on the phone until two or three, then she would return to her writing.

Although much of her preliminary work on the Indian book was done by now, she had learned from the commanding officer at Fort Robinson that their daily records for the two years from 1876 to 1878, years vital to events in her book, were missing, and she needed to locate information for that period from diverse sources.[19] She was also seeking information about that mysterious artist Robert Henri. Because Henri had deliberately obscured as much of his early life as possible, she found the search difficult, but Denver, she was sure, had some of the information she needed. She reported to a friend that summer that this work had gone very well so far; she had stumbled on some good material, if it could be proved.[20]

Now that she was writing *Crazy Horse*, she was thinking of future books. After *Son of the Gamblin' Man*, the Henri book, she was contemplating a fur-trade novel for her Great Plains series, the name she now gave to her projected multivolume work. Much of the research for the Indian books and *Old Jules* could be used for this one as well. With the fur-trade book she planned, she would have covered the history of the plains from 1804, the time of the Lewis and Clark Expedition, to the present.[21] She was thinking, too, about the possibility of two other books, one on the transitional period in Wyoming, with a ruthless man as the main character, and the other a contemporary novel on the sons and daughters of old frontier-tamers, an idea she had thought of in the thirties.

During the summer and early winter of 1940 Mari spent many hours in the archives of the Colorado Historical Society and the Denver Public Library. Her research notes and her three-by-five-inch index cards, usually written in the brown ink she preferred, became so bulky they would not all fit into her files at the apartment and she stored some in a Denver warehouse. Often after she had left the library, she would walk the few blocks downtown to the Bargain Book Store, run by Fred and Helen Rosenstock, to wander through the stacks until closing time. She seldom bought a book; she could not afford many. After the customers had gone, the Rosenstocks and Mari would go for dinner at the nearby YWCA. Fred Rosenstock, an avid history buff, was also interested in art, particularly the works of Charles Russell, and had already begun his western art collection that later became nationally famous.

Mari appreciated Fred Rosenstock's sense of history and discussed *Crazy Horse* with him, sometimes reading from her manuscript. He recognized the sincerity of her work and thought her judgment of events accurate, but he criticized the liberties he felt she took in assuming she knew the Indians' thoughts. In defense, Mari pointed out that she tried to be as true to history as she could, but in order to tie her protagonist to historical events she had at times to use imagination.[22]

With the fine research facilities and an interesting social life, Mari was happy, but she had not solved all her problems by her move, certainly not those with the Atlantic Press and Little, Brown. To Helen Blish she remarked that since her publishers advertised only eastern writers, she knew she would not be able to compete with Howard Fast's book. But though she fussed and complained to friends, she could not easily bring herself to actual battle; it was very difficult for her to make a direct confrontation. At last, however, she decided the break with her publishers could come only if she bluntly charged, to Weeks himself, their lack of interest in her. Although he protested that *Capital City* had sold so poorly the publishers had taken back eight hundred copies from the booksellers, she declared she assumed she was now free from the clause in the contract that gave the Atlantic Press first option on her next book. When the press replied that they considered the option still to be valid, Mari dramatically told her agent, Jacques Chambrun, they had maneuvered her into a position that would prevent her from getting anything more published, because she did not want them to do her Indian books. "I'm heartbroken about my Indian books," she announced. "For them I gave up everything that usually makes life tolerable at all; for them I spent so many years trying to get some mastery over the printed word."[23] She considered writing a few short stories, "something to keep me busy until I can reroute myself." She also reported having received a good job offer; perhaps she would take it and get out of writing. Finally, she put together a collection of her short stories, calling it "The Devil's Lane." If the Atlantic Press accepted it, she had another book to her credit. If they rejected it, she would then be free. The Atlantic Press accepted the book, but their contract for it gave them an option on her next book, and Mari refused to sign it. She was now free to go to a new publisher.[24]

Meanwhile, her friend Paul Hoffman, who had joined Alfred A. Knopf in New York, a house with an impressive reputation, also heard her complaints. Hoffman, a sensitive, intense young man from New York state, the son of a Hessian minister, reared in the rich "Deutsche Kultur," and a graduate of Harvard University, was a fine editor. He now suggested that if she was dissatisfied with the Atlantic Press, Knopf would like to publish her work. Mari was amenable, but she required several stipulations in the Knopf contract. She wanted to be sure she could get her manuscript back if they did not agree on revision, a problem she had had with the Boston firm. "Once they had a manuscript I could either fight for it or let them butcher it; under no circumstances could I get it back," she complained.[25] The details were worked out to her satisfaction.

Alfred A. Knopf himself intended to sign up the new author, but plans were changed and instead it was Hoffman who went to Denver. In January 1941 the contract was signed in a suitably historic setting, the famous old Windsor Hotel, where H. A. W. Tabor and Baby Doe and other famous characters of the region once stayed. Mari and Paul signed the papers "in the old bar, with the water-stained old ceiling still untouched, under a bullet hole and a picture of Calamity Jane."[26] Now she could write seriously on *Crazy Horse*.

Organization of all her material was, of course, of prime importance. Mari had been gathering information even during the upheaval when she ostensibly had neither book nor publisher. In December 1940 she surveyed her file cards for the running story and to spot holes she needed to fill from further research. By the end of March 1941, she had put them in chronological order and begun sorting, evaluating, and writing, a process that would take more than a year. Always a perfectionist, she cared particularly that *Crazy Horse* be done just right. Her special mystic feeling for her Indian biographies was more intense than for her other works. The spiritual debt she felt she owed the Lakotas, and Crazy Horse himself, was too great to allow her to compromise on that book for any reason. It required meticulous attention and responsible judgment. As she often remarked, every quality of character and even the thoughts of the individuals must come from historical sources.

As always, she depended heavily on maps, those from private and government sources, but primarily those she made herself. For *Crazy Horse*, she covered the walls of her apartment with maps showing the land from the time of the Spanish period to the present, marking in the information she thought pertinent. She had made a large detailed map of the area from the Cache la Poudre to the Milk River (Colorado to Montana) and from the Sweetwater to the Red River, giving the old Indian and trapper names for the rivers and other landmarks, as well as the contemporary designations. In this way she could reconcile the contradictory names given for battle and camp sites by the various participants. Later reproduced in the book, it was the most accurate map anyone had made of the area, according to the author.

Crazy Horse was unusual, both in point of view and in style of language. The language is consistent with Indian points of reference. The author associates her word-pictures with the time and region: the prairie and its grasses, the rivers, the sandhills, and the rhythm of the seasons are depicted as the Indians experienced them, rather than from the standpoint of their white adversaries. For this book she has developed a language form, carefully integrated with her material, which is different from that of her earlier books. Much superior to her earlier attempts, the Indian-like style and idiom are well controlled for the first time in *Crazy Horse*. Late in her revisions, she rewrote the manuscript all over again to tell the story from the Indian point of view. She later spoke as if the final version came to her almost as a revelation: "And then suddenly it came to me, that this was a book that I could put into various sections, with various parts. And then I would also change the writing of it. I worked with it until the writing got a sort of stylistic thing to it. It did what I wanted it to do, or as nearly as one ever gets anything."[27] Just how dependable the author's memory is here, is a matter of speculation. She said, for instance, that she did not remember writing any Indian fiction other than "The Birdman" before *Crazy Horse*, omitting any mention of the many efforts using the Indian treaties or the work she may already have done on her Cheyenne book.

Mari appealed to Helen Blish to assist her in filling in gaps and resolving apparent discrepancies in the family relationships of the Smoke and Bear clans of the Oglalas, "aggravated by later contributory splits such as the killing of Grattan [and] the breed feuds as that between the Janis and Richard factions, up to the killing of Crazy Horse himself,"[28] information she had not been able to clear up even after a year of intensive research. She wanted to go to the Pine Ridge again, mostly for the Indian atmosphere and environment. By April 1941 her index to the Crazy Horse material exceeded five thousand cards.

As usual, Mari still found time to read manuscripts sent to her by hopeful writers and to forward names of prospective authors to her publisher and her agents, a task for which she continued to have unending patience and for which she never charged a fee. She continued to lecture, too, until she began to suspect she should be on a regular circuit. That summer she served on the staff for the Twelfth Annual Writers' Conference at Boulder from July 21 to August 8, with other advisers who included Wallace Stegner, Hudson Strode, Harry Shaw, Louise Seaman, Witter Bynner, and Eric Knight.

She was not too busy to notice when Fast's book came out in the fall. Weeks's protest had deterred Simon and Schuster, but it was published by the new firm of Duell, Sloane and Pearce. A Little, Brown editor wrote her consolingly, "I see that Howard Fast beat you to the draw, but his book doesn't seem to have made much splash; at least I judge so by the absence of advertising put out by his publisher." Ironically, her royalty check for the first six months of 1941, included in the letter, was the munificent sum of $29.30. A contemporary review spoke of Fast as a good technician, "although his knowledge of the plains country is a little synthetic,[29] and the book was a Literary Guild selection. Fast's action rankled the rest of Mari's life. She was not surprised when, a few years later, another writer sued him and his publishers for plagiarism and received a substantial settlement.[30]

In the fall of 1941 Mari took her *Crazy Horse* manuscript to scenes important in the book, a custom she followed with all her historical works, traveling the Indian routes, making a final round to the Indian campsites along the Powder and Tongue rivers and to the Devil's Tower region and Fort Phil Kearny in Wyoming. In November she traveled with pack horse through the area to see what the Sioux camps must have been like when snowbound. She wanted to be sure she understood these areas in winter as well as in summer, that her descriptions of these places was accurate.[31]

By now most of the old-timers she had talked with in the thirties were dead. She and her two friends, Helen Blish and Eleanor Hinman, had more accurate records than most of the Indians now alive. Therefore, these later trips to the reservations were more important for the atmosphere she could absorb than for the information she could gain in interviews. She liked to do her summer interviewing when the whole family and all the neighbors were sitting in the shade of the pine shelters, the women doing beadwork, children and dogs everywhere, the old men sitting to one side, smoking, listening, interrupting, contradicting, and adding. This communal arrangement was a natural and easy situation, and it gave Mari a sense of the Indian social life she wanted to express in her books. The feeling she hoped to capture was important because she was working with another race, a vanished culture, and a period full of conflicting accounts that had to be examined for the information most probably correct psychologically as well as historically. There is no doubt she enjoyed this aspect of her research. As she wrote an elderly Indian woman whom she wanted to interview, she was eager to collect and preserve all historical material; "I'm so interested in Indian history it will be great fun for me."[32]

Mari had returned to Denver by December 1941, when the Japanese bombed Pearl Harbor, and feared more than ever that fascism would succeed as she had anticipated in *Slogum House* and *Capital City*. Even though she had some requests from Washington to go into war work there, she felt she had done about all one person could do to alert people to the menace: she had, she wrote to friends, stirred up local Nazis and Silver Shirts when she wrote *Capital City*.[33] And now she was right in the middle of her Indian project.

Throughout the writing of *Crazy Horse* Eleanor Hinman continued to send material, to point out inconsistencies and ambiguities in the historical research, and to share ideas and insights. Besides supplying information on Sioux myth and folklore, she reminded Mari that Crazy Horse's religious background was as important to his biography as an understanding of medieval Catholicism was to a biography of Joan of Arc or an understanding of the Moslem faith to a biography of Saladin. She sent her notes from Helen Blish's investigations of the Thunder Cult, to which Crazy Horse belonged, explaining the symbolism and religious significance of his battle dress and paint and the meaning of the rites he participated in: "He Dog points out that the outstanding forces invoked symbolically in the rite (the Sacred Bow ceremony) were all death-dealing agents: the lightning, the wind, the hail, the smoke, the bear: they show no mercy."[34]

It was Eleanor to whom Mari turned for help in attempting to determine the hero's physical characteristics. Since diligent and persistent research had not produced any photograph known to be that of Crazy Horse, Mari had to rely on descriptions by those who knew him. Many referred to his appearance, but not with the intimate detail she was seeking. Eleanor had talked with persons who had seen him, and she gave this information generously from her notes: "I have the honor to present to you Coffee and Black Elk, both cousins of Crazy Horse and said by the Indians to resemble him in person and features." Coffee, the Indians thought, looked more like Crazy Horse than any other man then living. Eleanor observed that he was slender, lightly built, of middle height, with a very light complexion. His narrow, pointed face, straight nose, and long, expressive eyes were well proportioned, but she felt he lacked the fire of his cousin's personality. Black Elk, whom she had met on the reservation in 1930, she described as taller and darker than Coffee, with one of the most expressive faces she ever saw on any man: "For just that fraction of a second I *saw* 'Tashunkeh Witco,' reflected in his cousin's face as in a mirror. When a man has chosen to carry deeply in his heart the tragedy of his nation, and to live with it, this does not make for simplicity nor 'outgoingness,' and the impression is not easy to describe. But the shadow of Crazy Horse fell on Black Elk at that moment."[35]

After reading a preliminary draft of the manuscript in early 1942, Eleanor commented that she was haunted by it, adding "I can't possibly tell you how pleased I am with it." But she expressed concern about Mari's feeling toward the book, its protagonist, and herself. If anything Eleanor had said implied that she still had any emotional claim on the story, she had not meant it: "It is true that I got somewhat emotionally involved in this yarn, partly because my feeling about CH was to some extent a reflection of my feeling about a certain Mari Sandoz; I liked some of the same things in both of them." She also gave encouragement. "I can't see how people can help but be stirred by it. I can't see how the completed book can do otherwise than justify the enormous expenditure of time, labor, and spirit which you have put into it."[36]

Several years later, in 1947, Eleanor asked Mari for notes from her files to aid her in writing a story about the chief from the viewpoint of his third, mixed-blood wife, using the idea that the wife had tried frantically to persuade Crazy Horse to save himself from the plots and intrigues at Fort Robinson. Mari sent her notes from the files, but when Eleanor learned that rather than helping him there was a possibility that this wife shortly after his death had an affair with Lt. William P. Clark, who both women believed was largely responsible for the chief's fate, she felt too loyal to Crazy Horse to write a story whitewashing a "really hateful woman."[37] By then Helen Blish had died, but the charismatic chief continued to attract both Eleanor and Mari.

In May 1942, late as usual, because she felt it needed more revising, Mari bundled up the manuscript and mailed it to Knopf. Torn apart and rewritten many times, it was now in the idiom she hoped would be authentically reminiscent of the Plains Indians' language and life. The "Indian feel" had been developed over a long period of time, reflecting the author's changing point of view toward the Indians over the years. She had known them from the time she was small and was sympathetic with them, but her writing of the early thirties sometimes shows the condescension characteristic of many whites living close to an Indian reservation and indicates that at first she considered the search for information on the Indian heroes a lark. The journal she kept on the 1930 trip with Eleanor includes their discussions of Indian peculiarities and particularly exasperating characteristics. She noted the difficulties encountered in their first attempt to interview He Dog, the old friend of Crazy Horse, and when they learned something important about the Oglala chief, she wrote jubilantly that they had caught a "whiff of our ghost." Her notebook also describes events that were funny, silly, or, on the other hand, touching and dignified, such as her observation of a young Indian washing his shirt in a stream so that he would have clean clothes for church services. Her later recollections stressed the dignity of the Indians. He Dog, for instance, no longer showed the obtuseness or irascibility she had attributed to him in her 1930 notes; the gaudy and incongruous costumes she observed on some of the young women in 1930 she accepted in her later writing as reasonable wear. More than one person pointed out that she had grown both as a writer and as a person between the writing of *Old Jules* and *Crazy Horse.*

The first publication resulting from her reservation trips of 1930 and 1931 had been an article in the *Lincoln State Journal* of 27, September 1931, titled "Black Hills Become Stake in a $700,000,000 Lawsuit." Recapitulating the government takeover of the Black Hills from the Indians, it reflects her sympathy for the Sioux but is in the language of an investigative reporter. At the time the article appeared, Mari was also working on other Indian material, already experimenting with Indian locutions. In July 1932 she attempted to publish her work, written from an Indian point of view, on the Lone Tree Council held near Fort Robinson in 1875. She advised the *Saturday Evening Post* then that she was beginning a novel with an Oglala subject (almost certainly this was Young Man Afraid of His Horse). Sending one version of "The Great Council" to *Country Gentleman* in 1932, she pointed out that she had tried to reproduce history as faithfully as she could on the basis of her research, and she also noted that she had tried to stay within the Indian language and feeling for words as much as possible.

In 1935 Mari sent a manuscript of "The Great Council" to Collier Young at Brandt and Brandt, but this version had as a main character a fictional Indian, No Voice. Everything in the story was authentic except for the main character. None of the versions sold, and the historical matter was later incorporated into *Crazy Horse*. For several years the author continued to experiment with the Council manuscript, using at least three perspectives, that of the fictional No Voice and those of two of the actual participants, Young Man Afraid of His Horse and Little Big Man. She had made a study of the Indian personalities involved and of the tribal conflicts. Clearly, she was working on Indian material as early as 1931 and it occupied her at intervals throughout the thirties. But over the years a change in her attitude toward the Indians had taken place: in 1930 she felt sympathy; by 1942 it had become empathy.

In the spring of 1942, *Crazy Horse* was complete except for the bibliography and notes. The map to be inserted in the front, painstakingly drawn by the author from her own collection of nearly two hundred army and topographical survey maps of the area, was not quite finished. There had been last-minute problems—one typist got the measles, a second an abscess on an eye; and when the typewriter broke down there was no repairman available in wartime Denver. Exhausted by the tension and pressure, Mari went to bed to catch up on weeks of missed sleep.

Before long, rumors reached her in Denver that convinced her that someone was trying to plagiarize the book. She heard that a member of Knopf's staff had sent her manuscript to an expert on Indians to verify its authenticity (which in itself she considered an insult, since she thought no one else was as knowledgeable as she on the subject); and she feared that the expert was attempting to use her material to write his own version of Crazy Horse's story. She refused to send her bibliography until she could be certain no unauthorized person could get it, for she could not bear to lose this book.

Whether she really had grounds for worry is hard to determine. Her publishers had sent her book for evaluation to a well-known western historian who had already written one Indian biography and had apparently written several chapters of a projected biography of Crazy Horse. Despite Hoffman's assurances that her manuscript was not in danger of being plagiarized, Mari was incensed and certain that the danger was real. She insisted on an early fall publication in order to beat any rivals. She told acquaintances that through influential friends in the historical field, she did what she could to scotch any rival work. Whether it was this pressure or whether the rumor was only that, no competing book appeared.[38]

Mari put aside her publishing difficulties for a few weeks in July and August in order to appear at the 1942 Boulder Writers' Conference. Soon, however, author and publisher were at it again as they strove to reach agreement on the final form of the book. Her relationship with the Atlantic Press had been strained by the editor's attempts to excise westernisms from her books; the same problem threatened to cause her to sever her association with Knopf.

It was most disappointing that Paul Hoffman now saw flaws in *Crazy Horse*. He had been enthusiastic about *Old Jules* and sympathetic about her earlier publishing problems. Now he suggested she may have flattered her reading public by assuming it had previous knowledge of the Sioux wars (a charge several critics later made also) and recommended that she define Indian expressions more clearly, since readers might not know the meaning of such terms as *Lakota* or *counting coup*. The book was too diffuse and discursive, he felt: "After all, in essence yours is a story with the intensity of an American *Iliad* and although I know it's a bromide, intensity can't be sustained unduly."[39] Hoffman's reaction to the manuscript was a blow to Mari because it indicated that he missed the point she had worked so hard to make, that the story was an attempt to simulate the Indian perspective. She did not think intelligent readers would be satisfied with the bare story; she wanted to make her book credible, a good book.

In her mind, the differences between herself and the publishers were too great. Having reconsidered the whole matter, and her spiritual debt to Crazy Horse and her old Lakota friends, she felt she could not make the compromises Knopf thought necessary. The language, the idiom she had used, was not sim-

ply a stylistic device; it was a literary means to convey her
vision. Hoffman protested her change of heart and went to Denver to talk about it. His was the difficult assignment of persuading Mari to cut thirty thousand words—words she wanted left in.
Although Hoffman was acting on his employer's instructions,
his action seemed to Mari a personal betrayal and she argued
bitterly.[40] Any spirit of compromise disappeared when this book
was involved, but if she wanted it published by Knopf she had to
accept his decisions, though she continued to object to the
changes.

When she saw the proofs in September, she was really angry;
the book had looked beautiful at first glance, but on closer
examination Mari found it "hacked and cut as with a knife." Her
method, as she stated in her foreword, was "to use the simplest
words possible, hoping by idiom and figure and the underlying
rhythm pattern to say some of the things of the Indian for which
there are no white-man words, suggest something of his nature,
something of his relation to the earth and the sky and all that is in
between." A great deal of damage had been done to her manuscript, she believed; by changing all the *lays* to *lies*, the *ways* to
way, and inserting many *hads*, the editor had nearly destroyed
her style, and all without any consultation with her. Hoffman,
recalling Mari's battles with the Atlantic Press, remarked, "Well,
it's like old times, isn't it—being 'at it again,' if you know what I
mean?" Later he apologized, with some pique, for their difficulties: "And I'm sorry—for the fourth time!—about your 'disillusionment.' That I was largely responsible for it, I suppose, goes
without saying. But I might add that I have been somewhat
disillusioned myself. If I thought anything constructive could be
accomplished by doing so, I'd try and try hard to go back over the
whole business and straighten things out; but I'm discouraged."[41]

Once publication had been determined, another phase began
that was to be repeated time and again for Mari, the difficulty of
marketing the book. She was always an active promoter of her
work, although she did not enjoy posing for the publicity photographs. Still self-conscious about her appearance, she usually
delayed making appointments with the photographer as long as

possible. This fall, nonetheless, she made autographing dates with several midwestern book stores in conjunction with the publication date. Notified that the book would be late coming off the press, thus throwing off her elaborate schedule, she also learned that some stores could not get the quantity they wanted. Later she complained that Knopf had used their paper supply, limited because of wartime shortages, for William L. Shirer's *Berlin Diary*, which came out at the same time, thus limiting the number of copies of her book printed.

After publication, Mari thanked Paul Hoffman for his part in getting the book finished on time and agreed that it was handsome (it won a bookmaker's award). The friendship was broken, however; the two were not reconciled for several years. The difference in their point of view, Mari believed, was due to Hoffman's lack of understanding of man's identity with the earth. He had championed *Old Jules*, not on the basis of such considerations, but on the basis of her depiction of Jules as a character.

In spite of the difficulties and emotional upheavals, there had been happy moments during the writing of the book. Mari knew as she worked that her biography was important, that this was not just another Indian book. When Knopf's editor questioned the sales potential of the subject, she replied that thousands of people had requested information about Crazy Horse when she worked at the Nebraska State Historical Society; she could not imagine that literate people could not have an interest in this strange, doomed man. The implications of the story extended far beyond the group of Lakotas defeated on the plains during the last century. As she had written Helen Blish earlier, "The story is tremendous, with all the cumulative inevitability of a Greek tragedy, and I feel small and mean and incomplete, although I've done my best to get at the truth. If I can only pin it down on paper."[42] To find the truth and to portray the timeless tragedy of a small nation overwhelmed by a large one, and of a leader, an honorable man, caught in a web of fate from which he could not escape, made her long efforts and difficulties worthwhile.

Mari had a sense of the importance and rightness of her

writing about this man, a vital symbol to his people, whose death at thirty-four ended all hope for the Oglala Sioux in their struggles against the enemy. She remarked that the book gave her a peculiar sense of physical power, the feeling that she could tear down a butte top and throw it into the next county, or blow the clouds from the sky. At the same time, she added, nothing had ever broken her heart as this story.[43] Crazy Horse was always her favorite work because she thought it came closer to achieving her own literary standards than any other, and because of her affinity with its hero. They seemed to have similar psychological natures, for Crazy Horse could not tolerate violent emotions and neither could she. She also felt a mystical, perhaps psychic, tie between them. After the book was finished, she missed "her Indians" so much she was tempted to take up the Cheyenne book soon.[44]

Crazy Horse was not a best-seller. The time of its publication may to some extent have lessened its impact on the public. In 1942 the United States was involved in a world war as a heroic defender against aggressors intent on acquiring territory and wealth. Very few Americans were bothered then with either conscience or consciousness of any dark past of their own. Nor were they particularly interested in Indians. The fact that Crazy Horse was an Indian was undeniably a factor in the book's appeal. (John G. Neihardt's Black Elk Speaks, published in 1932, sold so poorly that the author bought the remainder from the publisher. Frank Waters's The Man Who Killed Deer, published in 1941, remained relatively unknown for twenty years.) The critic for the Los Angeles Times pointed out both problems in his review: "But, sadly, I do not see how this great book can become a best seller. It starts out with the disadvantage of being about the American Indian, to whom the modern American public is indifferent. . . . Miss Sandoz appears to be pointing a moral for today: that we must not imitate our own past in treating with minorities here or abroad." The review further compares the groups in the book with the Allies and the Axis powers. Stuart Rose, a Saturday Evening Post editor and Mari's staunch friend, commented in 1954 on the market for Indian books: "The finest book I've ever read involving the Plains Indians is Mari Sandoz's biography of Crazy Horse. In my estimation, it is one of the best biographies ever written by an American, but when it was published, customers ignored it in great numbers."[45]

The reviews were mixed. Clifton Fadiman, the most critical reviewer, wrote in the *New Yorker*, "Mari Sandoz . . . has been carrying on a fervent historico-literary affair with a dead Indian, the consequence of which is a curious, half-interesting, uneven book." He called it "half history, half historic epic, and not entirely successful as either," and damned it further: "Whenever she is able to extricate herself from the quagmire of detail Miss Sandoz writes with great drive and passion—more, perhaps, than the average reader will think the theme deserves."[46] Some critics assumed that she had romanticized the biography. Her use of detailed descriptions of places; minute details of the characters' dress, gestures, and conversations; dialogue; and dramatic narrative form suggested that she used her imagination to create situations or events of which she could have only general knowledge. She might be true to the spirit of the period, they commented, but could not be chronicling events literally.

The reviews were often colored by the individual critic's own preconceived ideas of the primitive Indian culture. Some could not accept the idea that Indian warriors—like members of any society venerating battle—believed death was not a thing to be avoided, that for the Indian men part of their life was the enjoyment of tribal wars, the *gaudium certaminis* of George Bird Grinnell's *Fighting Cheyennes*; some doubted that a "barbarian" could have the philosophical concept that the Lakotas expressed, "A people without history is like the wind on the buffalo grass." The fact that the Siouan culture differed from that of the whites was a stumbling block for some critics; the fact that there might be some similarities seemed inconceivable to others.

The author's use of language, while one of the book's strong points, certainly limited her audience. In attempting to recreate the psychology of another race and another time, she used locutions with which few readers were familiar. Although many of the reviewers were considered western history experts, or at least were reasonably familiar with the subject matter, the most frequent criticism of the book was that the language was too esoteric. Even Mari's commonplace terms were foreign to many, for example: "the winter called White Beard Is Holding" (the Indians used one major event to identify each year); "the buffalo were leaving before the lengthening shadow of the whites" (meaning the buffalo became scarce as the number of whites in the country grew); "down along the Holy Road there was a cow-dying sickness this summer" (along the Platte River trail there was a cattle disease). These Indian metaphors or references baffled some white reviewers and readers.

Sharp criticism also came from those who felt Mari had taken undue liberties in her use of direct dialogue. Both Thomas Hornsby Ferril and Fred Rosenstock had argued this point with her while she was writing the book. In his "Childe Herald" column written at the time of her death, Ferril recalled their many discussions on the issue of invented dialogue in historical writing. While the two agreed that an author could put his own words into the mouths of people long dead, Ferril objected to this treatment of contemporaries or people of the recent past. "Mari would always hold her ground: what she caused an Indian or cavalry officer to say was not only plausible but truer than any documented record because, she would argue, it fitted the nature of the man in the context of the situation; and in this matter of context her knowledge was based on far more historical research than many authors are willing to undertake."[47]

The book's impact on the literary world was limited by its uncommon subject matter and style, although western writers such as Wallace Stegner, John G. Neihardt, and Jack Schaefer admired it. Very few writers had attempted to recreate life as it must have been in that period, for that culture and those protagonists. The work had a more obvious influence in other fields; within the still rather exclusive group of those interested in western and Indian life, it is well known. Scattered throughout the important books about the plains are acknowledgments or references to *Crazy Horse*. Years later, a *Colorado* magazine reviewer stated that as the portrait of an Indian it came as close to reflecting the Indian world-view as any work written by a non-

Indian could hope to do, and rated it among the best works of American biography.[48]

The mail Mari received was gratifying in tone if not in quantity. One reader shared his recollections of several characters he had known personally—Red Cloud, Old Spot, Little Big Man, and "that skunk Frank Gruarde [sic]"—for he had grown up on the Pine Ridge Reservation. A relative through marriage of one of the Larrabee women wanted more information on her and her later history. Another reader, interested in the death of Logan Fontenelle, agreed that her version seemed the most probable of any he had found. Mari sent him her sources for verification. She heard, too, from her friend Wallace Stegner, himself a western writer of note, who found *Crazy Horse* "a marvelous fusion of fact and the method of fiction, and the whole book has a grand epic sweep. I found myself comparing Crazy Horse with Hector, which makes you automatically Homer."[49]

Still another group, the history enthusiasts who make the study of the plains their concern, indicated their approval. They were, in a way, the hardest to please, for they often had frontier or Indian acquaintances; some had spent a lifetime ferreting out the very kind of detailed information Mari had, and they could be very severe about what they considered inaccurate information. M. I. McCreight, with whom she shared information, wrote her his reaction: "Just finished reading it. Took me six days and a part of most nights. Lived with Crazy all the days—and all the places you took him—every fight he was in, experienced his every mood, grieved with him at the baby scaffold. It is a marvelous work! No equal as a history of the long disgraceful Sioux war. I want you to know that one who knows something about Indians in the old days, appreciates the enormous job you have done."[50] He noted one error in the narrative: Mari wrote that Crazy Horse carried a Winchester in the Custer fight, but McCreight owned the actual gun, a Springfield carbine 1873 model, and identified the markings on it, including a split gun butt. She answered that some stories said Crazy Horse had two guns in the battle and ran out of ammunition.

Even more rewarding was the response of the Indians, many of whom revered Crazy Horse almost as a messiah. One Oglala,

Chief Standing Bear, remarked that the author wrote "just like the good old Lakotas spoke." From Lone Eagle, the son-in-law of Luther Standing Bear, author of *My People the Sioux*, and related by marriage to a nephew of Crazy Horse on his mother's side, she received this praise: "I recently read your splendid book 'Crazy Horse' and must say, without thought of flattery, that your writing is by far, and far, the finest work ever composed on this famous Dakota. I am also very happy, and much surprised to learn that you knew so many of the old timers (Sioux) that I have also known. It was like reading a story of my friends to note the many many people you mention that were friends of my family many years ago."[51]

Occasionally during the following years Indians, not always Sioux, called on Mari as a matter of respect. Once, after she had moved to New York, a group of young Flatheads and northern Lakotas, most of them soldiers, stopped by. While they sat in a circle, one gave a harangue in what she thought was Lakota; then they read bits of the book, using sign language. Before they took their formal leave, they gave her the double handshake, first the right hand on top, then the left. She was pleased and a little shaken by the experience.[52]

Eight
New York

After the publication of *Crazy Horse*, Mari made her last major change of residence, this time moving to New York. She wanted to be nearer the important archives and museums in the East and to her publishers. After years of trying to work out details of her books by telephone and mail, she finally conceded that difficulties between publisher and writer multiplied when there was so much geographical distance between them.

In January 1943 Mari left the mountains for the East, keeping her autographing dates in bookstores as she made her "slow march eastward," leaving much of her material in storage in Denver. Despite her dislike of the East, she expected to be in New York for two, possibly three, years. "I'm only in New York, not of it," she often remarked. She was to write propaganda for the war effort, and that too, could be done best near those she worked with. Perhaps a change in surroundings would give her the impetus she needed to write *Son of the Gamblin' Man* as well. She had moved to Denver in part because of that book, but it was proving a difficult matter.[1]

Housing in wartime New York was scarce, but eventually she found an apartment she liked, fine accommodations really, at 23 Barrow Street, "a little stub of a street" in Greenwich Village. Situated in a colorful Italian neighborhood, the fourth-floor walkup had three large windows facing the street, a fireplace, and, most important, large closets for storage. Nearby were houses associated with famous people—Edna St. Vincent Millay, Bret Harte, Mark Twain, William and Henry James, Edgar

Allan Poe. Some of the buildings in the neighborhood dated from the time of Thomas Paine and Washington Irving. Although Mari often spoke disparagingly of the lowlands of the East and of its inhabitants, before long she was interested in local politics and gossip. Fiorello La Guardia was mayor of New York City, and his benign influence was strongly felt. In the Village there was a friendliness and small-town neighborhood atmosphere that appealed to her; she had her morning coffee at the same drugstore every day, along with the other regulars, often fellow writers and artists. She ate in the small neighborhood cafes and revised her writing in one of the pubs or taverns, sitting in a booth "while a juke box blared, drunks fought, and glasses clinked," as one of her friends remembers.[2] It was in such a setting that Marguerite Young, future author of *Miss MacIntosh, My Darling*, first saw Mari and declined to be introduced to her, sure she was some kind of a poseur. (Later the two did meet and became close friends.) All through her writing career Mari continued to use public meeting places for her work of revising manuscripts. To her, it was the modern equivalent of the wine cellars of France and the coffeehouses of England in times past.[3] Besides, working where others so obviously pursued other activities kept her ego from becoming inflated.

Mari did not make much money from *Crazy Horse*. When she was offered an original Remington painting, "Attack on Crazy Horse," for $750, she had to refuse it; her kind of writing did not allow for expensive hobbies. It was all she could do to pay for photostats of unpublished maps and other materials and her travel expenses from one archive to another. She had already decorated her apartment, anyway; she had hung her old cowboy hat on one wall and on another had stretched her six-by-nine-foot map of the High Plains country on which she had for many years been recording the movements of the Plains Indians during the period of which she wrote.[4]

Though it was not rewarding financially, *Crazy Horse* had established Mari's reputation—to a small audience, it is true—as a historian as well as a writer. Just the same, it was shortly after her move to New York that she wrote in her little penciled notebook that she planned to keep track of events to prove there was a pattern in her life, that good things happened only when things happened only when they were anticlimactic and bad when she was already depressed.

Her depression was due in part to moving to New York. World affairs, too, perturbed her. She was beginning to realize that some of the Allies' organizations in the United States were devious and self-seeking. She had welcomed the Russians as allies against Hitler, although she had never been personally interested in the communist movement. Her eventual recognition that some communist groups were using war activities to promote their own ideology was a distinct shock.[5]

Concerned about what she saw as neurotic, even psychopathic, aspects of wartime society (and foresaw for the postwar period), she put aside the troublesome *Son of the Gamblin' Man* once more and began to write her third thematic novel. She called it *We'll Soon Have You Back Again*, but later changed the title to *The Tom Walker*, a nickname for one who walks on stilts. The title was meant to imply that the aggressions stirred up in wartime could continue after the war and could vault national boundaries "as casually as a boy on stilts goes over a rut."[6]

Although *The Tom Walker* kept Mari busy throughout 1943, late in the year she was again planning to work on *Son*. She was also thinking of her projected fur-trade novel, to be part of her Great Plains series, and the possibility of an autobiography sometime in the future. She had an accumulation of rough sketches of the silly things that had happened to her or to others around her, jotted down so that, with her "leaky memory," she would not forget them.

Having resumed the long working hours, self-discipline, and almost monastic life of her Lincoln years, Mari once more established for herself that her work was her life. Often she slept only four or five hours at night. When tired, she would take a five- or ten-minute catnap, shower, and then return to work. She had time for friends who visited her from the West and for a few acquaintances in New York, but it was difficult to cajole her away from her writing. She made herself a large sign for the telephone, "Be Brief, Be Ruthless," and the old "Busy" card often hung on her door. Once in a while she would call Marguerite Young, Sidnee Livingston, an artist friend, or someone else she was fond of. They would go to dinner, a play at the nearby Circle-on-the-Square Theater, a ride on the Staten Island Ferry, or an art show, but she did not stay away from her work for long.[7]

In those early years in New York Mari became friends with Kay and Joe Rogers, both journalists. Although they admired her and often invited her to dinner with their friends (they seldom met hers), Joe had difficulty in understanding Mari's absolute seriousness about her work. Kay often accompanied Mari on the long walks necessary to work off the dizziness and nausea caused by the Gynergen shots she took regularly for her migraines. The two spent the night of President Roosevelt's death walking through the Village, talking out their grief. Most often the Rogerses and Mari would dicusss world affairs and politics, but the long-into-the-night sessions she had enjoyed in Denver were no longer her pattern. Often she would arrive at social gatherings late and leave early to return to her work, sometimes with a noticeable theatricality.[8]

She knew many people in publishing and maintained her interest in the arts, but she steered clear of social commitments. Her friends simply had to accept her overwhelming interest in her writing. When she felt people getting too close to her, too intimate or too demanding, she had ways to keep them at a distance. She would blow up over a trifle, such as a house plant that had been overwatered or a typewriter a secretary must have misused. She often used insignificant, mundane, inanimate objects as an excuse for ending a relationship. She was generally considerate of any working person and paid her secretaries well, but they often did not stay with her long. Sooner or later she would find some inexcusable mistake. And yet there were intervals when she suffered from loneliness. One secretary recalled that sometimes Mari would come into the room in which she was working and talk for hours. She was a compulsive talker at times and could discuss in depth almost anything that came to mind, from jazz to banking to sports to home remedies for illness. At first the secretary was concerned that she was not earning her money, but eventually she realized the author was willing to pay for the companionship. The secretary did not interrupt, nor did she contradict; Mari did not expect to be wrong.[9]

Though she was now a mature person, there was a part of Mari that was eager to please and to be recognized, just as when she was a little girl. Sometimes overly grateful for recognition and commendation, she found herself giving too much time to people she had no obligation to. She read many manuscripts, not only from writers she knew but from complete strangers as well, answered too many letters in too much detail, took on too many worthy causes. She could keep her personal life clean and un-cluttered through subterfuges, but she had difficulty in saying no to those with no real claim on her.

Fretting to her friend Mamie Meredith that *The Tom Walker* was pressing on her like a double migraine, and wondering why she could not get things done as quickly as others, she nevertheless had time to write a short story, "Sit Your Saddle Solid," for the *Saturday Evening Post,* a task that relieved the tedium of working on longer novels or histories. She also produced an article on juvenile delinquency, though it was not published. She had definite ideas on how children should be reared and emphasized the effect of a child's place in the family on his behavior.The oldest son, for instance, may be subjected to too much protection and coddling by his mother, whereas the oldest daughter may suffer from her mother's sexual jealousy. Mari often observed that one must suffer and overcome as a child in order to handle the world when he grew up. A child who has too easy a time of it has no protective shell when facing the vicissitudes of an adult world. And a child must learn a sense of responsibility if he is to be a responsible adult.[10] Many of these ideas later found a place in her works, especially in her novels for young adults.

Mari made time to examine and identify as original several Alfred Jacob Miller paintings an acquaintance had found in an attic; she helped Martin Schmitt, editor of General George Crook's autobiography, supplying him with references and suggestions. She suggested to one neophyte writer that with his knowledge of the lumber business he could write a revealing book on the lumber barons. She advised him to select or invent a typical figure and let him stand for the whole group, the method she used for her thematic novels, apparently unaware or unconcerned that her novels written with that method had not met with success. She also shared her artistic philosophy with a painter mourning the departure of the friend he considered his inspiration. Although she agreed it was important to have someone near who was stimulating or challenging, what really mattered was the artist alone in his world, with nothing but his craftsmanship to help him in the tests his imagination and material set for him. Essentially, an artist must depend only on himself.[11]

Nor was Mari too busy to write Governor Dwight Griswold of Nebraska of her concern for the Nebraska State Historical Society. The society, which was being crowded out of the state capitol, was finally to have a building of its own, but on the university campus, and she feared that the university would dominate the society. She was concerned about any possible threat to the Historical Society. Most of the state historical societies in the midlands were great because they were independent institutions, she pointed out, reiterating that the trans-Missouri region offered the most complete and comprehensive records to be found of modern man's arrival in the area, and that the Nebraska Historical Society was one of the great repositories. She did not win the argument, however; the building was constructed on the campus.[12]

Knopf rejected an early version of *The Tom Walker* in March 1944. Mari was not surprised; it merely proved, she said, that she was ahead of her readers, as a good novelist should be. Properly finished and presented, the book might save society from the chaos toward which it was certainly headed unless those who knew the dangers pointed them out. This speaking out in times of stress had always been a basic premise of her philosophy.[13]

When she had finished revising *The Tom Walker* to her satisfaction, Mari determined to aid in the war effort more directly by joining the Women's Army Corps. She hoped to enter as a private and go overseas. That way, she could pay back a little of the debt she and her family owed for Walter Reed's medical service to her father back in 1884, after his fall into the well. In spite of her age—she was forty-eight—she easily passed all the physical examinations except the eye test. Rejected because of the eye blinded in the snowstorm so long ago, she was furious, perhaps in part because Eleanor Hinman was a WAC serving as a psychiatric social worker in an army hospital. Turning her frustration back into her work, she concentrated on research for three books she had in mind for her Great Plains Series.

Then she became ill. Potsdam disease, a type of flu, struck many people in 1944 and 1945, and Mari was among them, too sick to work much of the winter. A scheduled reprinting of *Old Jules* was cancelled because of the wartime paper shortage. For the first time since 1935 it was out of print, except for a paperback Armed Services Edition, small enough to fit in a uniform pocket, for which she received one-half cent a copy. Little, Brown had notified her earlier that the government wanted the metal from obsolete book plates; unless she wanted the plates for *Capital City* they would melt them down. She bought the plates and sent them to be stored in Lincoln, carefully specifying that the book title not be printed on the outside of the box. She still feared repercussions.

Her finances low, Mari turned to short-story writing again and sold "The Spike Eared Dog" to the *Saturday Evening Post*. She could always make money now if she wrote about horses, dogs, or children, but producing light fiction no longer gave her a sense of accomplishment. Once she had wanted simply to be a writer, a good one; now she considered herself a historian as well, and her serious work always involved the art and science of history as well as the craft of writing.

To Mari, restless and unwell, her apartment in the spring of 1945 had all the charm and convenience of a Wyoming home-stead shack. Adding to her depression, she heard that Orin Stepanek, a close friend at the University of Nebraska, had wanted to propose her for an honorary degree but had been told it was not a good idea. She advised him not to waste his energy on the plan. She knew that her liberal politics had angered some of the regents, and *Capital City* had not helped her cause.[14] Her close association with the English Department, which was considered unruly by many administrators, would not help her chances.

It was at this time, too, that A. E. Sheldon, her old friend and mentor from State Historical Society days, died. As one early interested in her writing career, he may have been the one who suggested that she concentrate on the trans-Missouri series. She had worked and corresponded with him so long that she felt as if she had lost a member of her family.[15]

Eventually both her spirits and the tempo of her life began to pick up. She regained enough energy to defend herself when a reader complained of the profanity in her books. "Many things in life offend me, man's inhumanity to man, for example, but as a writer dedicated to the portrayal of life as honestly and wholly as I am able, I cannot cavil at profanity, or anything else that I find intrinsic in human character."[16]

Mari spent the summer of 1945 at the Lazy VV Ranch in Colorado, revising *The Tom Walker* and probably also working on two long recollections, "The Neighbor," about the bachelor friend of the family, Charley Sears, and "Martha of the Yellow Braids," about the daughter of a family of settlers who stayed with the Sandozes for several months while Jules located a claim for them. Martha was everything Mari was not: plump, cuddly, affectionate, and friendly, a pink-cheeked girl with long, thick, blonde braids. Though the two made an incongruous pair, they became close friends, a relationship Mari treasured. She, like the other children at school, now had a best friend to talk to, confide in, and play with; Martha's friendship remained a happy memory. Both articles were later published in the *Prairie Schooner* and collected in *Hostiles and Friendlies*.

Mari continued to lecture frequently. At the Indiana University Writers Conference in the summer of 1946, she was in the company of a number of distinguished writers, among them Marion and Walter Havighurst, Robert Hillyer, MacKinlay Kantor, and Mary Jane Ward. Her principal lecture, on the writer's responsibility to his material and his work, stressed two points she acted on all her life. First, all writers are public servants to the extent that the public pays them, and they owe it something. Thus, when she spent so many hours working with young writers, when she answered readers' letters at length, or when she appeared at autographing sessions, she was fulfilling what she considered part of her duties as a writer. Second, writers have the stern obligation to avoid any word or implication that might encourage human injustice.[17] This strong sense of morality, the most persistent quality in her writing, appears in all her books.

Mari had long since overcome her hostility toward the Atlantic Press and exchanged amiable letters with Edward Weeks, sending him names of potential writers, on several occasions including articles she had written with the *Atlantic* in mind. Although they did not publish any of them, they were interested in *The Tom Walker*. In August the fiction editor accepted it, but Weeks asked for more time to read the manuscript and kept it for some time. It was an old story; Mari recalled they had held up both *Slogum House* and *Capital City* for months. She thought no publisher should hold a book longer than two months, and she turned the matter over to Harold Ober. Weeks rejected the book later that month, calling it implausible. Ober said that while the idea of the book was excellent, it was not ready for publication. Miffed at his criticism, Mari asked Jacques Chambrun to take over all her agent's duties and sent the book on to Edward Aswell, formerly of the Atlantic Press, now at Harper and Brothers.

Harper's had already accepted a book with a similar theme, but Dial Press, to whom it was submitted next, took it immediately. Postwar events so closely paralleled some of those in *The Tom Walker* that the Dial Press wanted to publish as soon as possible, even postponing another book already at the printer's. Mari hoped *The Tom Walker* would make people aware of the mistakes made in the hysteria of a postwar period. The atomic bomb tests and what she saw as lack of concern for the war veterans worried her: "First we send them out to die for our mistakes of the post-war period, then we give them no homes, and now no future."[18] If enough people got mad, the situation could be remedied.

There was no time to go through the manuscript for errors;

Mari had to catch them in the galleys. Surprisingly, under these rushed conditions, she was pleased with the galley proofs. Once more, however, she had to reinsert the westernisms removed by the publisher and give the authority for her usage, even though she had been consulted on almost every collection of westernisms in the preceding twenty years. She also insisted on leaving in one episode of sodomy, since it was important to the plot.

The book came off the press in the spring of 1947, well in time for the author to teach an eight-week Writers Workshop at the University of Wisconsin. It gave her an opportunity to combine her love of teaching with her sincere desire to help aspiring writers. She succeeded so well that although the university's usual policy was to bring in a different writer each summer, she returned for nine years. This first summer her course was called Writing of Fiction, Biography, and Novel. In succeeding years, the course was narrowed to Writing the Novel. Mari did no writing of her own during these weeks, but divided her time between class lectures and individual conferences. Her lectures were stimulating, and her students learned that her interest in their work extended beyond the eight weeks of the course. Whenever they sent their manuscripts to her she would go over them painstakingly, encouraging any signs of talent, patiently indicating ways to improve their writing. When a work showed promise, she sent it to her agents, publishers, or editor friends. She also used her influence in securing grants for several of her students.

At the Lazy VV Ranch after her teaching stint in the summer of 1947, she worked on the light novelette set at the ranch. At first it was called "Masoud," after Lynn Van Vleet's favorite Arabian stud, but the title was later changed to "Foal of Heaven."[19] She based it on the people she had known at the ranch, attempting to picture the ranch owner and his complex relationship with his family, working crew, friends, and guests. "The Boss," as Van Vleet was called, was in many ways a Napoleonic figure such as had fascinated her for years—small, domineering, and sometimes belligerent, irascible, or tactless. He was a financial tycoon, wielding power egotistically and tyrannically, according to some, but he could also be a good friend, generous, thoughtful, and considerate. He and his family liked Mari. She recognized that his personal characteristics were similar to Old Jules's, but she enjoyed her friendship with this man, a person as ruthless and domineering as her father, but one who was, by contrast, delighted in her knowledge and creative ability. He was important in her life at least in part because of comparison with her father.[20]

The father image may have interfered with the novelette. Certainly Mari restrained her writing because so many of the characters were based on real people, still alive. She was reluctant to write a *roman à clef,* although the material lent itself to just that sort of treatment. The plot revolves around a small boy, the horse, and "The Boss." She would use the story of the young boy and the horse again in quite a different setting, in a different time, and in a different culture, for *The Horsecatcher.* Mari showed a strange ambivalence and a certain lackadaisical attitude toward "Foal of Heaven." It intrigued her imagination, without doubt, and she worked on it at intervals for several years, but primarily as relaxation, and she did not push its sale as forcefully as she did her other manuscripts.

There were times when she wondered if writing was worth her efforts. When *The Tom Walker* was published in the fall of 1947, her first book in five years, it was not well received. The public was not particularly impressed with her effort to alert them to the dangers of the postwar world. Once more she had a story with its bones too thinly padded to disguise the moral, with characters flat and wooden. It was the same problem she had with *Capital City* and much of her other fiction. The excellent historical background, powerful writing, fine descriptions of the country, and excellence of occasional scenes were insufficient to counterbalance the weaknesses. No matter how important the message, she could not hold her readers' interest with her allegorical writing. Readers liked novels with characters so well developed they could respond to them—sympathize with them, love them, or hate them. The characters in this book, written primarily from her imagination, could not elicit any such response. One reader summarized the problem: "Sandoz's interest in history and talent for historical presentation could not (or would not) be subordinated to the needs of the novel. The story teller's abilities which enabled her to make Old Jules live for the reader do not survive the self-imposed task of writing 'social criticism' in novel form." The critics were generally in agreement with the public. Although the *New York Herald-Tribune* saw that she had "the right feel for [the past], rich and warm and extravagant and deeply rooted in what her America has been and is," *Time* was more accurate as well as more succinct: "Small shakes as a novel, it is long on period history, melodrama, local color and wondrously rowdy soldier, sod-hut and ranch-house talk."[21]

To add to her woes, Knopf notified Mari that they planned to melt down the plates for *Crazy Horse* unless she wanted them, since the book was selling fewer than one hundred copies a year. She took the plates; she felt she owed it to her old friends the Sioux, as well as to herself, to do everything she could to preserve the book, but she was saddened that, only five years after its publication, it was not considered worth reprinting.[22]

Nevertheless, she decided to take up once more the Cheyenne book, dropped in 1939 because of Howard Fast's Cheyenne book, *Last Frontier,* and because she had felt it was the wrong time to write of the destruction of the Indian people when the whole world was coming unglued. After her 1947 summer writers' conference at the University of Wisconsin and her visit to the Lazy VV Ranch, she returned to New York. She had decided to write *Cheyenne Autumn* in the East.[23]

There were good reasons for her decision. One was the easy access to government documents in Washington and the fine collections of the New York City Public Library and other great archives in the East, such as the Smithsonian Institution and the Coe Collection at Yale. There was material vital to her story here. In the American Museum of Natural History she found an important ledger taken from the body of Little Finger Nail, one of the Cheyennes killed on the flight north, the ledger filled with pictographs of incidents on the journey. Besides, her research files had now reached monumental proportions. Some index material could be used for more than one book, but each history had its own considerable volume of research cards and papers. It was easier to stay in the East than to move the bulk of her papers west. Her material in Lincoln was left in storage, but that sent from Denver, together with her current research material, filled her New York apartment—work room, closets, and even the kitchen—chairs, table, and all. The only spot not covered with boxes and files was the kitchen sink. One visitor even reported files in the fireplace.

Mari took time now to correct a longstanding historical error having to do with two Sioux chiefs named Sitting Bull, one friendly to the whites, the other hostile. She pointed out that historians, the *Encyclopaedia Britannica*, and even a biographer of the northern, better-known, hostile chief, had confused the two. Slipshod historical writing, which had produced a mythical hero like Buffalo Bill and made a hero out of the small-time badman Wild Bill Hickok, bothered her so that it broke her heart, she remarked more than once; for with a persistence and a desire for honesty, an author could still find authentic records and tell the true story. So before she began to settle down seriously once more to her Cheyenne book, she wrote an article on the two Sitting Bulls for *Blue Book*, a magazine "the adventure boys liked to read." A Pawnee artist, Brummett Echohawk, illustrated the article. The two corresponded about Indian writing, art, and ideas for several years, Echohawk eventually visiting the author in New York.

Much of Mari's time in 1949 was spent in trying to find publishers. She offered the *Foal* novelette to the Atlantic Press, suggesting that it be one of a package of three books, along with *Cheyenne Autumn*, which she hoped to have ready in 1950, and *Son of the Gamblin' Man*, to be written by 1952, all three to come out together. The Atlantic Press rejected the horse story as too light, though they wanted to see the Cheyenne book as soon as she had a sizable portion of the manuscript ready. Knopf was not interested in the horse story, either, and released her from her contract in May.

That fall she put all such problems behind to spend ten weeks on a research trip she could thoroughly enjoy, exploring again the region she was writing of in *Cheyenne Autumn*. She once said that she had an impractical desire to own a helicopter so that, armed with her beloved maps, she could hover over any or all spots that seemed interesting to her out in the sandhills.[24] She had to do without the helicopter, but her explorations were detailed and she found much valuable information in the country between the Washita River in the South and the Yellowstone in the North. Housed in the recently abandoned government hospital, she spent five weeks at the Cheyenne Agency at Lame Deer and at nearby Birney, Montana, tracing the extremely complex family lines of many of the Cheyennes who would appear in the book. (The information she obtained would become even more important in the future, after fire destroyed the agency records.) From Montana she went to Darlington, Oklahoma, the southern agency from which the Indians fled in 1878, to see that area again, review the records, and interview agency personnel and Indians. She then retraced the Cheyennes' route from south to north, walking over every great Cheyenne battlefield except one that had been washed away since the battle.[25]

Her own old neighborhood on the Niobrara provided the most exciting and rewarding discoveries. She and her brothers and sisters located sites important to both Cheyenne groups, that of Dull Knife and that of Little Wolf, including the valley in which they believed Little Wolf and his people had wintered while Dull Knife's group was imprisoned at Fort Robinson. Mari had been given a detailed map of Lost Chokecherry Valley, drawn by a Sioux who had slipped into the valley to visit his Cheyenne wife during the winter of 1879. Now she looked at all the little lost valleys until she found one that fit exactly the map of the place where the chief had hidden his people from the army. It was so perfectly camouflaged that even though the valley was remarkably lush, with wood and water and grass enough for the pony herd, one would not know how to find it unless one knew every foot of the country. Once more her story was affected by her sense of place, her need to experience the land physically. Lost Chokecherry Valley was on her brother Jule's ranch.

Later, Mari went to the Fort Robinson vicinity and followed the path that Dull Knife's starving, poorly clad band of men, women, and children fled over for thirteen days in freezing

January weather. It seemed fitting to her that the gully where the final massacre took place was a break in a great bluff-walled saucer, with the buttes of the Nebraska badlands rising here and there from the bottom, steep, gray, and foreboding.

From Stratton, a small town in southwestern Nebraska, Mari was guided by H. D. "Doc" Wimer, whom she had known through the Nebraska State Historical Society. In this area she did her most diligent research, investigating two related massacres on the Sappa River in northern Kansas. In 1875, according to her information, the Cheyenne keeper of the sacred arrows, Medicine Arrow, also known as Stone Forehead, and the chief Bad Heart and their village were killed by soldiers and buffalo hunters. In 1878 came the retaliation, the killing of nineteen white settlers by Cheyennes under Dull Knife and Little Wolf as they passed through the area on their way north. These events are the basis for chapters seven and eight in *Cheyenne Autumn*, "Sappa—Meaning Black," and "To Make the Bad Heart Good." Wimer, a lifelong resident of the region, had information on the incidents gathered from old newspaper accounts, memoirs of survivors, neighborhood gossip, and his own interviews with the white participants whom he had known. His material, together with the already extensive research Mari had done, gave her details hitherto not used by historians.

Mari had been interested in the Sappa fights for some time. The official army report of the 1875 skirmish gave little information. The lieutenant in command of the party gave no details of the killing of the Indians, but Wimer's sources, including several eye-witnesses, did. Mari used much of Wimer's material to show that the army account was inaccurate. His evidence certainly strengthened her belief in the Indians' cause. It was on this trip also that an old-timer named Rice showed Mari an Indian pictographic book, borrowed for her from Mrs. John Prowers, a full-blooded Cheyenne and the niece of Medicine Arrow. It depicted the 1875 massacre, showing two chiefs, one known to be Medicine Arrow, being shot by the whites as they held a flag of truce. The book has since disappeared.[26]

Some historians believe Medicine Arrow was not killed at the Sappa, but died peacefully the next year in the North. But it was known that he did move north of the Washita in 1875, trying to keep the sacred arrows away from battle, as was his duty. Mari based her conclusions primarily on the Prowers manuscript and other privileged information. She also had the story Wild Hog had told her father, that the group had stopped in 1878 at the bend of the Sappa, where Medicine Arrow's body had been placed in a hole in a bluff. And she had heard Old Cheyenne Woman verify this one evening when the Cheyennes stopped to visit Old Jules. The Cheyennes never wanted to talk of the Sappa killings; but on the reservation, she confronted the old-timers with her material, telling them she would write the story with what information she had unless they told her what really happened. Then they told her about the killing of Medicine Arrow and the reason for the killing, three years later, of nineteen settlers, a settler for every Cheyenne man killed in 1875. She was told, "There is no way to pay for women and children killed."[27]

The details of the Sappa massacres, the information found in the Little Finger Nail pictographic book, and the fate of Yellow Swallow, allegedly Custer's son by a Cheyenne woman, were the facets of the story Mari focused on most intently during her research. Although certain aspects of her interpretation are still being argued by historians, she never felt her version to be in error.

During the trip to the reservations Mari found another cause to champion; this one became a crusade. Appalled at the misery of the Indians, particularly at the Lame Deer Reservation in Montana, and the lack of local aid, she became active in Indian affairs. A very bad blizzard in 1948 had killed much of the Indians' livestock; it was followed in 1949 by a heavy infestation of grasshoppers. Moreover, government appropriations had been cut, and the closing of the reservation hospital was only one bad result. Mari served on committees, attended the Institute on American Indian Self-Government; corresponded with President Truman, Alexander Lesser, chairman of the Association on American Indian Affairs, Senator Mike Mansfield of Montana, and Toby Morris, chairman of the House Subcommittee on Indian Affairs; and often attended hearings in Washington, D.C. She also kept up a regular correspondence with people on the reservation, including Wilbert and Geraldine Harvey, who operated the Birney Day School. Later she recommended Geraldine Harvey for a John Hay Whitney Foundation scholarship. Mrs. Harvey was perhaps the first Indian woman to attend graduate school through such a grant.

Back in New York in the fall, Mari pursued the Sappa battles vigorously by letter, tracking down the survivors, both Indian and white. She also followed up the matter of Yellow Swallow. She traced his name in medical records, in agency rolls, and through the memories of the Indians who had fled north. She was sure he had started on the flight and at first thought he must have died on the way. She wrote Charles Brill, whose *Conquest of the Southern Plains* discusses Custer's relations with Monahsetah, the boy's mother, to ask if Yellow Swallow could have been among those killed in Dull Knife's band. According to medical records, Brill replied, the boy had died of syphilis at the age of seventeen, while living at the southern agency. Despite the records, Mari was reluctant at first to let go the romantic idea that he had died on the freedom flight, killed by soldiers avenging the Custer battle, and she hinted at all these ideas in her book.

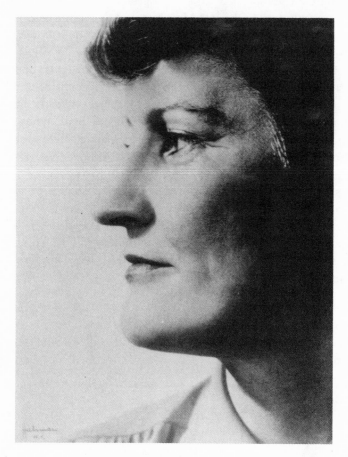

*When success finally came, Mari wore
it well, although never lightly*

Nine
The Middle Years

The next few years were busy and productive for Mari. There were still major battles ahead, but she would achieve considerable success and recognition, although they never came easily. The high point of 1950 came in June, when she was awarded an honorary Doctorate of Literature by the University of Nebraska. The degree meant a great deal to her; it removed the stigma of her missing high school education and made up for the lack of a regular college degree.[1] Louise Pound sent her a circumspect note in March: "MM [Mamie Meredith] and I hope you have had good news from Lincoln recently. I can't be more definite at present." Later her friend gave more details. Mari had been proposed by members of the English Department because of her books, but the determining factor in the award was her teaching at the writing institutes. This was suggested in the citation read when the chancellor of the university conferred the degree: "Mari Sandoz, distinguished Nebraska historian, biographer, novelist, story writer, authority on Indians of the Nebraska territory and neighboring states . . . widely known teacher in creative writing at several state universities."[2] The author herself took special pleasure in her recognition as a storyteller.

In the same month, Mari was featured in Flair, a stylish new picture magazine. The epigraph from Old Jules—"One can go into a wild country and make it tame, but, like a coat and mittens that he can never take off, he must always carry the look of the land as it was. . . ."—was used as the unifying theme of the article, which was illustrated with photos of Mari with Masoud, the Arabian horse. The profile brought a request from Carl Sandburg, whom she had met during her Denver days. He asked her to contribute a folk song for a folio he was publishing that fall. "The very rare and superbly American Mari Sandoz," he called her. "Some of her books will be standing and in use when the best sellers of the period are in the dustbins of oblivion."[3]

Just at the time the article appeared in *Flair*, the Atlantic Press told Mari they no longer planned to reprint *Old Jules* and sold her the plates. According to her thinking, it was typical of the bad timing of events in her life. Edward Weeks had returned her early-draft chapters of *Cheyenne Autumn* that spring, saying that in the first chapter she had taken too much for granted, had not worked hard enough to keep the focus clear, to make the reader feel in sympathy with what was to happen. And if it were to have anything like a general audience she would somehow have to overcome the initial reluctance of most Americans to read about Indians. In July, after reworking it, she dropped off her latest revision at the office of Jacques Chambrun, to be sent off once more to the Atlantic Press.

That summer, after her eight weeks in Madison, Mari returned to the Lazy VV Ranch for her last visit. The Van Vleets were closing the famous Arabian horse ranch, for "The Boss" was no longer able to tolerate the altitude of the mountains north of Boulder. Thereafter she would visit them at their Denver home, but the pastoral interludes of the mountain meadows were over. It closed what had been for her a romantic and rather fabulous epoch, in which she had enjoyed glorious scenery, beautiful horses, opulent surroundings, stimulating people, and in which she had been able to relax and use her imagination for fun and pleasure.

On her return to New York in September, she found the Atlantic Press had rejected *Cheyenne Autumn* again. The editors could not overcome the chronological difficulties that made the story so hard to follow. Soon she discovered the cause of some of the problems. Always working against a deadline, she had rushed her manuscript, together with her historical maps and pictures explaining the book, to Chambrun's office in the same taxi in which she left for her summer course at Wisconsin.

But when the agent delivered the manuscript to the press, the maps and pictures were left in his office. The publishers were not aware that fine comprehensive maps of the region existed in the missing papers, maps bringing the high points of history together and showing relationships no other historian had been aware of.[4]

Other publishers were interested in the manuscript, however, and since she now had the plates for *Old Jules* and *Crazy Horse*, she hoped to work out an arrangement for the three books. Acting as her own agent, she offered the package to Paul Hoffman, by then at Westminster Press in Philadelphia, for the two, having made up their differences some time before, were once more good friends. Mari would have liked to work with him better than anyone else, but Westminster turned down the offer, perhaps because some of the material did not seem suitable for a church press.

She also changed agents. At one time she remarked that selecting an agent was, next to choosing a spouse, the writer's most important voluntary human association, and there were about as many opportunities for bad choices.[5] She had had three and considered several others. Margaret Christie had lasted a year, back in 1929–30. Both Harold Ober and Jacques Chambrun had been her agents for several years, but Ober had not been very active on her behalf for some time, and when he criticized *The Tom Walker* she began to deal with Chambrun exclusively. The fiasco of the misplaced maps for *Cheyenne Autumn* indicated to her that Chambrun was not interested enough in her work either. In December 1950 she arranged for McIntosh and Otis to represent her. The agency was made up of women; Mary Abbot, who dealt primarily with novels, eventually worked most closely with her.

Giving the agents a short résumé of the publishing history of her Cheyenne book to that point, Mari told them she was still working on the manuscript and would try any changes a publisher might like, provided the book was not cheapened below the standards set for her six-book series about the coming of modern man with gunpowder and iron to the High Plains.

As lack of money began to plague her again, she turned to

"light stuff" to pay her bills, writing from December 1950 to March 1951 on "bread and butter" fiction. The result was "The Lost School Bus," written in two months but on her mind since the great blizzard of January 1949 had struck the Midwest. Her niece Celia, a country school teacher in the sandhills, and her pupils were in a school bus that overturned during the storm. Luckily, they found protection and provisions in a nearby shack, where they remained twenty-three days until rescued. Mari speculated on what would have happened if the shack had not been there, and created from this situation a story in which the teacher and seven children, aged six to twelve, are stranded in a willow clump for eight days. Once more she used the opportunity to write an allegory. Each child represented a different type of upbringing, giving the writer an opportunity to elucidate her ideas on child care, but few readers recognized it as such. Many found it, instead, an interesting character study of individual responses to a difficult situation. In this novelette, Mari was able to make the children believable and the story less noticeably didactic than in her allegorical novels. The *Saturday Evening Post* bought it for three thousand dollars and published it in May 1951.

Although Mari's negotiations with film companies at various times in the past had come to nothing, she was still interested in selling a script to Hollywood. She outlined for the film star Greer Garson a script about a woman frontier doctor, fiction based on a composite of several women who had practiced medicine in western Nebraska in the 1870s and 1880s. When this movie did not materialize either, she decided to write the story as a novel and signed a contract for *Dr. Fix,* as she called it, with Edward Aswell, formerly of the Atlantic Press and Harper's, now at McGraw-Hill. She needed money and she did not expect to make much on her serious books. It had taken until 1949, she figured, to be repaid for the direct expenses of her research on *Crazy Horse,* with no compensation for her time.[6]

Meanwhile, *Cheyenne Autumn* was sent from one publisher to another. Once more the author had a book they seemed reluctant to accept, but she was not as disturbed as when *Old Jules* was making the rounds. She could afford to wait until she could arrange a three-book deal, because she knew her three biographies were important. Her summer workshops at Wisconsin and the short, light pieces she published periodically kept her from being as poor as she had been while waiting for *Old Jules* to be accepted. *Cheyenne Autumn* was rejected by the Atlantic Press; Westminster; Duell, Sloan and Pearce; Dial; Viking; T. Y. Crowell; Norton; and Scribner's. Several tentative arrangements failed to materialize. In October, when she signed with McGraw-Hill for her book about the woman doctor, her Cheyenne book was still not contracted for.

The Korean War had some effect on Mari's feelings about publication. She wrote Elizabeth Otis of McIntosh and Otis in October 1951 that she thought the book should be held up until the war was settled; the Korean women and children running from the soldiers were similar to the Cheyennes running from the soldiers in 1878. Another, and rather novel, concern was the possibility of saturating the market, since the doctor book was already contracted for and her snowstorm story, which had appeared in the May *Saturday Evening Post*, was to be reprinted in the *Best Post Stories for 1951*, to be published in 1952. But if by chance the Cheyenne book should come up during the discussions about the doctor book with Aswell, perhaps he would be interested in it.

Concentrating on *Miss Morissa*, as she retitled the doctor book, Mari traveled that fall through the Black Hills and western Nebraska to get a sense of place. She had forgotten how exciting the area of the gold trail from Sidney to Deadwood was. She stopped at every old stage station she could locate, from Water Holes on the Sidney tableland to Deadwood. She went to the Wright Gap region; up Pumpkin Creek and across the Wildcat Range; on to Scottsbluff, Mitchell Pass, and Mitchell Valley; down toward the old Bosler Ranch; to the rock crossing on the Platte River, where freighters used to cross before Henry Clarke built a famous bridge; and to Chimney Rock.

Aswell took the *Cheyenne Autumn* manuscript under consideration in May 1952 and after some time agreed to publish it as well as *Miss Morissa*. As for Mari's qualms that the Korean War made the book untimely, she decided that since the war might go on for another twenty years, she would go ahead with publication. Now her problem was to determine which should be published first, the Indian book or the one about the woman doctor. She chose *Cheyenne Autumn* (*Miss Morissa* would be published in 1955). Perhaps one reason for her choice was the reception of her article "What the Sioux Taught Me" in the May 1952 *Reader's Digest*, written to bring the attention of the American public to the fine characteristics of an Indian culture of the past. Many readers discovered the author of *Crazy Horse* and an interest in Indians for the first time.

Mari hoped the article would draw attention to the current problems of the Indians. Since her 1949 reservation trips, she had continued her interest in Indian affairs, writing congressmen, appearing on TV shows, speaking at meetings of the Association for American Indian Affairs. She was concerned about many issues, from discrimination against the Sioux in the border towns of Nebraska to the damage the peyote cult was doing among the Northern Cheyennes, to the maneuvers of the big oil and coal companies to secure contracts on reservations, forcing the Indians off their lands, cheating them of their grazing, mineral, and timber rights.

It was to Brummett Echohawk, the Pawnee Indian who had illustrated her article on the two Sitting Bulls for *Blue Book*, that she first wrote of her ideas for two Indian books for the twelve- to sixteen-year-olds, books about men who excelled in something other than fighting (she believed in nonviolence herself.)[7] She considered the problems and role of a tribal historian such as Amos Bad Heart Bull, the Oglala Sioux. And she wondered about two famous Cheyenne peace chiefs she knew of, both named Elk River. What had their childhood been like? How had they resisted the pressure of a culture built around the glory of warfare?

Mari's career took a new turn in the fall of 1952, when her current agent, Mary Abbot, arranged a meeting between Mari and Walter Frese, president, and Henry Alsberg, editor, of Hastings House, a company interested in Americana. It led to Mari's longest association with one publishing company. Walter

Frese and the writer had not met before, but Mari had known Henry Alsberg, who was editor of the state guide book series and of the Historical Sites and Records Survey during the WPA and FERA days in the 1930s. The two men commissioned her to write a book, *The Buffalo Hunters*, as part of their historical American Procession Series. She hesitated; she had never thought to write a book at a publisher's request, but Alsberg appreciated the richness of western America history. Unlike other eastern editors, he knew something of trans-Missouri life.

Suddenly it was a very busy time. Although Aswell at Mc-Graw-Hill had not yet set a date for either *Cheyenne Autumn* or *Miss Morissa*, she now had two requests in one week—the buffalo hunters book and her autobiography. The autobiography she would write when she had no energy for anything else, but she accepted the contract for *The Buffalo Hunters*, although she did not then intend it to be part of her own Great Plains series. Work on the revisions and her introduction to *Cheyenne Autumn* kept Mari in New York during the summer of 1952, except for her eight weeks in Wisconsin. It was the first summer in many years she did not go west. She complained, as she had with her other biographies, that the publisher was demanding changes that destroyed the meaning and the Indian feel of the book.

Edward Aswell, scheduling publication of *Cheyenne Autumn* for 1953, assigned the manuscript to a young editor who, Mari recognized apprehensively, had no western background at all. Nor had the copy editor. Her arguments with the copy editor were lengthy, as she once again spelled out her theories of language. Publishers never followed the author's spelling of proper names, she had discovered. In her concern for language, she had gone to great lengths to be as accurate as possible. Earlier, when writing of the Sioux, she had gone over all the Lakota words carefully with the few old men she could find who had the vocabulary and pronunciation of the prereservation days, and she was just as concerned about the language of the Cheyennes. She was particular in her choice of words where white characters were concerned, too, and attempted to suggest the vernacular characteristic of the region and the time.[8]

Noting the copy editor's aversion to her use of participial forms, Mari pointed out that although people from villages and cities tend to drop those forms from their vocabulary, persons who are aware of the continuous changes of life use the -*ing* form. The Indians, she said, were the extremists, particularly the Cheyennes, who had a pervading sense of the present, as their names often indicated: Flying Hawk, Sitting Man—even Dull Knife, which, translated literally, means Knife-that-isn't-cutting. Participial forms are indispensable to this sense of life as a continuous thing, an endless, flowing stream, Mari argued, and for that reason she objected to the editor's attempt to eliminate them.[9]

The arguments became so serious that Aswell finally stepped in, recognizing that the editor he had assigned to the manuscript was the "most thoroughly limited Easterner of his whole staff." Removing the editor, he also announced there were to be absolutely no editorial changes without his approval. The copy editor acquiesced to Mari's use of language, asking only that she add a paragraph in her introduction to explain her use of the Indian idiom and simplicity of expression.

Once Aswell made his point, things went smoothly for a while. Agreement was reached on the placement of the essential map and on footnotes and index, which were much more detailed than those in Mari's earlier books. The author had one more dramatic confrontation before the book was published, this time after it was set in type. When she saw the first galley proofs, she discovered that the text of the first few pages had been altered. Charging into the publisher's office, she demanded that the text be printed according to her manuscript or she would stop publication. Her original text was restored.[10]

After the book was published in the fall of 1953, Mari complimented Aswell and his staff on its handsome appearance. That Christmas he presented her with a hand-bound leather-tooled copy to convey their pleasure in publishing it. It looked like an old classic and she was delighted with the gift, even though she could not forget those months she had spent defending her ideas until Aswell had finally sent down word to let her alone.[11]

Although *Cheyenne Autumn* has to do primarily with the lives of two men, Dull Knife and Little Wolf, who were leaders in their own culture even before they challenged the United States government, it was also intended to portray "the destruction of a whole way of life and the expropriation of a race from a region of 350,000,000 acres" by the whites.[12] The book stresses the heroism of the fleeing Cheyennes, their idealism, and their view of life, which was almost destroyed by the government's animus. The material, combined with the author's vision, dictated an epic treatment: a long narrative in elevated language, a wide landscape, the story revealed through a series of events rather than through a tightly constructed plot, and characters of high position performing actions important to the history of a nation or race. Many people have recognized that the Indians' way of life on the plains was the very stuff of legend and myth. Through her knowledge of John Neihardt's beliefs and her friendship with folklorists who subscribed to the theories of Frazier's *Golden Bough*, and also as a historian, Mari recognized the recurrence of events. What had happened to the Jews fleeing Egypt, to the Greeks in Persia, and to the Mongols on the steppes of Russia could happen again.

A unifying factor in *Cheyenne Autumn* and one of its strengths is the aura of everyday Indian village life and customs which envelops the entire story. Only through a minute knowledge of Cheyenne attitudes and mores could the author have captured this sense of life as it was. She knew, too, the importance of their religion—the significance of Sweet Medicine, their culture hero, and the importance of their religious objects, the sacred arrows and buffalo hat. "The Cheyenne religious beliefs, rituals and practices," she wrote, "once permeated every thought and act of this people and made them, although numerically a small minority, one of the great tribes of the Plains."[13] Such high levels of personal and public virtue, courage, and integrity could come only from remarkably effective philosophical and religious culture patterns, such as those centered on the Cheyenne religious objects and the high standards required of those in charge of them.

As in all her Indian books, Mari used Indian perspectives and

Indian language patterns as nearly as she was able to render them. As she explains in her preface, "To convey something of these deep, complex, and patterned inter-relationships which I myself sense only imperfectly, I have tried to keep to the simplest vocabulary, to something of the rhythm, the idiom, and the figures of Cheyenne life, to phrases and sentences that have flow and continuality." She thought that the language of the Cheyennes was the loveliest of the Algonquin languages, soft and flowing—the Cheyennes never raised their voices, even in political oratory. She used in all her Indian books the precursive Indian sense of place, which is described in relation to the speaker himself—his relationship to the universe, his sense of the individual in his world, of being one with nature—and his sense of time, both past and future existing forever in the present. Given her fascination with words, it is not surprising that she worked at language continuously. She wrote a friend who asked about the naming of Buffalo Tongue River that at one place it supposedly made a gurgling noise that reminded early Indians of the curious sound buffaloes were supposed to make with their tongues. She was not sure that was true, however; she had sat out close to the buffaloes around Denver for many hours and had not been able to detect anything like the noise the Indians talked of.[14]

Like her other books, *Cheyenne Autumn* was affected by childhood influences. In the preface Mari speaks of the stories she heard then: "In my childhood old trappers and Indian traders or their breed descendants still came to visit around our fire on the Niobrara River. The Indians told stories too." Her acknowledgments of help begin with Old Cheyenne Woman, who had been on the flight and was one of the few participants still living when she was pulled from the last battle hole near Fort Robinson, close to Warbonnet Creek—one of the "seven women and children alive but wounded, one woman to dying." The aunt of the young artist Little Finger Nail, she had carried a child on her back during the long trek. She had also been wounded at Sand Creek and the Sappa. Ironically, Mari points out, the woman survived the terrible ordeal only to live out her life among strangers: "She nursed many white children through the diphtheria epidemics and finally died, a pauper and alone, in a little white-man town." At one time Mari considered dedicating the book to Old Cheyenne Woman and Little Finger Nail. She acknowledged, too, all the other Indians who helped but who wished to remain anonymous because it was contrary to Indian custom to talk of those who have died, and perhaps because they still feared reprisals for the Sappa killings. Her end notes, however, make it clear that she checked oral information against written records.

She had another unique source, her father's friend Wild Hog. One of Dull Knife's headmen, captured and held hostage while the rest of the band fled from Fort Robinson, he attempted suicide so that his family would be able to remain in the North with their Sioux relatives. He recovered and later told his story to Old Jules, who took notes of their conversations to send to his Swiss sweetheart, Rosalie. Although Wild Hog died before Mari herself could hear his tales, she had over two hundred pages of those notes, most of them regarding the government's Indian policy and Wild Hog's belief that the Cheyennes were all to be killed—to be "wiped out."[15]

Her later reading also influenced Mari's views of the Cheyennes and their fate. Both the ironic humor in Franz Kafka's parabolic novel *The Castle* and the immorality of the political policies described in Hitler's *Mein Kampf* seemed to her to be pertinent. She subtly paralleled the government's Indian policy to Hitler's persecution of the Jews, an implied comparison many readers noted. She also emphasized the immorality of an inimical bureaucracy's constant frustration of the Indians' attempts to return to their homeland. Once more she repeated her theme that the United States had destroyed much of its potential for greatness because of its treatment of the Indians. She saw the flight of the Cheyennes not as an isolated incident but as a typical result of colonization that might have happened at any place in the world to which settlers were sent to convert a wilderness into a market for capital and manufacture; it was an area of exploitation for the homeland, in this case for the eastern vested interests.

Mari was never happy about the structure of *Cheyenne Au-*

tumn. The publisher insisted on the two expository sections, "The People and the Time" and "Gone Before," following her acknowledgments and foreword. She often stated she had ruined the book at their insistence, by putting such a mass of exposition at the beginning rather than inserting it as necessary in the text: "All my life I'll be ashamed of the mutilation that was demanded of me before McGraw would publish *Cheyenne Autumn.*"[16] Aesthetically she was undoubtedly right, but for those not entirely familiar with the history of the Indian wars the early information is essential.

Cheyenne Autumn received more critical acclaim than *Crazy Horse.* Few readers objected to the long explanatory sections, and there was much less criticism of Mari's use of idiom, although some reviewers still found it a pseudo-language and therefore neither authentic nor of literary value. Inevitably, some made comparisons with Howard Fast's book. Oliver La-Farge, himself the author of a Pulitzer prize-winning book about Indians and long interested in their literature, commented in the *Saturday Review of Literature* that Fast had taken the point of view of the whites attempting to deal with the Indians, so that the Indians, though actually the heroes, were cast in a negative light. "It remains a good book, a surprising one to come from a devoted follower of the Communist line, but it lacks internal view of the protagonists. Mari Sandoz has gone inside the Cheyennes."[17] She, of course, agreed with the reviewers that hers was the more authentic version.

Readers responded favorably, too. Not only had the earlier *Crazy Horse* prepared them for the Indian locutions, but the subject matter, the heroic flight, caught the imagination of many. Helen Mary Hayes, a writer for the *Lincoln Sunday Journal and Star,* expressed her admiration privately: "*Cheyenne Autumn* is a cracking good yarn and could stand alone on that basis. It's so much else that I'm glad I don't have to analyze it for an English class or something. About four times in the course of every page I think, Who else would know that? Who else would bother to find it out? Who would put it down just that way? The law of averages says I don't catch everything, but believe me, I get an awful lot besides what is printed."[18] Another friend,

Mamie Meredith, also praised the work: "I thought *Crazy Horse* could hardly be surpassed, but the Cheyenne story is much bigger. The geographical details alone would be a tremendous problem. Digging out, from so many records, the sequence of events, causes and effects, is your greatest achievement so far. No one who has not worked with conflicting tales from many records can begin to appreciate your accomplishment."[19] In England, Hugh Brogan, in the *Manchester Guardian Weekly*, compared the book's theme to that in William Golding's *The Inheritors* and Cecil Woodham-Smith's *The Great Hunger*, an account of the English government's guilt in the Irish potato famine of the nineteenth century. Even Mari's use of fictional techniques in writing history was dealt with more kindly than by reviewers of her earlier books.

Perhaps the most enthusiastic and thoughtful review was that of her friend Thomas Hornsby Ferril in his "Childe Herald" column in the 5 December 1953 *Rocky Mountain Herald*. "A new book, *Cheyenne Autumn* by Mari Sandoz, has demoralized me," he began. He became so engrossed in the book that he searched out several sources to track down more information. Beginning to read the book over the weekend, he finished it between midnight and five o'clock Wednesday morning. He admitted he believed that in *Crazy Horse* Mari had gone too far in inventing dialogue for historical characters only recently dead—a point they argued continually. Yet she used the same method in *Cheyenne Autumn* and he did not object to it. She had so saturated her spirit with the Indian culture that her imagined words for Wild Hog and Pretty Walker were as true as the speeches she had documented in her notes. Ferril admitted she had her sentimentalities and prejudices that annoyed him, but he could only express his gratitude for "this book which has nailed me down and cluttered my library with so much collateral inquiry." He was well qualified to judge the book and ask penetrating questions: his antecedents were pioneers (his grandfather rode with Jim Bridger and General Patrick E. Connor in the Indian campaigns in Wyoming in the 1860s)—and he is a foremost western critic and a noted poet.

A further accolade came from Rufus Wallowing, a tribal

council member of the Northern Cheyennes, who asked Mari to write a sequel covering the period from the group's arrival in the North until about 1884, when they "finally found a country and settled down" on the Tongue River Reservation. But not all Cheyennes agreed about the book; some criticized the inclusion of the reflections of Little Finger Nail, believing the author could not know his thoughts. That criticism would not have bothered her, however, for she often asserted that modern-day Indians knew less of their own history than researchers such as she.

Cheyenne Autumn was listed by the *New York Times Book Review* as one of the best 275 of the 11,000 new titles published in 1953, not one of the best-sellers, but attracting a respectable audience. It was noted by persons in the scientific, historical, and anthropological fields.

A young Episcopalian seminarian, Peter J. Powell, was so impressed with *Cheyenne Autumn* that he has made Cheyenne religious life his major research interest. Father Powell first called on Mari at the University of Wisconsin in 1953 to tell her of his admiration for her earlier *Crazy Horse*, beginning a friendship that lasted until her death. Their mutual tie was their concern for the Cheyennes. She gave him help in his initial search for information, introduced him to people on the northern reservation, and counseled him on many points of Cheyenne custom. She also recommended him for several research grants, though she would not take credit when he received them. Such good things, she said, come because they are worked for and wished for by those who have nothing personal to gain, once more indicating her Whitman-like belief in a sea of good-will from which such things could be drawn.[20] Father Powell considered *Cheyenne Autumn* the greatest of all source books on the Cheyennes and his two-volume study, *Sweet Medicine*, is studded with footnotes crediting her book or information from her.

With *Cheyenne Autumn*, Mari finished the third of her projected six-book series of the plains; she was just past the midpoint of her thirty-one-year publishing career. In *Old Jules*, *Crazy Horse*, and *Cheyenne Autumn*, the first and the last published eighteen years apart, she remained remarkably consistent in her ability to recreate a man and his time. The biographies also allowed her strong didactic sense to function without overwhelming her characterization, as often happened in her fiction. As her real heroes acted out their fate, the moral issues could be recognized easily enough.

Although these books have recognized value as history, the author's great achievement in the biographies is her literary art. Her imagination could work best with this kind of material, her strong sense of place making it easy for her to identify with events occurring not far from her childhood home and with people who had lived in her region. This factor—her identification with the people and the region—is the key to the unity and strength of these three biographies.

At the Van Vleets', 1947.
One of their horses inspired a
novel that Mari never published

Ten
The Harvest Years

Mari Sandoz's relationship with Hastings House followed what seemed by now to be a consistent pattern. She blew up early in 1954 over *The Buffalo Hunters*, baffling editor Henry Alsberg and publisher Walter Frese, who to this point had found her affable. The first time they offered criticism she thought unwarranted, she resisted like "a granite wall." She was sorry, she wrote Alsberg, if she had deceived them into thinking she was malleable. She had agreed to write a commissioned book only because she considered both men sound in their field. The granite wall would stand.[1]

Now, at last, Mari seemed to have the upper hand with editors. In resolving their differences, Hastings House deferred to her a good deal more than her earlier publishers had. Alsberg wrote of his pleasure in her approach to her subject: "Somehow you have made the buffalo almost human, a great stupid, blundering animal that nevertheless arouses the sympathy of the reader, a sort of Ajax of the Plains."[2] He thought too that she had managed to expose the folly and wickedness of the white man's treatment of the Indians without resorting to preaching. Indeed, Hastings House liked her writing so well they urged her to sign with them for the remaining books of her projected Great Plains Series, although the publication of *Cheyenne Autumn* by McGraw-Hill seemed to eliminate that possibility. Mari was also under contract with McGraw-Hill for *Miss Morissa* and felt she owed Edward Aswell first chance at the rest of her series.

Now that her latest battle with publishers seemed to be settled, a number of personal difficulties confronted her. Don Hollenbeck, a friend whom she had known since college days, committed suicide. He had called her shortly before but was unable to reach her. When another acquaintance had killed himself some time earlier, she had regarded it as an irresponsible act and blamed it on his lack of maturity. About the death of Hollenbeck, a nationally known journalist and radio commentator, however, she felt differently. She believed he had been driven to suicide by the hounding of Jack O'Brian and Senator Joseph McCarthy during the Senate "witch hunts" directed against Communists. She feared McCarthy's power and was angered at the Senate's inability to stop his egregious actions.[3] His blatant leaking to the press of secret information from his investigating committee and his callous persecution of those he investigated made him much like the demagogues she had portrayed in *Capital City* and *The Tom Walker*. Her fiction was now being played out in real life.

Mari was facing a more personal crisis as well. In May, she went into the hospital for removal of her right breast. She vowed she would not let this cancer terrorize her—as a child she had had a gun pointed at her twice by her maddened father and now she would not allow herself to panic.[4] And she did not. She took a private room in the hospital, an unjustifiable expense except that she needed quiet to write, working until the moment she was taken to the operating room and throughout the eight days she remained in the hospital. Within a day after the operation, she had her secretary in her room, dictating to her a story she had had on her mind a long time, a fantasy about a little man in the sandhills of Nebraska who fell in love with a huge female dragonlike creature living in an alkali lake. The story had its genesis in tall tales she had heard as a youngster in the hills, and although it was written with a light touch, she referred to it as allegory. She called it "Ossie and the Sea Monster."[5]

The cancer seemed to have been detected in time and did not require further treatment. Mari was up and moving briskly about within a very short time. When she decided her wound was not healing as fast as she thought it should, she resorted to a method she had learned that Colonel Grenville M. Dodge used on the Kansas prairies in 1870. He had put soldiers with stubborn wounds out into the air and wind with the wounds bare. Since she could not go to the Kansas prairie, she adapted the treatment to her New York environment, sitting before a fan until she had a good, tough scab.[6]

Her operation and recuperation had interfered with her supervision of the printing of *The Buffalo Hunters*. She had not seen the final proofs or the galleys of the bibliography, and she was incensed at the inaccuracies she later found. One of the illustrations was "pure hokum," and the cartographer not only had misspelled Bismarck, but had put it in Minnesota instead of North Dakota, necessitating a change in the map after the first copies of the book had been released. She corrected such errors as she could, but to change them all was too costly. The copy editor responsible, whom Mari thought insufferably officious, was discharged, but the author was still unappeased. Such slovenly work hurt the author's reputation, not the publisher's or the copy editor's. Once more someone had botched the maps and illustrative material she felt so crucial to an understanding of her work. Hastings House wanted to publish her history of cattle in North America, but she vowed to her agent, Mary Abbot, that there would never be such a book unless she could see every word in proof, and the proofs for the maps and illustrations as well. The cattle book was to be one of her Great Plains series and she would not stand for such errors in it.

As a concession to her convalescence and in order to do research for forthcoming books, Mari did not teach her usual Writers Workshop in Wisconsin that summer, thus reducing her taxable income for the year to less than one thousand dollars. She did continue to work with six or seven students from earlier classes and to encourage others with ability, but the thought of her absence seems to have distressed several faculty members as well as the students. One professor protested: "One of the things that you have done best for the Writer's Institute is to infuse the feeling of urgency: writing is worth doing, worth giving one's best efforts to. Even those with little talent have felt the force of this belief. The word 'inspiration' has been trivialized but what it used to mean is what I mean that the students have got from you."[7]

In late summer, Mari went west to promote *The Buffalo Hunters*. The book went on sale 23 August in Lincoln to celebrate Nebraska's territorial centennial. The day was also designated Mari Sandoz Day by Governor Robert Crosby and appropriate festivities were held. The same week, Mari's picture appeared on the cover of the *Saturday Review of Literature*. Ignoring her recent operation, she scheduled a grueling six weeks in Iowa, Nebraska, and Colorado, autographing in stores, giving interviews, and appearing on TV and radio shows.

The Buffalo Hunters, with an animal as its central figure, traces the effect of the bison on the history of the West and employs the organization she used later in *The Cattlemen* and *The Beaver Men*. The foreword gives a brief panoramic sketch of the bison, its habitat and life patterns, from the early sixteenth century to the time of its near extinction in the late 1800s. The author brings in her own association with the subject, as the reader might anticipate, but only briefly, as she retells a myth a Pawnee Indian once told her of the buffalo's role in the beginning of the world.

The approach is anecdotal: events are related in terms of how they affect or are influenced by particular men on the scene. This approach gave the author an opportunity to gossip about the historical figures and other old-timers of whom she disapproved, men often built up as heroes but who she believed did not deserve that appellation. Wild Bill Hickok and General George Custer are treated with the most acerbity, but General Philip Sheridan also comes in for criticism. Mari had been investigating Hickok since she was a young teacher in 1922, and she considered him a true badman, a psychological killer. Custer's overweening ambition and severity with his troops, she thought, did irreparable harm to the Indians as well as to those around him; she never forgave him for the battle of the Washita, an Indian massacre similar to those at Sand Creek and Wounded Knee. General Sheridan, too, she considered a small man for the big part he was expected to play in history.

Buffalo Bill Cody is another frontier figure who fares badly at her hands, but her feelings about him were somewhat less hostile. She objected to the legends created about Buffalo Bill—about his prowess as an Indian fighter and scout—whereas he was actually a notorious drinker, more often in saloons than in the field. She recognized Cody as a great showman, but she knew too much about him from his former acquaintances and from local newspaper accounts from North Platte, his home, to allow the fanciful hero image to stand.

Most reviewers spoke approvingly of The Buffalo Hunters, but some commented that using a species of animal as hero made it less interesting. Several complained that a proper bibliography, index, and annotation would have made it more valuable as a reference book. (The author's illness undoubtedly contributed to this omission.) The most consistent criticism was directed against the use of invented direct dialogue. Carl Coke Rister, for example, in the 21 August 1954 Saturday Review of Literature, the issue with Mari's picture on the cover, criticized "the overuse of imaginative fill-in dialogues," ruling the book out as the definitive history of the American buffalo primarily on this count. Once again Mari defended her work on the grounds that every characterization of a person, a time, or a practice in all of her nonfiction came directly from contemporary sources. Furthermore, she argued, her use of direct dialogue helped give a sense of the character of a region at a particular time as nothing else could. Using authentic idiom was an artistic principle with her.[8]

Almost all the reviewers praised the detailed descriptions and the panoramic view, acknowledging the novelty and drama of her approach to history. Orin Stepanek, a longtime friend at the University of Nebraska, praised her style in a way that confirmed her own belief in her writing: "The book reads well aloud, and that's the infallible test of style. The breath pauses are where they should be; your sense of prose rhythm is biologically right."[9] A young man named James Carr, reading her work for the first time, was so impressed that he asked if he might meet and talk with her about The Buffalo Hunters. His request began a lasting friendship. Later, as a bookseller and publisher, Carr brought out several of her works in leatherbound limited editions. In 1962, at his request, she gave her manuscript of *These Were the Sioux* to his alma mater, Syracuse University, the only book manuscript she gave away in her lifetime. During her final illness, he was one of the few people she allowed to see her.

In September, after her promotional stint for *The Buffalo Hunters*, Mari spent a short time in the sandhills with her family, then made another excursion to southwestern Nebraska, Kansas, and Colorado with friends, including the Wimers, who had given her so much material for *Cheyenne Autumn*. They once again visited Cheyenne Hole on the Sappa, where the 1875 massacre of the Cheyennes by soldiers and buffalo hunters had occurred, and Mari, scuffing in the sod nearby, found a homemade buffalo hunter's kerosene lantern, which she took as one more indication that her version of those events was correct.[10]

After her brief holiday, she went on to Colorado to promote *The Buffalo Hunters* and to speak to the Denver Posse of the Westerners. She was a charter member of the New York Posse of that national organization dedicated to promoting the literature and history of the West. Her subject was "Some Oddities of the Plains Indians." Much of the material in her speech later appeared in the little book called *These Were the Sioux*.

Returning to Lincoln once more before going east, Mari gave another major address, "The Look of the West,"[11] for the Nebraska territorial centennial meeting of the State Historical Society and received the Distinguished Achievement Award of the Native Sons and Daughters of Nebraska for her "sincere and realistic presentation of Nebraska as it was." The honor was a surprise and one she cherished, for it confirmed to her that she was giving an accurate picture of western history. It was a fine way to end her western tour.

The six weeks of strenuous activity in the West worried her friends. She seemed determined to ignore that she had undergone major surgery, but several people noted her severe fatigue on her return to New York. When she was eulogized at a surprise meeting of the New York Posse of the Westerners held in her honor, she began to feel almost as if she had already died.[12] But, regaining energy quickly, she once more became involved in a variety of projects. Preparing *Miss Morissa* for publication, she also went to Philadelphia several times that fall to work with her friend Paul Hoffman, trade editor at Westminster Press. With his aid she was putting together a collection of short stories and reminiscences that would include "The Lost School Bus." Due to come out in November, the book would carry the story's new title, "Winter Thunder." Paul and Mari had returned to the easiness of the "klatches" of old times. At his invitation, she often came as guest of honor for author-editor parties. She recalled that it had been nineteen years since Paul's enthusiasm had convinced the editors at the Atlantic Press that they should publish *Old Jules*.

Paul Engle offered her a teaching position at the University of Iowa Writer's Workshop, but she was too busy to accept a full-time job.[13] Now writing a good deal of fiction, she was putting the final polish on *Miss Morissa* and was behind schedule on a short novel begun some time ago for Paul Hoffman at Westminster. This one, intended for a young adult audience, she called *The Horsecatcher*. It was the book she had first mentioned to Brummett Echohawk several years earlier, fiction but based on the youth of two actual famous Cheyenne horsecatchers. Mari was still thinking about *Son of the Gamblin' Man*, too, now outlined for twelve years. Sometimes she was appalled when she stopped to realize how much of her time she spent on books that had no place in her original scheme of things.[14] She was eager to start on the serious writing of the cattle book to be included in her plains series, but it was hard to keep up the pace.

Slogum House was again being mentioned as a possible play or film, but Mari felt its chances in either form at that time were slim. Someone suggested, too, that *Capital City* be made into a movie so people could see the excellent exposé of fascism and McCarthyism, but no serious offer from the film industry came through. An option on *Crazy Horse* had expired in 1951 and another, signed with Gregory Ratoff in 1952, had also run out, but *Old Jules* was once more of interest to several companies. Little would come of it, she suspected; she had a low opinion of Hollywood's ability to produce authentic history in movies. Some years earlier she had complained to Cecil B. De Mille, director of many of the spectacular films, about historical inaccuracies in the movies. She had received a polite but firm refutation of her charges.[15]

Of more immediate concern, Mari learned that Greer Garson, for whom she had first conceived *Miss Morissa*, was now making a movie for Warner Brothers called *Strange Lady in Town*, about a woman doctor in the 1800s. The setting was New Mexico rather than Nebraska, but the story appeared to be much like hers.[16] She was worried about the similarity, especially since she had given permission to Hal Kantor, well known scriptwriter for movies and for the George Gobel television show, to write a film script of *Miss Morissa* independently, hoping to sell it before the book was published. The threatened competition from *Strange Lady* could ruin the chances for *Miss Morissa*.

She was worried, too, about *Crazy Horse*. She had heard rumors for some time that Universal-International was filming the life of the Indian chief, starring Victor Mature, John Lund, and Suzanne Ball. Mari heard the script had, without authorization, borrowed liberally from her book. Friends in the studio reported they saw scriptwriters using her book, and the synopsis and production notes, sent to her surreptitiously, confirmed her suspicions. She believed the movie to be an outright steal of her material. Her film agent and other friends advised her to wait until the picture was released before taking any action. Then if she found portions of the movie that could have come from nowhere else, she would have every right to sue.[17] She was concerned not only about the matters of copyright violation and of money, but also for the damage the film might do to the image of her favorite hero. Her Lincoln friend, Helen Mary Hayes, sympathized; it would be a "nasty dirty deal" if the company robbed Mari and a shame if they ruined the name of a great hero with a "lousy film."[18]

Lousy was indeed the best description of the film, according to Mari when she saw it. She wanted no credit for the story. A pointless fabrication, it did not even pretend to be true to history. Crazy Horse's wife in the movie is the daughter of Spotted Tail, his maternal uncle, a relationship that would be incestuous by Sioux standards. Little Big Man was made a mixed-blood rather than a full-blood Indian, and in the film he is the villain who actually kills Crazy Horse, whereas in many accounts, those that Mari accepted, the chief died from a wound from a white soldier's bayonet. Refusing to have her name associated with the film in any way, Mari did not bring suit against the company.

To continue her record of failure with films, neither Kantor's script of *Miss Morissa* nor any of her negotiations for *Old Jules* came to anything. On the other hand, there were always readers who found her books worthwhile. She was amused and pleased to start 1955 with an unusual award—five dollars sent by a man because he had found *The Buffalo Hunters* so fine. The year before he had started his own private awards program for authors who pleased him; she was the second recipient. He assured her that the amount of the check was based on his bank account rather than the value he set on the book.[19]

Mari's schedule continued to be heavy in 1955. She was behind on manuscript delivery dates, as usual, because she could not stop revising and because she continued to accept new commissions. She had to postpone the delivery date for *The Horsecatcher*, hoping to get it to Westminster by fall. Mary Abbot urged her to continue work on *Foal of Heaven*, the story of the Arabian horse and the Lazy VV Ranch, which had been rejected by two or three publishers, but Mari had not been able to refuse requests for two magazine articles, one for *American Heritage* on the South Dakota artist Harvey Dunn and the other for *Holiday* about Nebraska, part of its series on the states written by famous authors. In the first she would be able to combine her two greatest interests, art and Great Plains history, and in the other she could make known particulars about her native state. She would mention the Platte River, the real highway to the West, but she could also point out the north-south trails crossing the eastward-flowing streams that were like rungs of a great ladder. She was also asked to write a book about General Custer, but this she refused. The subject had been so mauled, so pawed over and warmed over, that she was not interested.[20]

In May, after a short trip west to gather material for the *Holiday* article, she returned to New York to finish preparing *Miss Morissa* for publication. The usual battle ensued with an editor attempting to remove her idiomatic expressions and, even more infuriating, to rewrite her plot. At length, an appeal to Edward Aswell solved the difficulties. Satisfied that the book would be ready for fall publication, Mari turned to other writing and to her summer teaching.

Events both at home and abroad continued to concern her. Albert Einstein died, and although she had not known him, she felt his death marked the end of an age of intellectualism and integrity. The following months saw the abortive Hungarian revolt against Soviet Russia. There were the hydrogen bomb tests in the Nevada desert, the social dangers of which she had already suggested in *The Tom Walker*. The fate of the Indians discouraged her, too. She sometimes felt that neither her work as an individual nor as a member of a group was of much benefit to them. She had written hundreds of letters over the years in her efforts to help them obtain decent educational and health facilities, but as far as she could see, they were now worse off than ever. During President Truman's administration, she wrote to a friend, her activities had helped to get a commissioner of Indian affairs she considered inept dismissed, but now replies from congressmen were often rude suggestions that she mind her own business.[21]

Yet she worried, she told another friend, particularly about the rapid "unlanding" of the Sioux in recent years and their gravitation to the edges of the big cities. Their income was inadequate and they were unfitted and untrained to cope with the discrimination they encountered. She was not sentimental about it: she recognized that there were both good and bad Indians, with most of them simply trying to be as decent human beings as possible. What bothered her was that white people so seldom acted like human beings toward them.[22] Nevertheless, she continued to try to help, both through correspondence and through public lectures.

Miss Morissa, published in the fall of 1955, is characterized by the strengths and weaknesses of much of the author's fiction. The physical scenes as well as the language and mores of the people are meticulously and often fascinatingly described. Most critics, while praising the historical aspects of the story, found the fictional elements less commendable. The characters are not as believable as the scenery. They seem to move at times too obviously in response to the author's purpose; too often the machinery employed is apparent. W. R. Burnett, writing in the *New York Times*, expressed the feelings of a good many when he noted that the book was a mine of information regarding the period and place, but "the potentially interesting story of the young woman doctor gets lost completely, while one unrelated, or barely related, incident after another is told. The central character becomes increasingly difficult to believe in." The author's major problem, according to one student of her work, was her difficulty in integrating atmosphere with the complications of plot; she lacked the fusing power of imagination.[23]

Undoubtedly the major difficulty was her use of source material. She had the lives of three frontier women doctors from which to draw her story. Her proclivity for history may well have overpowered her skill as a novelist in this case. With such a wealth of material, she was not as diligent as she should have been in selecting the events to work into the fabric of her fictional heroine's life.[24] The public, however, seemed eager to read the book in spite of the weaknesses the critics found.

When *Miss Morissa* came out, Mari made the usual arrangements to promote it, particularly in Nebraska and Colorado, and found there were no books to sell. Most authors complain that their publishers do not push their books hard enough; certainly that was Mari's constant cry. She had complained that McGraw-Hill was glacially slow in filling orders for *Cheyenne Autumn*, although it had been named a selection for both the *Military Science Book Review* and the American History Publication Society. When *The Buffalo Hunters* came out, several midwestern critics had not been able to review it because they were not sent advance copies, and supplies for the author's Denver autographing sessions arrived only after she sent urgent wires to Hastings House. Later that fall books were unavailable from October 26 to November 20; therefore, sales for that month were lost. With *Miss Morissa*, the advance publicity was adequate, but when Mari arrived at the western bookstores, not only were there no books to sell, but the publishers were out of stock. They had badly underestimated the market and were losing many potential sales. Although reorders reached three thousand the first week after publication, McGraw-Hill informed Mari they would not have books for five weeks. She demanded furiously to know whether the book would be in the stores she had scheduled for later autographings out west, or whether, after paying her own travel expenses, she would be publicly humiliated before her friends.

Harold W. McGraw, Jr., admitted responsibility for underestimating the demand and assured Mari that *Miss Morissa* would be in the stores at the later date and that the company would step up their advertising and promotion to make up for the weeks the book had been unavailable. He fulfilled his promise in time for her late autographing dates in October. Later, though *Miss Morissa* was one of ten books recommended in *Wings*, the Literary Guild review, and was the Sears Book Club selection for February 1956, Mari felt nothing could compensate for the month of lost sales.[25] In January, *Miss Morissa* was produced on the TV NBC Matinee Theater, but it was done so badly that Mari sent out a form letter to acquaintances disclaiming any connection with the "claptrappy" affair.

In contrast to the inauspicious introduction of *Miss Morissa*, *Old Jules*, which had been out of print for two years, was published in a Twentieth Anniversary Edition by Hastings House and once more was highly praised by reviewers. The response to the reissue of this book so long after its first publication was gratifying; Mari could now be sure it was not dated. Remembering how she had had to objectify her memories to write it, she thought back to the innumerable revisions she had made in the five years she worked on it to remove any connection between the small girl Marie and the author. Although some of the memories, such as her mother's attempt to take strychnine, filled her with grief, she knew that she had managed to write a good book, one that became more valuable with time. Mari heard from an old Nebraska pioneer, Charley O'Kieffe, who wrote her some of his recollections of her father and many other figures in her book. She urged him to write his own memoirs. He followed her suggestion, and in 1960 his work was published by the University of Nebraska Press in its Pioneer Heritage Series as *Western Story: The Recollections of Charley O'Kieffe, 1884–1896*.

Another accolade for her achievements helped to soothe Mari's feelings about the inadequate handling of *Miss Morissa*. The Chicago Corral, the parent group of the Westerners, after polling the members of all the "posses" in the country to select the one hundred best books about the West, announced in November 1954 that she had four on the list—*Old Jules, Crazy Horse, Cheyenne Autumn*, and *The Buffalo Hunters*—more than any other writer.

Eleven

Ties to the West

Now well established as a western regional writer and historian, Mari was in demand as a public speaker and spent most of 1955 shuttling back and forth across the country at a rapid rate, returning to New York briefly to work on *The Horsecatcher,* then going west again for a series of lectures. She spoke at universities and colleges, book-and-author meetings, book fairs, historical societies, and symposiums. Her fees for these appearances were substantial, but when the Omaha Friends of the Library learned she was to be in Chicago and asked if she would speak to them also, she rearranged her schedule to accommodate them, asking only her travel costs from Chicago to Omaha and back. Anything having to do with a public library was close to her heart; she was very conscious of the debt that she owed the libraries and historical repositories of the West.

Her 1955 schedule allowed her to spend her first Christmas since 1933 with her family in the sandhills. The visit came between speaking engagements at nearby Scottsbluff and in Gordon, where she was guest of honor at the annual chamber of commerce banquet. Most of the area residents had long since overcome any hostility they may have felt toward her writing and now took pride in the famous author. Gordon's highway signs, which had formerly read "The Home of Jules Sandoz," now read "The Home of Mari Sandoz."

Upon her return to New York, Mari spent much of the winter working on *The Horsecatcher.* Then, with that book nearly finished and work on *The Cattlemen* underway, she turned once more to the Cozad story she had first become interested in during the 1930s when she was working on *Slogum House*. Although she had known parts of it since she was a child and had been gathering information and writing on it intermittently for years, many aspects of the Cozad family history still could not be verified. There were writing problems as well, for she was attempting to make the father the foil for the son. The former, respected founder of the town bearing his name, was at the same time a big-time gambler in the East, a fact not known to most townspeople. The son, eventually learning of his father's nefarious activities, assumed leadership of the family and later achieved success as a painter under the pseudonym of Robert Henri.

After her attempts to pin down proof of some parts of Henri's life had been frustrated in Denver, Mari had brought her materials to New York, thinking she could write the book there. But she had put it aside time after time. Some of the difficulty was caused by the secrecy that had surrounded the father's activities when he lived in Cozad. She also feared that descendents of the Cozads might be hurt by exposure of events that had been secret so long. But then a lawyer from nearby Lexington, Nebraska, wrote her of his knowledge of those events, and at about the same time Harry B. Allen, a local sleuth, published in the Cozad paper important leads to the mystery of the family's disappearance. The story was featured in the *Omaha World-Herald* and was now public knowledge.[1] As soon as the cattle book was finished, she would work again on *Son of the Gamblin' Man*.

Harper and Brothers asked her to write a book about Nebraska for their projected series on the states. Hesitant at first because she was already writing or planning several other books, she eventually agreed, providing Harpers were willing to wait until she could get to it. Thirty years earlier her story "Fearbitten" had won honorable mention in *Harper's* Intercollegiate Short Story Contest, her first encouragement on a national level. It had given her confidence to continue writing. Now she could repay that early impetus to her career. It appealed to her sense of loyalty.[2]

Another old loyalty also claimed her attention. In 1956, the *Prairie Schooner*, the University of Nebraska's literary quarterly, was feeling a financial pinch and Lowry Wimberly, the editor since its founding, was ill. Some time earlier, Mari had suggested to the University of Nebraska Press that they establish a Lowry C. Wimberly Award for Creative Writing. Now, anxious that her old professor receive recognition and that the *Prairie Schooner* be kept alive and a first-rate publication, she helped in several ways. She sent letters to former contributors and friends of the magazine soliciting contributions of money. She also established a Mari Sandoz Fiction Award, and helped in the search for a new editor (it would be the poet Karl Shapiro, whom she had known through a writing workshop).

The *Schooner* staff used the money she helped raise for a thirtieth anniversary issue dedicated to Wimberly. When they asked for an article from Mari, she was pleased to contribute, not only to help honor Wimberly, but for another reason as well: the *Schooner* had published her short story "The Vine" in its first number. She sent a long recollection, "The Neighbor," first written eleven years before at the Lazy VV Ranch as part of her projected autobiography. The subject of the essay was Charlie Sears, a quiet, gentle bachelor who had shown interest in and consideration for his little neighbor girl. He was a good man, she wrote, "who lived in complete inconspicuousness, but he made my life as a useful and happy member of society possible, despite my heritage from the violent frontier region and family into which I was born."[3] She thought the piece might help single people realize the good influence they could have on children if they concerned themselves about them. In addition to portraying Charlie Sears, the author reveals a great deal about her own childhood and family life.

In June, when the first Mari Sandoz *Prairie Schooner* prize was awarded, the response from the young woman who had won, Ann Gerike, brought back memories. She wrote, in words that seemed to echo Mari's own, that the award was a tremendous morale booster, the first public recognition she had ever had, and the first visible proof that she had some talent. Mari understood those emotions, recalling how much the fifty-dollar award from the Omaha Women's Press Club had meant to her in 1930.

Mari was in the Midwest all summer. She spent her usual two months at the Wisconsin Writers Workshop—her last stint at this work—and then went to Texas once more to do research for the cattle book. When she returned to New York that fall, she found that her two favorite editors had left their companies, Aswell at McGraw-Hill and Hoffman at Westminster. She knew editors changed jobs often, but this seemed almost like musical chairs. It was disconcerting, not only because she liked both men, but also because she was uncomfortable unless her business affairs were settled.[4] Paul, in particular, she would miss. She had followed him from the Atlantic Press to Knopf to Westminster, but this time she would not move with him. She had too many other contracts: she now had four publishers and four deadlines to meet, which complicated her life considerably. Her cattle book for Hastings House, being late, bumped *Son*, contracted for by McGraw, which in turn bumped the Harper book on Nebraska, and so on down the line.

The Horsecatcher, published in 1957, received very good reviews. Writing in the style she first used in *Crazy Horse* and *Cheyenne Autumn* to portray the world of a Cheyenne boy and his tribe in the 1830s, Mari relied on the Indian point of view and language. The protagonist, Young Elk, was patterned after an actual person, a man of peace and a great horsecatcher, but since her information about him was incomplete, she wrote the story as fiction.

It irked her that this small book, which had taken so much less time and effort than her larger works, was more successful financially—it was a *Reader's Digest Condensed Book* selection. In this novella (a form that is neither short story nor novel), she synthesized the historical background with a believable young hero. One critic noted that the work did not suffer from the author's usual insistence on introducing too much detail through digressions that seem to have little to do with the story: "It is the fusion of the simplicity of eating, sleeping, and tribal habits with the complexity of his personality which makes this

book a little classic."[5] Most reviewers found it beautifully written (although the *New York Times* called the prose "frequently
turgid") and most of them easily understood the message. Several spoke of the humor, the gentleness, and the quietness of the
story, and almost all remarked on her thoughtful examination of
the Indian mind and the Cheyenne culture. Although it was
intended for adolescents, most reviewers recommended it to
adults as well. More than one called the slender but beautiful
little book a classic and praised the author as a creative artist of
the first rank.

Mari spent much of the rest of the year on *The Cattlemen* and
on lecturing, often in the Midwest. When she was in Lincoln, she
was approached by the University of Nebraska Press about the
possibility of their publishing a collection of her short writings.
The editors thought such a book might ease their troubled financial state. Eager to help, Mari agreed to consider the proposal,
although she doubted the wisdom of publishing her early short
stories, which now seemed an inadequate gauge of her later
writings. In fact, she told Virginia Faulkner, an editor at the
press, that on close examination of those stories she felt the
writer had no business giving up all the usual things in life for a
career that produced such results.[6] About the only good purpose
she could see for the book would be as a collection of her
research articles, but if Virginia could work out some unifying
scheme for the assorted short pieces it might succeed.

Mari was not afraid of the evaluation posterity would put on
her nonfiction, she said. Good or bad, it was unique, and those
who came after her would have to depend on it to a very large
extent. Her nonfiction had had critical acclaim, even when not
always understood. And upon consideration she thought the
short story "Mist and the Tall White Tower" was worth reprinting. She also recommended "The Smart Man," not published in
the early years but making the rounds of magazine editors when
she burned her stories in 1933 and thus saved from their fate.
Both of these stories illustrated the allegorical aspect of her
work, which critics and the public had neglected.[7]

The author's continued interest in allegory is amply suggested by a list of her favorite books at this time. She included

the grim and epiclike *Independent People,* a novel of Iceland by Halldór Laxness; *The Fable* by Faulkner, because he touched some ancient and deep-lying symbolism in racial memory; *Roots of Heaven* by Romain Gary, a powerful allegory of France and the world; and *The Castle* by Kafka, the book she returned to perennially, always before starting any new book herself, to refresh her sense of man's search for wholeness and identity.[8] She was sure that the dreams and underlying symbols found in the human mind from earliest infancy revealed man's racial heritage. She had read Jung, Fromm, and other psychologists and was interested in experiments like those of Aldous Huxley with peyote. She disapproved of excessive use of such drugs, however, which she feared was happening among the Northern Cheyennes.

The happy fate of *The Horsecatcher* did not befall another of her novellas. *Foal of Heaven,* about Masoud, the Arabian stallion, was turned down by Hastings House early in 1958. Uncharacteristically, Mari did not fight for this book. Once intended as a serial, it had been sent out only a few times and revised only three or four times, but she did not work with it again, apparently feeling it was not worth her while to rewrite it. *Foal* was one of her few longer works not published in her lifetime.

She directed her energies instead toward finishing *The Cattlemen.* When it was ready for publication, she took time to find a new apartment, something she had contemplated for several years but was too busy to do. The owner of the apartment building at 23 Barrow Street had sold it to a syndicate, one she suspected was involved in illegal activities. The immediate effects were an increase in her rent and a series of restrictions that emphasized the impersonal ownership by a corporation rather than the personal landlord-tenant relationship she had enjoyed with the previous owner.[9] The neighborhood, too, had changed since the years in which LaGuardia had been mayor and his benign influence had pervaded the city. Petty criminals and drug pushers were operating in the area and the comfortable Italian families had left the neighborhood. Now the apartment dwellers were merely anonymous tenants.

Even more nervewracking had been the fire in her apartment two years before. The night after she had returned from the West in January 1956, the apartment above hers had caught fire. Although she was in robe and slippers, as soon as she was aware of the fire, Mari began to pile her most valuable files on the fire escape. As the water from the firemen's hoses began to come through the cracks in the ceiling and walls, she continued to collect her material. The other apartment dwellers dressed, grabbed their valuables, and left, but Mari's first concern was for her research material.[10] She wanted then to move to a place with greater security, and she put as much material as she could into storage for safekeeping, but she was too involved with writing and speaking commitments to look for a new home at that time.

Now, after fifteen years at 23 Barrow Street, she moved to 422 Hudson, still in the Village. The building had only two apartments in addition to the owner's. Mari's had large, spacious rooms, three closets, and space for her files and writing materials. But she had chosen the building mainly because it was brick, practically fireproof, and had vaults in the basement where she could store her material. Soon she had her effects as she wanted them, the large rooms almost overwhelming her few pieces of furniture. But even here the sink was the only spot in the kitchen not covered with boxes, and there were files and typewriters in both the study and the bedroom.[11]

The owner, who lived on the floor above, sometimes found her tenant difficult. Mari's appearance was quietly elegant, her clothes always in hues of brown, her shoes particularly attractive, but the landlady discovered that she was capable of bitterness, flaring temper, even occasional malice. She thought Mari a fascinating woman, but not necessarily one she could like.

After she was finally settled in her new home, Mari enjoyed several memorable events. In Cincinnati, Charles Mills composed a *Crazy Horse Symphony* inspired by her book. Much earlier she had tried to convince H. L. Mencken, among others, that the Indians of the West would be a fine subject for opera or other serious music, but no one had paid attention.[12] Later in the year, she received a second award from the Nebraska State Historical Society. In acknowledgment of her historical achievements, the society presented her with its first honorary life membership.

There was sadness, too, at the death in June of her friend and teacher Louise Pound. Since her undergraduate days when Louise Pound had encouraged her in her work, they had shared an interest in linguistics and folklore. Louise Pound had often used Mari's knowledge of sandhill colloquialisms in her lectures. Mari had appreciated her friendship and enjoyed her erudition and wit. Her influence had weighted heavily in the university's decision to confer the honorary doctorate that meant so much.

The Cattlemen, published in May 1958, followed the same general plan as *The Buffalo Hunters*, using an animal as the focal point, and contained some of the same strengths and weaknesses. In her foreword, Mari recalled her own early association with the cattlemen and described her first glimpse of a rancher riding by their home on the Niobrara when she was a little girl: "He sat his saddle so the fringe of his gauntlets barely stirred in the long easy trot, his horse a fine star-faced, well-coupled black." She also stated her aim in writing the book: to dispel the romanticism that pervades the popular western tales of cowboys and cattle. Once more some of the famous gunmen appear: Wild Bill Hickok, Bat Masterson, Wyatt Earp, and others. In *The Cattlemen*, however, Mari provided more information about important persons than she did in *The Buffalo Hunters*, and to that degree *The Cattlemen* is a better book. It has an index and rather substantial bibliography, which *The Buffalo Hunters* lacked. Though she repeats her earlier practice of retailing gossip, she brings in solid verifiable information about such people as Charlie Goodnight, B. H. (Barbeque) Campbell, and Senator Carey "Kit" Carter. She offers a grim picture of the Olives, unscrupulous cowmen, bent on building an empire, who were responsible for the brutal murder of two Nebraska homesteaders. Although she resorts to innuendo occasionally, her statements about the Olives usually have the ring of authenticity.

After a long excerpt about the Olives appeared as "Tyrant of the Plains" in the *Saturday Evening Post*, Mari heard from the descendants of several people involved in the lynching of the two homesteaders, Luther Mitchell and Ami Ketchum, who were seized while under a sheriff's protection, hanged, shot, and their bodies burned by a gang led by Print Olive. The son of the sheriff of Kearney, Nebraska, who had held the two settlers in jail for safekeeping (not of the sheriff from whom they were taken) confirmed the author's account and furnished her with corroborating details. A niece of Ami Ketchum wrote of the effect of the killing on his brother (her father), and gave some details of the family's reaction to it. When the daughter of the judge who released Print Olive from jail insisted that the allegations Mari made about him were incorrect, Mari sent her her references and refused to change her opinion. "When I say a thing in my books of nonfiction it's to the best of my knowledge, wholly true," she told William D. Aeschbacher, the superintendent of the Nebraska State Historical Society.[13]

Most reviewers liked *The Cattlemen*. The *New York Daily News* made it their book of the week, calling it an admirably compact narrative. On the other hand, Lewis Nordyke and J. Frank Dobie found much to criticize. Dobie, in particular, though he had previously praised her books, was critical of this one. While giving credit for her description of the "Big Die Ups"—winters in which thousands of cattle died—and of events on the Northern Plains, he said he was tired of "the same old dance to the same old tune" and hoped for something fresh in treatment. Mari attributed the objections of Dobie and Nordyke to their being Texans who resented any non-Texan writing about their state. Then she delicately pointed out to Lewis Nordyke errors she had found in one of his books.

In honor of the publication of *The Cattlemen*, there was another Mari Sandoz Day in Nebraska in May, and she made speaking engagements from Cleveland, Ohio, to Norman, Oklahoma, to publicize the book, paying most of her own expenses. During this publicity tour Mari joined battle once again with her publishers over marketing. Although *The Cattlemen* was on the *New York Times* best-seller list right after publication, as so often happened there were not enough copies in the stores where she was autographing. Moreover, the printers would be closed for vacation during the month of July, which meant no more books could be printed until August. Even the libraries in the Midwest would not be able to get the book until fall, although in many small towns the library was the only place potential buyers could see it.

Both the publisher and the salesman had promised a shortage would not happen. In a blistering letter to Mary Abbot, Mari threatened to quit writing. "If this were the first time this happened, or even the fifth or sixth, or seventh. But it always happens. Either my books are not worth keeping in good supply or all my publishers are fools." The two books she had under contract she would finish, but that would be all. Unless the problem could be solved, she would give up writing and take a job offered to her by Mutual Broadcasting as a regular panelist. Mari was an interesting conversationalist with encyclopedic knowledge. She would sometimes spend hours, even days, tracking down some minute detail that excited her interest. Precise, definite, and confident of her knowledge, she believed she could talk at length on almost any subject and would be a popular panelist. Much as she would like to finish her series, she was through battling with publishers.[14]

The threat was effective. Her agent and representatives from Hastings House met and agreed that Mari was to have a vote from then on about the size of the first printing, as well as a weekly stock report in writing to keep her up to date on the availability of her books. The mollified author admitted that she preferred doing what she had been training herself for so long—writing. Later sales of the book were good.

In Lincoln often in 1958 to promote *The Cattlemen* and do research for *Son of the Gamblin' Man*, Mari also concerned herself with the problems of the University of Nebraska Press. During 1957 Virginia Faulkner had been working on the organization of the collection of short works, titled *Hostiles and Friendlies*, but internal difficulties at the university had frozen production at the press for months. Mari liked the organization of the material so well she believed that if the press could not publish the book, a commercial publisher would take it.

The press's difficulties were resolved, and by June 1958

Virginia Faulkner noted with some pride that she believed they had a book which, apart from its intrinsic merit as literature and as history, would be a blessing to those who wanted to study, write about, or simply enjoy the Sandoz canon. As Virginia Faulkner wrote in her introduction to *Hostiles and Friendlies,* "The various pieces fell naturally into three categories, of which the first two—Recollections and Indian Studies—pertain to sources of the author's material. . . . In the fiction group [the third category] we see the two kinds of source material in action, so to speak—applied to achieve an artistic end. . . . This 'sources-and-uses' line largely determined the plan of the book—to show how the author's subject-matter and point of view are rooted in her own experience, and to give some idea of the research preparation which enables her to write so surely and circumstantially. . . . In addition to the pieces selected to be run *in toto,* autobiographical sidelights and bibliographical data were extracted from occasional pieces, speeches, interviews, and letters."[15]

When Mari saw the galleys that fall, she approved them heartily, with one or two exceptions. The criticism she did make was sharp. "Never use 'milch' cow in any copy of sandhill material of mine," she admonished. She felt some of her early stories showed appallingly bad writing, but on the whole the book was much better than she had any right to expect, for she had been diffident about this one from the beginning. She complimented Virginia Faulkner as she seldom did an editor, "You did your work magnificently," and praised the appearance of the book as well.[16] Publication was set for the week of 2 May 1959, to coincide with the centennial of the city of Lincoln. Mari would be there for personal appearances in connection with the celebration.

The reviews, too, congratulated the press on having done an admirable job. W. H. Hutchinson of the *San Francisco Chronicle* spoke of fragments that allowed even the dullest reader to "grasp something of the singing voice and nobility of soul this woman has brought to her writing." The *Library Journal* admired the selections, "in truth adult Western fare," and "Miss Sandoz' compressed and iron-biting style, which cuts to the bone."[17]

In addition to launching *Hostiles and Friendlies* in Lincoln that spring of 1959, Mari agreed to make two seven-part series of telecasts for the Nebraska Educational Television network, the series to run concurrently. Because she would be in Lincoln for some time, she took an apartment in a rather shabby part of town, not one a successful author would be expected to have, but she had never cared what the public thought about such things.[18] It was within walking distance of the downtown area, the university, and the Nebraska State Historical Society.

The series of lectures called "Mari Sandoz Discusses Creative Writing" were adapted from material she had used in her writers' workshops at the University of Wisconsin. Noting that her approach was based on Melvin Van den Bark's ideas, she discussed techniques and methods for beginning writers. She also revealed her attitude toward her own work. To her, the most intriguing form of writing was what she called the "facet form." The story has already happened, but the reader is given many versions of it, each section becoming more meaningful until, when the story is finished, it is a beautifully illuminated jewel. Conrad, her favorite author and the first whose work she had read, wrote that way.

Mari spoke, too, of her fondness for the novella, or novelette. A good, true artistic novelette, she believed, dealt with a kind of isolation. In addition to her own *Winter Thunder*, she spoke of other examples she thought especially fine: *Ethan Frome, The Heart of Darkness, The Secret Sharer, Fontamara, The Old Man and the Sea*, and her favorite, *A Death in Venice*, "one of the most beautiful novellettes in the world." In discussing experimental writing, she used *Capital City* as an example. Although her portrayal of a unit of society, the city, as the main character, with each individual representing an aspect of the city, had not been successful, yet she thought that kind of experimental allegorical writing was worth a try. She had been attempting to dramatize her theory that man was no longer an autonomous individual, that from the time he had learned that survival depended on group cooperation he had started to lose his individuality.

She discussed the methods that worked best for her own writing, pointing out how she took voluminous and constant notes on everything that might possibly end up in her books—conversations, events, impressions, ideas—which she wrote on any scrap of paper handy and stuffed into shopping bags hanging on closet hooks in her apartment until she was ready to sort them out for a particular book. She explained her methodical approach to a new work, each time typing the thesis or theme sentence of the entire book and taping it to the wall over her typewriter in order to keep it in mind at all times. She also spoke of her method of revising, redoing some parts of the work as many as fifty times before she was satisfied. A slow, painful, perhaps inefficient way to write, but her mind was not the kind to create otherwise, she declared.

The second television series, "Mari Sandoz Looks at the Old West," amplified her idea that "people without a history are like the wind on the buffalo grass." Designed to entice the audience to view the people and events of the past and present from a new perspective and to create healthy skepticism concerning received, written history, it was presented in Mari's favorite method, that of the storyteller. The series followed a format rather like her books, anecdotal and full of references to specific people and events on the frontier, all illustrating a serious theme. She wanted to stress without stating too baldly that people rather than events were important, and the solid people, not the violent ones, conquered the wilderness. She reminded her audience, too, that one can best understand a great deal of the human story by knowing and understanding the story of one's own community.

Writing, television appearances, and research kept Mari commuting between New York and the Midwest throughout the spring and summer of 1959. She returned to New York to receive an award from the New York Posse of the Westerners for *The Cattlemen*—in their judgment, the best nonfiction book on the West. The award, a statue of a buffalo, was one of the last pieces Frederic Allen Williams did before his death, and for that reason as well as the honor it represented she treasured it. Returning to

Nebraska, Mari conferred regularly with Bruce Nicoll, the recently appointed director of the University of Nebraska Press, for she had added the press to the causes she thought worth supporting. She wanted to help build the press's reputation and increase its sales. Nicoll and his staff were planning a new venture, Bison Books, a line of quality paperbacks which would include reprints of western classics. In 1960 very few scholarly presses published paperbacks, and Mari thought the Bison Books would fill a need, particularly in the fields of history and literature. On every visit to Lincoln she spent time with Bruce Nicoll and his staff, advising about western Americana titles; the press's files are full of her notes and letters calling attention to possibilities for reprinting. Whenever she dropped in at the press there was great excitement. Everyone wanted to meet and talk with her. Her interest in their new venture and her genuine concern for the welfare of the press was evident. One editor recalled that a visit from Mari was "like a shot in the arm."

One of her first suggestions for the paperback line was John G. Neihardt's *Black Elk Speaks*, which she considered one of the three best first-hand accounts of American Indians with any flavor of the old days. Moreover, she wrote to Nicoll, "the people who wrote books and articles trying to 'interpret' Black Elk's mysticism and medicine dreaming expose the shallowness of their preconceived Christian notions. Neihardt had sense enough to let Black Elk speak for himself."[19] Her own copy, picked up long ago at a secondhand store for forty-nine cents, was now worth much more because of the scarcity of copies.

In addition to recommending out-of-print books, Mari occasionally evaluated original manuscripts for the press. She also gave permission for a Bison Book edition of *Crazy Horse*, which the press published in 1961, and the following year authorized a reprinting of *Old Jules*, even though other publishers, among them the University of Oklahoma Press, were interested in the rights. But Nicoll could not persuade her to write either a book on the Wounded Knee massacre of 1890 or her autobiography.

Visiting Fort Robinson again in the summer of 1959, Mari felt the time was right for a companion book to her successful novella for young people, *The Horsecatcher*. It would tell the story of an Oglala Sioux, a boy patterned after Amos Bad Heart Bull, the artist whose pictographic history Helen Blish had analyzed in the 1920s and 1930s. But the fictional hero would have to be placed in an earlier time than his prototype in order for him to participate in the Indian wars. Amos Bad Heart Bull had been born too late for that. The fictional hero, as a band historian, would be required to subordinate his desire for action to his task of observing what was happening, listening to the stories of his people, and practicing the skills necessary to portray events in drawings as well as possible. Mari was not one to indulge in self-analysis, but the idea could well have appealed to her because the book's protagonist would reflect to some extent her own early life. With her own tremendous energy held down for one reason or another as a child, she too became an observer, a recorder.

In Nebraska once again that fall, Mari spoke to the Nebraska Writers Guild at Red Cloud, the home of Willa Cather, whose style she had always admired. She complimented Mildred Bennett, president of the Willa Cather Pioneer Memorial and Educational Foundation, which was undertaking the eventual restoration of places important to the Cather canon: her home, the depot, the bank, and churches described in "Old Mrs. Harris," *O Pioneers!*, *My Ántonia*, *The Song of the Lark*, *A Lost Lady*, and other of Willa Cather's works. Mari recognized the significance of Mildred Bennett's efforts, "so much more important than anyone but you can see now."

Although Mari appreciated Willa Cather's work, there is nothing to indicate that the feeling was reciprocated. When confronted with the inevitable comparisons between the two women writing about the same state, Mari pointed out that they wrote of different times and different locales. Willa Cather's Red Cloud was quite different from the sandhills; it was more settled, closer to the railroads, and more populous in the 1880s than the western part of the state was when Mari's father arrived there in 1884. But the true difference, Mari said, lay much deeper than the material: it was the difference between an artist of Willa

Cather's caliber and an ordinary frontier historian with a desire to write. The two shared one major passion, however: their love of the land.[20]

The Nebraska book for Harpers was far behind schedule because of Mari's travels in the West. However, the editor, M. A. "Buz" Wyeth, got along exceptionally well with her from the beginning. He was sympathetic to her views and, perhaps because of her many years of experience with editors as well as her solid reputation as an author, she quickly established that her ideas and language were not to be tampered with. Wyeth usually accommodated her wishes without argument, as Hastings House now did and as the University of Nebraska Press had from the first.

Mari's affairs were not, however, going well with another of her publishers, McGraw-Hill. Long angered at what she considered their mismanagement of sales of *Miss Morrissa*, Mari was incensed to learn the book was out of print only four years after publication. Then there was the matter of the book with the very long gestation, *Son of the Gamblin' Man*. It had been contracted for in 1955 when Edward Aswell was still editor at McGraw, but the present editor, Ed Kuhn, found flaws in the manuscript. In a long, carefully worded critique, he suggested changes in several scenes, but Mari would have none of it. Her experience and authority now enabled her to override her publisher's views. The book, she said, presented a step-by-step development of the painter Robert Henri in a family and a locale where such a talent was almost unheard of. She believed she had created a new variation on old forms, using a large, dark, and undefined background, with a sort of "mystic naturalism" for the figures in the foreground, a formal written approximation of a Henri painting.[21] McGraw-Hill was unable to see the treatment as she did, and Mari, in view of the fiasco with *Miss Morissa*, was relieved to have this contract cancelled.

Since she was still angry at Hastings House for their lapses in the marketing of *The Cattlemen*, and because her editor, Henry Alsberg, was now gone from there, she did not send her manuscript to them. She preferred not to be at the mercy of one firm.

Therefore, when Clarkson Potter, who was starting his own company, made her a tempting offer for *Son of the Gambling' Man*, she accepted, agreeing to publication in the spring of 1960.

To round out her year, Mari learned of two constrasting views of her work. She was told that *Capital City* had been banned by the Riverside Library in California. The California state legislature's Fact-Finding Committee on Un-American Activities, in a 1948 report, had included her name on their list of Communists and Communist fellow-travelers who had written books purchased by public schools. She was named along with such distinguished Americans as Sherwood Anderson, Pearl Buck, Oliver LaFarge, and Frank Lloyd Wright. At this late date a member of the Riverside Library Board of Trustees proposed that the library not buy or circulate books by those authors.[22] As it turned out, the board of trustees did not agree to the proposal; the books were not banned.

At about the same time, Mari received the first of many solicitations for the bequest of her research materials, this one from the Nebraska State Historical Society. While the charge that her books could be subversive would anger her, the fact that they were controversial would not. The fact that one institution considered suppression of her work while at the same time another respected institution was asking to establish an archive of her material made an interesting contrast.

Mari Sandoz and Melvin Van den Bark, ca. 1958

Twelve
Battles Won & Lost

The year 1960 started out badly with *Son of the Gamblin' Man: The Youth of an Artist,* published by Clarkson N. Potter. Mari's relationship with the firm was unhappy from start to finish. She seethed when she found errors in the biographical information on the dust jacket and thought the photograph they chose to run on the jacket in spiteful taste, although she never considered herself photogenic. She objected, for the only time in her career, to the picture, which emphasized her blind eye and showed her mouth open "like that of a woman screaming in travail."[1] The dust jacket episode presaged the debacle.

When she went on her spring autographing round in the Midwest, spending two weeks and paying her own way, she found the book had not been advertised at all, nor had Potter sent out review copies. The scarcity of review books and the absence of advertising, together with the imprint of a new and unknown publisher, made the book a scandal, she asserted; people would think she had gone to a vanity press.[2] Potter took out a full-page advertisement in the *New York Times,* but it appeared the Sunday after her tour was finished, a waste of money as far as the western markets were concerned, Mari thought. Once more she was disgusted with the entire publishing business.[3]

Son of the Gamblin' Man sold poorly for reasons other than badly timed publicity. Critics and readers found many flaws in it at first reading, and very few gave it a second one. "The inability to show action not simply as it *affects* the character but to show the character being affected, internally, by the action, to show action *through* the character, is a serious artistic flaw," according to one critic.[4] The author had gambled that the readers would appreciate her effort to sketch in the characters lightly, as an impressionist would paint, but almost no one understood the book in that way. Even her friend Caroline Bancroft, in her review for *Colorado Magazine*, could find little to praise: "Unfortunately, the story, even in fiction, remains too confused for the reader's satisfaction. As a biography of a man or a family too many loose ends are left dangling for any true understanding."[5] She softened her criticism by pointing out that the book was filled with wonderful pictorial scenes and authentic bits of high plains lore which would make it worthwhile to those interested in western ranch life and town development in the nineteenth century.

The Bancroft review was only one of the negative responses. Critics found less to like in it than in any other she wrote. *Time*, calling the author "one of the better sod sisters" for her regional writing, thought that since the story was true, she might just as well have told it as such, "instead of grafting stiff-legged dialogue onto striding narrative. Somehow, her Platte seems more vivid than her pioneers, and poor John Cozad looks a bit shrivelled and out of focus."[6]

The review by her friend Thomas Hornsby Ferril in the *Rocky Mountain Herald* disturbed Mari the most. Ferril thought the Cozad-Henri story would have gained had the author used fictitious names. Then he concluded: "The historical novel is always a problem and an opportunity. The writer who doesn't know historical facts writes wretchedly. The writer who knows history too well may let it get the upper hand. The best work is done by the writer who knows his period thoroughly, writes imaginatively and completes a work that gives real history something to live up to."[7] The two had argued before about the use of direct dialogue in her books, but the implications in this review made her more than irritated. Their friendship was no longer close.[8]

The task Mari had set herself was almost impossible, to write a "novel" that was wholly true to fact. In spite of intensive research there were many things about John Cozad that could not be even surmised. In Denver, for example, she had attempted to track down a murder in a sporting house on Larimer or Market street, but the looked-for details concerning Cozad had been hidden too well. Many of her investigations had ended as fruitlessly. By keeping only to the facts that she knew, she eliminated the possibility of creating scenes for their dramatic value, or of establishing motives for the characters' actions, as a novelist could do. The result, according to one critic, was "spoiled history."[9]

Some time after the publication of the book that year, the author wrote down her thoughts on the origins and writing of *Son of the Gamblin' Man*. The story had its roots in her childhood; she recalled having heard parts of the Cozad legend from several men in her own neighborhood who had once been involved in the notorious Olive gang. The outfit was headquartered in Cozad's neighboring town of Lexington but had moved up to northwestern Nebraska when the law came too close to them. Some of the men had talked at length about John J. Cozad, who, they said, had opposed the Olives and their illegal use of government land, just as Old Jules had stood up against the ranchers. The Olives, treated at length in *The Cattlemen*, were a large part of this book, too. This time, their domination of the county seat and the surrounding area made them antagonists to the community builder Cozad.

Cozad himself had written her father Mari noted, suggesting they cooperate in building a new town in the Niobrara River region, perhaps with his son Robert coming to start a colony for artists. Nothing came of the proposal, but she recognized the many similarities between Cozad and her own father. Both were determined community builders, both had raging tempers, both alienated others with their absolute certainty of their own importance—"violent visionaries," someone had called them.[10]

She recalled that the story had been on her mind since Dr. Robert Gatewood, a younger cousin of Robert Henri, had approached her in 1939 and offered her the family materials. She hoped to combine in the one story descriptions of the formation of a region, a community, and a youth, "the young painter up to the time when his course as an artist and a fighter for artists was established." Then she used a familiar metaphor, that of the jewel: "Such periods remind me of the growth of a garnet from its gray matrix . . . the pressures and heats put upon it, the crystallizations often partial and flawed, but now and then perfect, a well-faceted jewel." In a rare apologia, she admitted that a creative manuscript was never really done, that if she went through the book again she would make changes. Whether it would improve it she was not sure, but the revision "goes on just the same, in my mind, for this book and all the others." It was as close as she ever came to admitting that the crystallization of the jewel in this book was indeed partial and flawed.

Earlier books made up to some extent for the disappointment of *Son. The Horsecatcher,* which was a runner-up for the 1958 Newberry Award for young readers' books and was included on the *Hornbook* honor list, had earned over twenty-one thousand dollars in royalties as well as adding to her literary reputation. Hastings House issued a new printing of *Cheyenne Autumn,* which brought approving reviews. It seemed a bit ironic to Mari, who recalled that nobody wanted the book in the early 1950s. "If it hadn't been for a luncheon I had with Ed Aswell, the book would probably never have been published, so thick is the provincialism of Eastern publishers," she commented to her agent.[11]

An offer from another publisher also helped assuage her pride, wounded by the reception of *Son of the Gamblin' Man.* In 1960, Lippincott asked her to write on the Battle of the Little Bighorn as part of their Great Battles and Leaders series. Hanson W. Baldwin, military editor of the *New York Times,* would be general editor. Mari was flattered, but with five books already scheduled with five editors, she had to refuse. The Nebraska book for Harper's was due 15 May 1960; the beaver book, the sixth of her Great Plains series, for which she planned a research trip to Canada the next summer, was due 15 January 1962; the delivery date for *The Story Catcher,* promised to Westminster, was 1 September 1962. Then there was a novel promised to Hastings House for 1 November 1963, and an oil book, the last one of her series, due to them 1 January 1966. Most of her research for these projects was already done, but the writing was not, and she could hardly commit herself further.

Hanson Baldwin and Lippincott persisted, suggesting that she sign a contract for some future date. When Baldwin outlined his recommendations for the series, he could hardly have made it more attractive. He wanted the best account available of selected battles. The books were to be short, about two hundred pages, or 70,000 words. They should have three or four simple but accurate maps; the emphasis should be on good, dramatic writing, skillful characterization, and a selection of important episodes or turning points. The primary interest in the Battle of the Little Bighorn, he felt, would be its significance in the ultimate winning of the West. The book should center not so much on Custer as on the survivors—on the Indians Custer had faced and "the inexorable defeat which was implicit in their victory"—and should exploit the tremendous dramatic possibilities of the event and its importance as a turning point in history. He did not want too many details; rather, the principal leaders and participants should be personalized as much as possible and eye-witness accounts used when possible. In other words, he wanted dramatic narrative, with the final chapter or so the writer's own interpretation of what went wrong or right in the battle. Any famous controversies about the battle or leaders should be brought in.

Baldwin thought that no one else could deal with the Custer battle, its drama, the characters of the leaders, or the consequences as well as Mari Sandoz could.[12] Finally she agreed. Certainly the subject was one she had long been involved with. It was probably the most controversial battle in American history, and she had a great deal of information collected in 1937 and 1938 from the Adjutant General's Office records when they were housed in the old building on Virginia Avenue in Washington, material never touched upon in any account she had yet seen. Since she always had several books underway at one time, she could begin gathering this material into one file as she worked on other books. A book seemed to ripen in her mind as her file grew. She knew she would enjoy working for an editor who understood the fluid nature of frontier warfare. Then, too, signing the contract would permit her to stake a claim to the material, as she had not been able to do in the affair of Howard Fast and the Cheyenne story. Furthermore, finances were a worry since *Son of the Gamblin' Man* was such a disaster, and her next two projected books, the one on Nebraska and the beaver book, would not be the kind to pay for themselves.

While 1960 was financially worrisome, it strengthened her reputation as a western historian. Often consulted by historians and historical societies, she sent material to Michael Straight on the Sand Creek Massacre and to Alvin Josephy, Jr., On Plains Indians for the *American Heritage Book of Indians*. The Nebraska State Historical Society was interested in her opinion of the reminiscences of Luther North, who had assisted his brother Frank in training and leading the famous Pawnee Scouts in the war against the Sioux and Cheyennes in the 1860s and 1870s. Were the reminiscences credible, and were they of interest to the public? Mari had met Luther North, who had stopped by the society when she worked there in the 1930s, and she had heard him and others talk of their adventures. She recommended publication. She wrote that the book would be a valuable adjunct to the official military records of the plains, which showed amazing discrepancies, some of them inevitable because of the corruption of the period and the general laxity and outright disobedience of orders.[13] The University of Nebraska Press published the reminiscences as *Man of the Plains: Recollections of Luther North, 1856–1882*, edited by Donald Danker.

Otherwise 1960 was a bad summer. Her plans to go to Canada for research on the beaver book were postponed; instead she spent her time sweltering and miserable in New York. Mechanical difficulties, the sort that always made her impatient, delayed her there. The apartment building was being remodeled, and the installation of an air conditioner, a process she thought would take two or three days, caused the building to be torn up for several weeks, with workmen coming and going constantly. Always fearful for her research material, especially since she lived close to the center of drug traffic—an area of violence and theft—she felt she did not dare to leave. Then another tenant in the building committed suicide, and there was a flurry of people, excitement, and further disruption of her work.[14]

In June, her old friend Paul Hoffman died, a victim of the violence of the city. As he was moving into a new apartment, three men attacked and robbed him, leaving him unconscious. He died a short time later. Although Mari was no longer associated with him professionally, he had been her friend as long as anyone in the East. After their one quarrel over *Crazy Horse*, long since healed, she had maintained a staunch friendship with him, loyally defending him when others might question his actions or decisions.[15]

In the fall of 1960 Mari escaped to the West. She traveled much of the time that year, following the pattern she had established, five or six major lectures in the spring, then another junket in the fall, usually in October. Her lectures, research, and related activities delayed the Nebraska book once more, pushing its delivery date to January 1961. Apologizing to Buz Wyeth, she reported it was growing into something special, and she had found a name she liked for it: *Nebraska: Love Song to the Plains.*

Love Song to the Plains (Harper's chose to drop "Nebraska") was delivered a week past the deadline; once more last-minute revisions put the author behind. The subsequent discussions with the publisher went remarkably well, for Wyeth was a sympathetic and eager editor. Some revisions were major: 26,000 words had to be cut to keep the book within budgeted casts for the series, and the change in title called for the recasting of several chapters. The old problem with the copy editor reappeared, and Mari responded predictably. If one had something special to say, ordinary words had to have a special arrangement. The repetitions were threads woven to hold the divergent elements together. *Spouse* instead of *wife* was ridiculous. *Slay* was a word for Shakespeare, not for the wilderness. Even worse, a date had been changed, something that could ruin an author's reputation for accuracy. Then in large red letters, she wrote her ultimatum across her manuscript: "But enough of this: I will not go through this whole book on the original trying to correct all your errors. I don't care to have weeks of my time wasted trying to restore accuracy of my work."[16] Wyeth solved the dilemma by finding a copy editor she could work with, a young man from St. Louis who knew the West. The editor suggested a new procedure as well. The copy editor was to check the first two or three chapters, being careful not to tamper with facts, then go over them with the author to be sure they agreed, before going further. This simple and sensible method solved the problem for this book.

Harper and Brothers had good reason to placate the author, for *Love Song*, aptly named, contains some of her finest and most poetic writing about the Nebraska that to her was not a geographic and legal entity but rather a state of mind, a large and vague territory with a special kind of people.[17] One of the themes she develops had been used in her 1959 television series about the West, the idea that everything about the country appeared to fit the category of a tall tale. So many fantastic stories grew up about the region that it was difficult to separate truth from fiction, and often the truth seemed the more fantastic. She tells the stories to prove it. Her theories of the exploitation of the new territory are also reiterated. She stresses that the "gold" of the area, whether from the plews of the muskrat or herds of cattle or boxcars full of grain or the metal itself, flows down the rivers and to the East, where the money is. Repeatedly she ties the development of the plains to economic factors in the East: "The generals had all gone east. Army men might not grasp the Indian situation, but they all understood the possible effect of the panic of 1873 upon their investments, their military careers. Military curtailment would be ordered by the economy Congress and every man wanted to be in Washington to look after his interests. The hard times that drove the generals east sent thousands of the unemployed and the lawless west to the buffalo ranges . . . ." Sometimes she presents the Indian point of view: "All through the early settlement period there was the usual complaint against the Pawnees as thieves and beggars, meaning generally that they came hungry and ate up everything in sight, which seemed logical in the Indian eyes, since the land and the grass were theirs."

Many of the characters already familiar from other books

appear in *Love Song*. Wild Bill Hickok, Calamity Jane, General Philip Sheridan, and Buffalo Bill Cody are once more debunked, although Mari's remarks about Cody are milder than usual: "a man, who, it was said, never deliberately harmed another human being, unless, perhaps, one asked his wife Louisa, Lu, for an opinion." On the other hand, she seems rather to admire Doc Middleton, Nebraska's most notorious horse thief, who reformed to run a temperance bar. She once more suggests the idea of farm-factory units, small factories situated throughout the rural communities in the state, adjusted so the seasonal work of the factory would come at the slack time of farming, in order to give the farmer the additional economic assurance he needs for a steady dependable income and to give the factory worker a healthy place to live and raise his family.

Mari introduces new material in this book, as well as recapitulating ideas and events she had written of before, but *Love Song* stands out among the author's works because of its literary merit. She herself may have recognized this, for she dedicated it to Melvin Van den Bark, "teacher and friend of a writing lifetime." The land itself is the thread upon which the narrative is spun. From the first page, in which Mari describes it as resembling a giant hackberry leaf in shape, to the last, she continually reminds the reader of the look and the shape of the country. Her last sentence recalls the simile used in the beginning, "The Plains will lie like a golden hackberry leaf in the October sun, a giant, curling, tilted leaf, the veins the long streams rising out near the Rockies and flowing eastward to the Missouri."

The language forms that she fought for so long are never seen to better advantage than here. She comments in her foreword that even in her earliest writing she found ordinary words poor saddlebags for transporting her sense of the frontier: "I began to maneuver for special relationships, special rhythm patterns, the strings of words perhaps as abrupt as a cut bank or vagrant as a dry-land whirlwind."

For one of the few times in her career, Mari had a voice in selecting the art work for the book, recommending as the artist another woman with ties to Nebraska, Mary Bryan Forsyth, granddaughter of William Jennings Bryan. Several years earlier, the artist had brought the author a portrait of Crazy Horse, painted as she thought he would look from the description in his biography.[18] Mari liked the portrait, which she felt showed the sensitivity and mysticism of the man, and she now suggested Mary Bryan Forsyth as a logical artist for this book.

When *Love Song* appeared, Mari heard "rumbles in the east" about her interpretation of the history of the plains, but she believed that was to the good. There should be as much difference between Atlantic Seaboard and western versions of history as between British and Colonial versions, she wrote to her editor, Buz Wyeth.[19] Most critics praised the book unstintingly. Walter Havighurst noted the dual authority of participation and research apparent in nearly every page of *Love Song*, which he called a spacious and shining book. Victor P. Hass referred to it as a " 'mood book,' a lyrical and beautiful evocation of this lovely, undulating 'sea of grass' in which we live," and added, "But if *Love Song to the Plains* is the title of one of Miss Sandoz's books, it could also be the covering title of her entire shelf of books. For, in sum, that is what Miss Sandoz has been writing all her life—a love song to the plains."[20] Mari was not entirely satisfied with such praise. Even before publication Wyeth had called the book lyrical, a quality that seemed now to be discovered by practically every reviewer. Mari hoped her old "written with barbed wire on sandpaper" style would not be entirely overlooked.[21]

Now several Sandoz books were available simultaneously, for Hastings House had recently reissued *Miss Morissa* and *Crazy Horse* in addition to *Old Jules* and *Cheyenne Autumn*. In England, Corgi requested permission to publish *Buffalo Hunters* with some excisions. In the fall of 1961, Mari launched *Love Song* at a children's book fair in Lincoln, a week-long series of talks to grade school children in which she fascinated her audience, not only with her storytelling, but by performing Indian dances for them.

These Were the Sioux, also published that fall by Hastings House, was developed from three previous works: the 1952 article for the *Reader's Digest*, "What the Sioux Taught Me"; her speech to the Denver Posse of the Westerners in 1954; and a later article written for the *Reader's Digest* which they did not take. It was a small book, but an important one to Mari, for she could provide information about the Sioux, expecially their ethical and religious systems, that she thought modern anthropologists would never see. It was illustrated with pictographs by nineteenth-century Sioux artists, and both she and her agent congratulated Walter Frese on its appearance. It would be a good book for the Christmas market.

In it Mari describes the Sioux, primarily the Oglala band who were visitors to the Sandoz homestead when she was a small child. The foreword once again establishes her relationship with the subjects of the book:

The Sioux Indians came into my life before I had any preconceived notions about them, or about anyone else. . . . I was free to learn about our Indian friends as I did about the rest of our neighborhood of mixed beliefs, languages and origins.

To me the dress of the Indians was just another folk costume, their language no stranger than English to my German-Swiss ear. But there was something most engrossing about these Sioux and their tipis, their campfires, their drumming in the night, and their ways with thunderstorms, small children and the mockingbird in our wood pile.

The reviewer for the *Christian Science Monitor* stated, "It unobtrusively overflows with Miss Sandoz's lifetime love and respect for these plains pioneers, and with her careful insights into their ways." The *Kirkus* critic pointed out that "in the descriptions of the well established patterns of conduct, Sandoz gives a picture of an orderly, deeply respected way of life that no longer exists."[22]

Another honor came to Mari in the fall of 1961. The National Cowboy Hall of Fame awarded her its Western Heritage Award for the best nonfiction article of the year about the West. The prize was for the *American Heritage* piece on the South Dakota artist Harvey Dunn, which had appeared earlier in 1961. But even with two books and a major article published, Mari felt far behind in her writing, to the point that she at last refused to read unsolicited manuscripts. She would continue to work with former students, but she could not continue to evaluate other manuscripts.[23]

There was time, late that fall of 1961, for a visit with her family in the sandhills and a trip with her sister Caroline once more through western Nebraska and the Black Hills. They went to Bear Butte on the northeastern edge of the Black Hills, this time to refresh Mari's feeling for the expanse of prairie around it, the great campground where the seven bands of the Teton Sioux gathered every summer in the 1850s. Twenty thousand Indians could live two weeks of the year there, with enough grass on the hills for forty thousand horses.[24] This place was to provide an important scene in *The Story Catcher*. Then she hurried back east to get on with her writing; she had been out on the plains most of the last two years.

Nonetheless, Mari spent most of 1962 in travel. In addition to her speaking schedule in the spring, she made two trips to Nebraska in the summer. In June she was one of several distinguished members of a university sponsored symposium celebrating the hundredth anniversary of the Homestead Act of 1862, the first claim under which was filed in Nebraska Territory. Mari, the only lecturer who had actually lived on a homestead, spoke on "The Homestead in Perspective."[25] In July, she returned to teach a summer session at the university.

Her writing early that year was limited to work on *The Story Catcher* for Westminster and an introduction to a new two-volume edition of George Bird Grinnell's *Cheyenne Indians* for Cooper Square Publishers. Harper and Brothers, pleased with *Love Song to the Plains,* hoped to persuade her to write a children's book about the Sioux. She was interested, but she wanted most to get back to the kind of writing with the power to disturb, something current in the allegorical vein of *Slogum House* and *The Tom Walker*.[26] There was plenty to write about, what with the Cuban crisis, the civil rights marches and riots, and the gradual and frightening involvement of the United States in Viet Nam. But whatever she had in mind would have to wait until after her long-postponed research trip to Canada for *The Beaver Men*. Chronologically the first in her series, it would trace the coming of powder and iron to the Great Plains. Starting at

Montreal to see the archives for which she had prepared earlier
by taking French classes, she carried her manuscript with her to
Ottawa, then west to Winnipeg, then along the old north trails
through various Hudson's Bay Company posts, before turning
south down the Souris River to the Missouri. With this final
check on her rough draft for facts and description, she hoped to
have the book finished by 1963. Somewhat to her disappointment, she found that her earlier research in records in the
Southwest and the West, together with her study in archives in
New York, Washington, D.C., and at Yale University, had already provided her with much information the Canadian archives lacked.[27] The trip she had planned to last at least two
months took less than one.

On her return to New York that fall, she learned that the
Nebraska State Historical Society had acquired a famous man-
sion in Lincoln, the home of Bob and Peggy Ferguson, with
whom she used to have late-night coffee, across the street from
her old apartment in the Shurtleff Arms. Always interested in
Lincoln affairs, she took time to write the governor her congratulations and urged that the house be restored as perhaps the
finest example of residential architecture in the city. Mari also
continued to take an active interest in the University of Nebraska
Press. Among other recommendations she had urged Bruce
Nicoll to publish the pictographic history of the Oglala Sioux,
the drawings by Amos Bad Heart Bull that her friend Helen Blish
had interpreted in the 1920s and 1930s. It would be the most
important single volume published about the Great Plains, she
thought. It was the fullest Indian picture history in existence as
far as she knew, and it contained fine details and examples of
exceptional artistry.[28]

Nebraska continued to appreciate Mari, too: she received
another award, this for her Indian writing, from the Nebraska
Society of Children of the American Revolution. Both the Joslyn
Museum in Omaha and the University of Nebraska offered her
facilities for study and research if she cared to leave New York.[29]
But she had long since recognized, albeit reluctantly, the advantages of the East, both for research and for publishing. As she
told one friend, "An outpost in New York is very useful when

you have to talk editors down. From Lincoln or Denver you know nothing; from Greenwich Village you know it all, no matter how seldom one is there."[30]

Current Indian affairs also continued to be of concern to her and she used her influence to help in whatever way she could. Serving on the boards of several interested organizations, including the American Indian Society for Creative Artists, she often went to Washington for hearings or to talk with government officials. She had been distressed when, in 1953, Congress had passed a bill giving legal jurisdiction over reservation Indians to the states without the consent of the Indians.[31] Since then, she had objected to the exploitation of reservation lands. She regretted that thousands of Sioux were forced off their reservations to seek jobs in the small towns near the reservations and the larger cities, as far away as Chicago. For years she had corresponded with cabinet members and members of Congress, including Senator Sam Ervin, chairman of the Senate Judiciary Subcommittee on Constitutional Rights. In response to a questionnaire from Ervin, she replied with many details of the Indians' situation, contending that they were still deprived of rights guaranteed under the Constitution. On a more personal level, she sent money for the Little Finger Nail Art Award for children on the Northern Cheyenne reservation, in honor of the young artist killed in the Cheyenne outbreak in 1878.

The fate of individual Indians saddened her. She had corresponded with friends in Wyoming for some time about an old woman, the second daughter of Little Wolf, who was killed by a car when crossing the street there. She had made the long trek north with her people, and had married one of Wild Hog's sons. Later, a widow living in poverty in Sheridan, she was for years a familiar figure in the town, making daily rounds of the alleys looking for cast-offs and food, or standing by the radiator in the post office to keep warm. She received little help from the local welfare agencies. After her death, investigators found that she lived in an abandoned truck body on a hillside with two handicapped daughters, one a deaf-mute and the other partially blind, and two younger children, relatives they were raising.

Many of the survivors of the Indian troubles seemed to suffer such sad fates.[32]

Occasionally Mari could help make others aware of the Indians' place in history. She learned of the research of two men into the arms used in the Custer battle, research that made no allusion to the weapons of the Indians, who had, after all, won the battle. She called their attention to the omission and referred the embarrassed historians to Rufus Wallowing, chairman of the Northern Cheyenne Tribal Council at Lame Deer, Montana, for that important information. And she sent two long pages of sources and information to Harvey Little Thunder, a Sioux who wondered if she knew how he might trace his genealogy.[33]

Because of another of her crusades for the promotion of historical truth, Mari severed her relationship with the editors of the *Westerners Brand Book*, the publication of the New York Posse of the Westerners. She had been one of the charter members of the chapter and had worked enthusiastically and actively with the editors for years, so her decision was not made lightly. The subject of her ire was, not surprisingly, the treatment of Buffalo Bill. A member of the Westerners had published a book on the "hero" that she felt falsely depicted Cody as an Indian scout and fighter, perpetuating the erroneous image she so objected to. She had urged the editors to deny the accuracy of the book, but they had done nothing about it. When the July 1962 issue of the *Brand Book* carried an article on Cody by the same writer, she notified the editors that she could no longer lend her name and reputation to that part of the organization.[34] She had spent a great deal of time debunking the tales about Cody, abetted by such authorities as her California friend E. A. Brininstool, the western historian who had shared his information with her over the years, and Luther North, whose brother Frank had led the famous Pawnee Indian Scouts. The Norths had known Cody well and at one time owned a ranch in partnership with him. Luther North always laughed when Cody's name was mentioned in connection with any Indian battles. Cody was a good shot, a friend of the Indians, and a wonderful showman, but a war hero he was not.[35]

The Story Catcher was completed in the fall of 1962. Mari had promised this book and *The Horsecatcher* to Paul Hoffman as long ago as his Atlantic and Knopf days. They had talked about the idea while *Crazy Horse* was being written, but as soon as that book was finished Hoffman had left Knopf. She later promised the books to him again, orally, in 1953 when *Winter Thunder* was being published, but could not get to them then. Now the promise had been kept at last.[36]

There were the usual arguments during the publishing process. Mari called the Westminster editor a *hadophile,* "one who has a mania for the word *had* and sticks it into prose like telegraph poles along a railroad right-of-way."[37] More important was the argument about the timing of publication. Westminster wanted to bring out the book in the spring of 1963, but Mari insisted that they wait until fall. No one out west had time to read in the spring, and the West was where her market was; she could not name one bookstore in Manhattan that carried her most recent work. The markets she had worked to build up for twenty-six years were in the West and they would buy best in the fall. After a prolonged discussion, Mari got her way.

She was generally pleased with *The Story Catcher* except for the illustrations, which she found not only childish but grossly inaccurate in several cases. One had three errors. It showed a boy with a feather at the back of the head, although in actuality only the highest council chiefs wore feathers. He was also wearing a shell core choker, the kind worn by Cheyenne agency chiefs of the 1870–90 period, not by an Oglala Sioux boy of the mid-century. Mari had sent Westminster a great deal of material from the Amos Bad Heart Bull pictographs for guidance, but the artist had ignored it.[38]

The tribe she describes in *The Story Catcher* is the Oglala Sioux, who roamed the High Plains from the Black Hills down to the Platte River and north and west to the Bighorn Mountains. The hero is Lance, a young man growing up and learning his responsibilities in the tribal society in the 1840s and 1850s. In these years, the white man's encroachment is feared, but the major battles with the army are in the future. The conflicts, the wars described, are between the Oglala Sioux and their Indian enemies, the Crows, the Pawnees, and the Arikarees.

The author once again presents amazingly detailed glimpses of life in the Indian village and on the plains. In this book, as in her earlier *Horsecatcher*, she shows the action, rather than telling it, successfully fusing history and imagination. Some of the events come from her own earlier works or from legends or actual adventures recounted by historians. Once more the influence of *Black Elk Speaks* can be seen in details of the young boys' training and games, such as burning sunflower seeds on the wrist, stealing dried meat from racks, or the Throwing-Them-off-Their-Horses contests. The capture of the eagle appeared in "The Birdman," an earlier story of hers. And the episode of the wounded boy who managed to survive for months on the prairie before returning to his village apparently was based on an actual happening.

The hero does not seem to be in any way a vicarious image of the author herself, as her earlier intent hinted. She had thought to create a major conflict between the young man's desire to participate in village activities and the more passive role requiring that he remain outside the center of action in order to observe and record. In her own youth, she had lived in a violent and exciting society but only as an observer of the action, never as an instigator or central figure. Though her own experiences may be reflected in descriptions of the young artist's love of detail, color, and form, she gave Lance the opportunity for action and decisions such as she had never had. *The Story Catcher* was a co-winner of the Levi Strauss Golden Saddleman Award in 1963 and winner of the Western Writers of America Spur Award for the best juvenile in 1964.

With this book written, Mari could at last work seriously on the Little Bighorn book for Lippincott. She took an early draft along with her in September 1963 as she looked over the locale in Wyoming and Montana, walking miles of rugged country at all the important sites despite her sixty-seven years, and checking at the Custer battle site museum for new materials they might have received since her last visit. She did not believe in delegating her research to others; by seeing the original material, she asserted, she could determine the meaning of internal evidence.[39] Still the painstaking historian she had always been, she never trusted either her files or her research to others.

Mari's distrust of Hollywood was reinforced at this time by the movie version of *Cheyenne Autumn*. The idea of filming the flight of the Cheyennes had been proposed at various times for some years. As far back as 1950, a screen play called *Cheyenne Massacre*, based on Howard Fast's book *The Last Frontier*, had been sent to Mari to evaluate. Her reply had been six single-spaced pages of corrections. She found the script a shockingly erroneous picture of both the Indians and the military, false in many aspects, through both ignorance and intent.[40] The film was not made. In 1961, the *New York Herald Tribune* reported that Fast's *Last Frontier* would be the first production of a new team for Columbia Pictures, Paul Newman and Martin Ritt. Mari complained to their writers; whether this deterred them or not, they did not make the film. In 1963, when she learned that Hollywood was again contemplating a movie on the Cheyenne massacre and might use Fast's book as its basis, she signed an agreement with Warner Brothers to film her book, hoping that the result would have some basis in historical fact.

It soon became clear that she had sold the title of her book and little more. John Ford was to direct the movie, and the large cast included Richard Widmark, Carroll Baker, Karl Malden, Sal Mineo, Delores Del Rio, Ricardo Montalban, Gilbert Roland, Arthur Kennedy, John Carradine, Victor Jory, James Stewart, and Edward G. Robinson, but Mari continued to hear disquieting stories about the rewriting. When she read James Webb's script, after the film was made, she was aghast. She had not thought it possible that what she believed to be the greatest epic in American history could be reduced to a crashing bore. The important characters were deprived of personality, dignity, and integrity. Furthermore, Webb had inserted fictional characters and incidents; indeed, most of the Indians and soldiers were his inventions. Webb also introduced famous frontier characters, such as Wyatt Earp and Doc Holliday, never mentioned in her book. In defiance of all probability he inserted a love story between two white people, the captain in charge of the cavalry pursuing the Indians and a young Quaker schoolteacher who comes along in a covered wagon on the Indians' flight from Indian Territory. A covered wagon could not have survived the flight, and certainly a white schoolteacher would not have been allowed along. In one of the concluding sequences, Archer, the cavalry captain, hurries from Nebraska to Washington, bringing back Secretary of the Interior Carl Schurz to Victory Cave, somewhere in the North (in a locale never identified) where the Cheyennes under Little Wolf and Dull Knife are about to be slaughtered by army troops. Just as the army guns are about to fire, Archer arrives with Schurz, who halts the action, has a friendly meeting with the Indians, and makes arrangements permitting them to return to their homeland. All fiction. Dull Knife and part of the tribe had separated from Little Wolf in Nebraska and shortly afterward were captured and incarcerated at Fort Robinson, Nebraska. In an attempt to break out of their captivity there, most of Dull Knife's people were killed or recaptured. Only the followers of Little Wolf—about half of the original group—went on north. Dull Knife and Little Wolf did not join forces there, Victory Cave did not exist, nor did Secretary Schurz come west, visit the Cheyenne, or negotiate a treaty.

Mari was distressed by the many stock characters added— soldiers, gamblers, prostitutes, senators—the trite, boring scenes with no historical basis; the endless anachronisms in Indian clothing and religious symbols, army weapons and procedures, and people's behavior; all apparently deriving from the script writer's ignorance. Webb defended himself at some length, citing his research, but it only made her angrier. He had not used primary sources, but less accurate secondary sources. Furthermore, the introduction of spurious conflicts and momentary drama into the picture, particularly the incredible insertion of the white girl and her wagon on the flight, proved to her that no one had bothered to try to understand the real conflict of the book, the struggle to save the young people who might carry on the Cheyenne nation. She called the filming a "continuation of the sad run of circumstances" in which the book was caught even before it was published. When Webb asked her permission to turn his script into a novel titled *Cheyenne Autumn*, she refused vehemently.[41]

Mari's current research was giving her difficulty, too. Her work on *The Battle of the Little Bighorn*, delayed for one reason or another, was behind schedule again. She at last won an important concession from the National Archives, however, that she hoped would make her research easier. After years of insisting that certain files in the War Department records from which she had taken notes in 1937 and 1938 must still exist, she received permission to take a more comprehensive look into the material related to the Custer battle. Some records she had seen earlier had disappeared during the move to the new war records quarters; and when the material was microfilmed, many of the loose papers apparently were not recorded. Her suspicions that the records had been bowdlerized were confirmed when she was unable to locate certain papers from which she had taken notes so long before. The Camp Carlin medical records of the treatment of Wild Bill Hickok's failing eyesight were now gone, as well as some of the records revealing the drunkenness and cowardice of an officer involved in the Cheyenne outbreak. The letter admitting that Custer's Cheyenne son was with the fleeing Cheyennes, sent by the Cheyennes' agent to the commanding officer at Fort Reno and dated 18 September 1878, had been enclosed in document #8535, but was now gone, although Mari could refer to the file and document numbers from her earlier research.[42] The missing references on the Custer battle would delay her book further while she located other sources.

It was a disappointment, but there had been similar disappearances of records before. Sometimes the records were removed deliberately, she thought; sometimes it was a matter of carelessness or accident. In 1956, when Fort Robinson was made a Nebraska state historical museum, Roger T. Grange, Jr., the curator, had asked her help in locating some of their missing documents. Much of the archival material was destroyed at the fort during World War II, when it was a training base and prisoner-of-war camp. Grange believed that local citizens had taken some of the records, but he thought others might be in storage at army record centers. Mari remembered that in 1930 the post commander had taken Eleanor Hinman and her through the basement of the post headquarters, where the unorganized post records were stacked, but when she later wanted to use them for *Crazy Horse* she was informed that they had been transferred. Still later, she found much of that material among the records at the old garage on Virginia Avenue in Washington used for storage before the National Archives building was built. She suggested to Grange that the Fort Robinson letterbooks might be at Fort Crook in Omaha. No longer available was a collection of General Crook's letters that belonged to an Omahan whom she never knew and that was lent to her in confidence in 1939. As in the earlier experience, she was again reminded in 1964 that she had seen information no longer available to historians.[43]

Mari was also battling ill health, which further delayed her writing. Cancer had reappeared; she would need a second mastectomy. In spite of the prognosis she was optimistic. Her last operation had given her ten years, perhaps this one would too. She had six books to write; four had been planned for some time, two were new ideas.[44] Operated on in late January 1964, she was out of the hospital by February 1.

Although her recuperation was slower this time than in 1954, by June she was out west again, in Portland, Oregon, then went to North Dakota and Montana, once more checking information and sites for *The Battle of the Little Bighorn*. In the fall she again took an active part in publicizing her work, flying to Omaha and Lincoln for autographing and television appearances to promote *The Beaver Men*. Nebraska honored the new publication by declaring October 18–24 Mari Sandoz Week.

The author's foreword to *The Beaver Men* is rather more than the usual explanation of her ties to the subject, although she includes those too. She recalls that one of her first lessons on the old treadle sewing machine was making beaver sacks from discarded Levis, "to be filled with sand or earth and fastened to steel traps to drag the captured beaver down, drown him before he could twist his foot off and be lost, left a cripple." She also recalls the storytellers she heard: "The household of Old Jules Sandoz on the upper Niobrara River had heard a great deal about beavers from the Sioux. Practically all the old, old stories were concerned with the beaver or his disappearance." In this foreword, she offers what could be considered the philosophical justification for her entire Great Plains series, reiterating that as she grew up and discovered how the white man changed the plains, she learned that it was only a repetition of what men had done to regions elsewhere from the stone age to the present. In the older regions the process had been so gradual that the records were lost, but on the plains the transition was so rapid that tangible records remained for those willing to investigate and tell the story.

In an earlier, discarded version, she described the way in which her interest in the region had developed:

We grew up under the interest Old Jules Sandoz had in the development of the universe, including the geologic ages and the outcroppings of great fossil beds only a couple of miles from our house, beds where he had watched eastern expeditions remove wagon loads of carefully cradled remains of prehistoric animals, great relatives of the elephant and the camel, giant turtles, the great volcanic ash beds, the glacial remains, and the Indian hunters before the white man came, and since, to the industrial age, the iron trap and gun, the iron plow . . . the steam-powered threshing machine, the gang plow, the oil drilling in Wyoming, along the old Bozeman Trail that drew the neighborhood boys.[45]

As in *The Buffalo Hunters* and *The Cattlemen*, Mari uses the animal itself as the central figure. The themes of all her works appear here—the rapacity of the white people, the callousness of governments, the often ironic lack of Christian virtues in the missionaries: "In 1702 Father Carheil urged the complete destruction of the Five Nations as a way to protect western trade." She is obviously saddened at the unscrupulousness of big business, particularly its systematic debauchery of the Indians. Her sympathy for the beaver, an industrious, clean, ambitious, attractive animal that had lived for untold centuries in amity with his human neighbors, is similar to the feelings she had expressed for human minorities who had something others wanted and whose admirable qualities were sometimes the very cause of their destruction.

The people she had come to respect during her research were

the individual French traders and trappers who had first gone into the wilderness. She had contempt for the French rulers, Louis XIV, the Regent, and Louis XV, who exploited their American empire only for money and religious aggrandizement. Had they cared about the new land, she believed, the whole of North America below Hudson's Bay might have ended up French.[46]

While in Nebraska to promote *The Beaver Men*, Mari conferred with Bruce Nicoll, who wanted a special publication for Nebraska's upcoming state centennial. Asked to write something for the University of Nebraska Press, she offered him a short reminiscence, *The Christmas of the Phonograph Records*, an elaboration of the event described rather briefly in *Old Jules*, in which the improvident Jules spent much of his $2,100 inheritance for a stamp collection, guns, candy and peanuts for the children, a new Edison phonograph, and eight hundred cylindrical records, rather than paying his many creditors. The episode occurred before the family moved to the sandhills in 1910. Not only was the family changed for all time by their new phonograph, but much of the community felt its impact too.

Nicoll was happy to have the work and planned to publish it as a clothbound book, but he hoped Mari would write other things for the centennial as well. He again attempted to persuade her to write about Wounded Knee and continued to urge her to write her autobiography. Finally convinced that neither book was in her plans for the near future, he asked her opinion of Wright Morris, another author with Nebraska roots, for a centennial publication. His work was good, she thought, although she felt its style would become dated, something she had tried to avoid in her own work. Ever since her undergraduate days, she said, she had worked to avoid literary affectations of the moment, all the self-conscious artistic approaches. She tried to produce an experience for the reader, sometimes an evocation of something beyond the actual occurrence. She hoped that occasionally she had been able to stir the deep racial memory that lies in all. There was art that could do so, she knew.[47]

In October of 1964, while in Nebraska, Mari appeared at a day-long program at Kearney State College, speaking at workshops in the morning and attending a luncheon, a college-wide convocation, and a tea given by the English honorary fraternity. Friends at the college noticed her terrible fatigue. Several times during the day she went to the home of a cousin to rest. Her return trip to New York was one of excruciating pain, which she blamed on enteritis and an attack of lumbago, which her mother had also suffered from. Although her appetite returned shortly and the pain of the lumbago was eased by a hot pad and by sleeping in a sitting position, she suspected she should have a checkup anyway. The examination revealed cancer of the bone.[48]

This, too, she met matter-of-factly. When Bruce Nicoll informed her that the University of Nebraska Press would publish the Bad Heart Bull pictographs as she had recommended and asked her to write a 3,500-word introduction, she delayed her answer until she received the test results, then replied frankly. Her two malignancies promised very little for the future, but if she was alive she would be happy to do it. She had not been able to write for several weeks because of the pain, but this introduction would be a labor of love. She sent for her notes held so long in storage in Nebraska and went to the American Museum of Natural History to consult Helen Blish's manuscript of the pictographs. With her notes on the Sioux and with Helen's letters and notes she felt she should be able to write the introduction.[49]

Walter Frese and Mary Abbot attempted to protect the author, who had always fought her own battles. Mary Abbot was concerned about a young man writing a juvenile biography of Crazy Horse. Although he had been candid in asking for permission to use material from the book, Mary Abbot thought she needed protection against the pirating of her works. Mari herself was inclined to be more generous, for she believed every researcher built up a body of material for others to use.[50] Mary Abbot and Walter Frese also suggested putting together an anthology of her selected writings to celebrate her thirty years in publishing. Mari doubted its commercial appeal, but she recognized that the thirtieth anniversary of her first publication might be an appropriate occasion, and her health was not likely to get better. The title chosen was *Old Jules Country*.

Her illness did not destroy her interest in the world around her. On the international level, she was deeply concerned at the defoliation of Vietnam, surely an immoral act of the government. She still promoted her students' and friends' works to publishers and to institutions giving grants. Her friend Marguerite Young had been working on a gigantic novel for almost as long as Mari had known her, always with her encouragement as well as practical help in locating jobs or securing grants. When it was published at last, Mari was delighted with the critics' reception of the book, *Miss Macintosh, My Darling*. Nebraska friends were on her mind, too. She still corresponded with the Wimers and others from the southwestern part of the state, pursuing the history of Wild Bill Hickok when he lived in Nebraska, and she wished it were possible to go on another history jaunt with the group. She expressed her continuing concern for modern-day Indians by suggesting a project for the young Sioux in the Valentine, Nebraska, area that they could excel in; perhaps it could be in art, such as the project started for the Cheyenne children earlier.

Any criticism of her standing as an authority on western history still caused her to sputter. In 1965 the editors of *American Heritage* wished to publish an excerpt from *The Battle of the Little Bighorn* but commented that she could not have had access to Cheyenne tribal information about the Custer fight on the order of that in a manuscript (later published as *Cheyenne Memories*) by John Stands in Timber, a Cheyenne tribal historian. She pointed out that although Stands in Timber's work had some fine and valid information, she had gotten hers from the Northern Cheyennes who had actually been in the battle.[51]

In March 1965 Mari's health worsened; she suffered a severe hemorrhage and went into the hospital again for some time, suffering from pain "traveling from one end of her bone points to the other." She was anemic and had violent "traveling muscular soreness." Her back now hurt constantly. She would make no more trips. She made arrangements for power of attorney and a lawyer to help draw up her will. She also worked at persuading her doctor, who had survived a Nazi concentration camp during World War II, to write up his experiences.[52]

She was thinking seriously of the final disposition of her

files, correspondence, library, and working papers. A number of institutions had asked for them. Several years earlier, the universities of Wyoming and Colorado had battled politely over a chance to house them. More recently she had received inquiries from Brooklyn College, Texas Technological College, and others, including Boston University. But she had long felt that too much of the western heritage had gone to eastern repositories. With the exception of the manuscripts designated for Syracuse University, her collection should go to its own region, the plains. She began discussions with the University of Nebraska concerning the eventual arrangement and use of her material.

Nebraska organizations continued to honor her. The descendants of Buffalo Bill made her a Cody Scout for her achievements in early Nebraska history, surely an incongruous honor since she had spent so much time debunking his reputation. A long, friendly letter from Donald Danker at the Nebraska State Historical Society included much news of happenings there and a request that she speak at their spring meeting, but she was too ill for that.[53] Her one determination was to finish the introduction for the Bad Heart Bull book for the University of Nebraska Press. If she had time, she would finish *The Battle of the Little Bighorn*.

While Mari was in the hospital during the spring of 1965, her niece, Caroline's daughter, Mary Ann Pifer, came to be her secretary for a time. The zoning laws of the city of New York had to be changed to permit Mary Ann to live as well as work in the rooms below Mari's apartment, which were zoned for offices. A personal appeal by Nebraska's governor Frank Morrison to the city's building commissioner brought the special ruling.[54]

It was through the newspaper accounts of this episode that many of her friends throughout the country learned of the seriousness of Mari's condition, and her mail was filled with their letters of sorrow and consternation. Her old friend Mamie Meredith reminded Mari that when she had first come to Lincoln in the 1920s, a doctor had warned her she might have only six months to live. She had overcome that illness; perhaps she would overcome this one as well. Eleanor Hinman spoke of the memories of the young Mari that she saw everywhere in Lincoln:

A place where a young Mari Sandoz and a young Eleanor Hinman sit under a tree in Pioneer Park, smoking together, looking at the distant State Capitol tower, and discussing the universe. A place at the Muny Swimming Pool where a young Mari Sandoz slips out of her worries and frustrations into the water. A place down town where a slim Mari Sandoz whirls around the corner of Miller & Paine's, buffeted by the wind and leaning on it, walking faster than anybody else in town.[55]

Mary Ann stayed while her aunt was in the hospital, taking her mail to her daily and answering it as instructed. Often she typed on a manuscript in the evening. The following day Mari would read the material and "make corrections, corrections, and corrections." She would revise even short sections until Mary Ann knew them practically by heart. Later, when Mari returned home, Mary Ann stayed on for a while, but the writer was so weak she could not resume her regular writing habits and worked only a little while each day.

When her aunt was stronger, Mary Ann returned west and Mari was alone. Although her friends kept in touch with her by phone or letter, she would seldom allow anyone to see her, except for James Carr, her friend of many years, or her landlady, Mary Towner. Carr would stop late at night, for Mari had always been a night person, never going to bed before 2:00 A.M. He would bring her the late edition of the papers and visit with her briefly. Thus he could evaluate her health and keep her family in Nebraska posted on her condition. Medication was making her voice deepen and making changes in her appearance that caused her to seek seclusion. A private, intensely feminine woman who would not tolerate familiarity, she found the changes in her appearance difficult to accept.[56]

That summer, when temporarily free from pain, she worked on the Little Bighorn book for Lippincott. By August it was finished except for the maps. She thought she would be able to complete them, but if not she had the information in such a form that a cartographer could do it. And she insisted on seeing the copy-edited manuscript before it went to the printer.

In September she sent her introduction to the Bad Heart Bull book to the University of Nebraska Press. At times her pain seemed alleviated and she made plans for the books she wanted to write in the next few years if the disease could be arrested. One of her doctors was optimistic about being able to control the pain without the use of drugs, and unless the cancer spread she thought she might well have a couple of years to write. She signed a contract for the oil book, to be the seventh and last of the Great Plains series, and planned to write about the Dog Soldiers, the warrior society of the Cheyennes, after she finished the Sioux book for children for Harper's. She was slow with her work on the maps for *The Little Bighorn,* however, because her hands pained her. By October she could no longer make tea for herself because she could not hold the teakettle, but she remained in her apartment, alone except for her cleaning lady and, later, a visiting nurse.[57]

Until February 1966 Mari was still working on the proofs of *The Little Bighorn,* but at the end of the month she returned to the hospital. Her hair, always vibrant red-gold or chestnut in color, was now a snow-white braid. She permitted almost no visitors, but she did allow a visit from Ron Hull, a friend since 1959, when he directed her two television series in Nebraska. They talked of the sandhills. She was homesick.[58]

When she entered the hospital this time, Mari asked Mary Abbot to have the agency's bookkeeping department send her checks directly to her bank, no longer to her personally. And no fuss, no flowers, please. She did no more writing. She died 10 March 1966.

Mari Sandoz was buried, as she requested, on the family ranch in the sandhills, the place she always considered home, no matter where she lived. As she once said, "The self-reliance, often the fierce independence, of a homestead upbringing seems to stay with children brought up on a claim. They may wander far from their roots, for they are children of the uprooted, but somehow their hearts are still back there with the old government claim."[59] Halfway up on a hill north of the ranch, her grave faces the southeast, overlooking the orchard, the hay meadows, the farm buildings, and the "constantly changing tans and mauves of the strange, rhythmical hills that crowd away into the hazy horizon."[60] There one can stop for a little while, admire the prairie flowers, the grasses, and the yuccas, and think of this friend, as the Indians paid respects to their buried chiefs long ago.

John Neihardt with Mari Sandoz

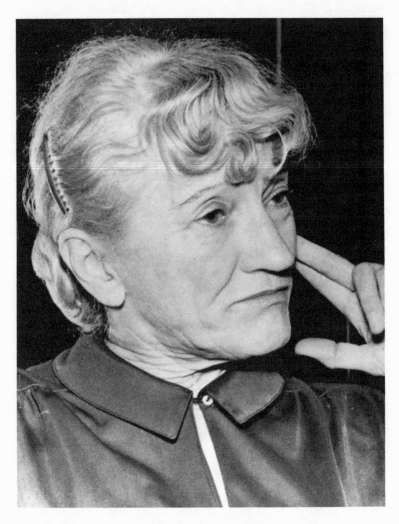

Ca. 1960, following the publication of The Cattlemen
and while Mari was working on The Beaver Men

Thirteen
Epilogue

Of her three books published after Mari Sandoz's death—*The Christmas of the Phonograph Records, Old Jules Country,* and *The Battle of the Little Bighorn*—the first, intended as a souvenir, or gift book, is the shortest, only twenty-seven pages long. Charming in its evocation of long ago and far away, it brings back one special Christmas on the Nebraska frontier, picturing with fine detail the excitement of that once-in-a-lifetime event— the arrival of the first phonograph to the neighborhood. Writing in the first person, Mari describes the extraordinary number of people lured from miles away to hear the music, hungry for music, both modern and classical. Night and day during the holiday season, wagons, buggies, riders on horseback, and people afoot streamed in and out of the yard, even the people who had had Jules arrested several years earlier. She reveals, too, details of family life. The Jules of this short recollection is jovial and generous, although there is one short dramatic scene in which he confronts his enemy, Freese. Certainly one of the most poignant moments is her mother's joy at the music and dancing. In this late piece, the author recognizes the deprivations her mother suffered through the years and sympathizes with her lot as the hard-working wife of Jules Sandoz. The book is handsomely made and illustrated, but not a major work.

Nor is *Old Jules Country*. Although copyrighted in 1965, it did not appear in bookstores until 1966 and could not have had much of Mari's attention. She made some of the decisions about the excerpts to be included, but there is little in her correspondence to indicate her further involvement in the book. Excerpts taken primarily from chapters in her Great Plains series are augmented by a few slight pieces and the article "The Homestead in Perspective."

The Battle of the Little Bighorn is Mari's last major work. At Lippincott, prepublication comments by readers asked to evaluate the book were jubilant; it "read like a dream," with the readability and suspense of a novel. The author obviously knew her subject intimately. One editor was nervous about what he saw as her anti-Custer view. Basing the entire battle on Custer's presidential aspirations, a hypothesis hardly mentioned in prior accounts, was a bold step, and documentation would be essential.

In recounting the events of the battle and what led up to it, Mari put together an enormous historical jigsaw puzzle, selecting and fitting the pieces together, picturing events from the Indian point of view as well as from the perspective of the many factions among the whites. Although she discusses Custer's role, including his refusal to accept the Indian scouts' evidence of a huge Sioux and Cheyenne encampment on the banks of the Little Bighorn, the writer concentrates on those who survived the battle: Reno, Benteen, Godfrey, Weir, and their men, and, of course, the Indians, the victors. She contends that Custer did what he did because he aspired to be president and could best win the Democratic nomination by a small victory over the Sioux. This contention she bases not only on the oral accounts of the Arikaree scouts to whom Custer allegedly revealed his ambition, but also on Custer's letters and documents dating back to his West Point days. As she tells the story, the motive is entirely plausible.

Many consider this her finest book, the apogee of both her historical and her literary career. Kathleen Walton asserts that the author's special rapport with the Sioux and Cheyenne gave her a better opportunity than any other historian to achieve accuracy. The distinguished historian Alvin M. Josephy, Jr., said: "Consider all the books that have been written on the Battle of the Little Bighorn. What writer would think it profitable to tackle that subject again? And yet this great Western theme was taken on by the late Mari Sandoz as her final book, and in the opinion of many people who have read it, the work is American literature of the highest order." In another review he comments that her analysis of Custer's motives sheds new light on an old mystery, and although it will be hotly debated, the book undoubtedly contains the most exciting, the most detailed and accurate account of Custer's and Reno's mauling by the Sioux.[1]

Praise was not unanimous. No one can write about Custer unscathed. Some critics objected to what they saw as an undue emphasis on scanty evidence and to her use of fictional techniques such as invented dialogue. The louder the controversy, the better she would have liked it; good literature was supposed to arouse, aggravate, stimulate. If this book persuaded anyone to look at history with a fresh perspective, if it awakened readers to the importance of the Great Plains and brought the realization that the shadowy figures in the conflict were individual human beings, she would be satisfied. If her mode of writing disturbed some historians, other critics believed that it fit her message.

It is the rare combination of Mari's knowledge of history and her attention to literary detail that brings praise from her admirers. A friend from her Lincoln days, Rudolph Umland, summed up both the book and the author's qualifications: "Her brain was the last repository of unrecorded minutiae of the Plains Indians and the pioneer whites. Nobody can ever again acquire the intimate knowledge she had of the Sioux, early fur traders, trappers, buffalo hunters and cattlemen. As she once said, posterity will have to take her word for some of it." Umland speaks in cadences that themselves sound Sandozian of "her style that sings like one of those Seventh Cavalry bugles, and an eye and ear that make a scene come alive," and of her words that "race along at times like raindrops making light running sounds over the dry earth of the prairies she knew so well."[2]

In the sandhills, early 1920s

Notes

The following abbreviations are used in the Notes and Bibliography:

NH
Nebraska History

NSHS
Nebraska State Historical Society

PrS
Prairie Schooner

WAL
Western American Literature

UN-L Arch
University of Nebraska–Lincoln Archives

Letters to and from Mari Sandoz and her unpublished manuscripts are in the University of Nebraska–Lincoln Archives unless otherwise indicated. Mari Sandoz kept a large collection of newspaper articles, which I
have used extensively. Sometimes they are not dated. When I used these sources, I did not attempt to locate the entire publication. Many of the author's ideas remained consistent throughout her life and can be found in more than one source, although I often cite only one.

Introduction

1. Mari Sandoz, "Stay Home, Young Writer," MS for speech to Chi Delta Phi, 1937, later published in *Quill* 25 (June 1937).
2. Mari Sandoz to Elaine Goodale Eastman, 1 March 1944.
3. Mari Sandoz, "Midwestern Writers," *PrS* 6, no. 1 (Winter 1932): 36.
4. Virginia Faulkner, review of *Old Jules Country*, *WAL* 1, no. 3 (Fall 1966): 226.
5. Reported by Eva Mahoney in the *Omaha World-Herald*, 26 November 1939, p. 2-C.
6. J. E. Lawrence, "Personal Views of the News," *Lincoln Journal and Star*, May 1948.
7. Mari Sandoz, *Love Song to the Plains*, p. 241.
8. Mari Sandoz to Robert Cumberland, 6 April 1945.
9. Mari Sandoz to Mamie Meredith, n.d. [1933?].
10. Mari Sandoz to Blanche Yurka, 7 January 1965.
11. Mari Sandoz to the Evan Stegers, 5 April 1941.
12. Mari Sandoz, address to Kearney State College (Neb.), 26 October 1964.
13. S. H. Butcher, trans. and ed., *Aristotle's Theory of Poetry and Fine Art*, p. xli.
14. *Book-of-the-Month-Club News*, July 1966, p. 11.

Chapter 1
The Father, the Family, & the Frontier

For this chapter I drew from Mari Sandoz's first novel, unpublished, written in 1928 and 1929, titled "Ungirt Runner," then retitled "Murky River," now held by the Sandoz Corporation, the home of Caroline Sandoz Pifer, Gordon, Nebraska. While it would be dangerous to assume her fiction is autobiographical, Mari's sister Caroline, for one, believes her imagination was the kind that worked only from actual situations. Mari herself admitted that her experiences were the sources for many of her early stories (Mari Sandoz to Hannah Folsom, 1 October 1963). It seems reasonable that events appearing, sometimes in variant forms, in both her fiction and her recollections were significant in her life. Myths attached themselves to Mari Sandoz at least from the time she first went to Lincoln; some of them she may have created deliberately. I have taken into account the risks inherent in relying too heavily on her fiction or her autobiographical material. Whenever possible, I have verified her writings with recollections of others before drawing a conclusion.

1. "Anybody Can Write," *Writer* 67, no. 4 (April 1944): 3.
2. Mari Sandoz to Mamie Meredith, cited in Sandoz, *Hostiles and Friendlies*, p. 2.
3. For material concerning Nebraska in the late nineteenth century, see James C. Olson, *History of Nebraska*, particularly regarding the schools, the railroads, the sandhills, and the Kinkaid Act.
4. Interviews with the Sandoz family; letters from Caroline Sandoz Pifer to the author 1969–79. Sources for Sandoz family history include Mari Sandoz to Thomas W. Wright, 6 November 1959; Sandoz family Bible; Mari Sandoz's autobiographical notes.
5. *Boswell on the Grand Tour: Germany and Switzerland*, ed. Frederick A. Pottle, pp. 161, 215, 236.
6. Mari Sandoz to the editor, *New Republic*, 12 April 1946; Mari Sandoz, *Old Jules*, p. 161.
7. According to some family members, Jules studied veterinary medicine at the University of Zurich.
8. *Crofton, Nebraska, 1892–1967*; Addison E. Sheldon, *Semi-Centennial History of Nebraska*; Jules's letters copied into Mari Sandoz's three black two-ring, loose-leaf notebooks in which she recorded information for *Old Jules*.
9. The very small cabin Jules and Estelle lived in still existed in 1978 on a farm near Verdigre and was at that time used as a hog shed.
10. Jules's friendly relations with the Indians were very important to Mari. She declared she had sheafs of notes he had taken from conversations with the Cheyenne Wild Hog and used in letters he sent to Switzerland (Mari Sandoz to "Neckyoke Jones" Sinclair, 12

October 1964; to H. D. Wimer, 19 April 1958). See also Mari Sandoz
to Fr. Peter J. Powell, 21 April 1961, about descendants of Jules's
Indian friends; Mari Sandoz to Frank E. Sibrara, 25 March 1954;
Sandoz speech at Gordon, Nebraska, December 1955.

11. Elmer Sturgeon to Mari Sandoz, 16 December 1935. His version of
the well episode is somewhat different from hers.

12. Sheridan County Historical Society, *Recollections of Sheridan
County Nebraska*, pp. 35, 37.

13. *Old Jules*, p. 33.

14. "Out of Old Nebraska," *Nebraska Farmer*, 6 April 1957, p. 35.

15. The Wounded Knee massacre is described in so many sources I
have not attempted to list them. For contrasting contemporary
accounts see the *Kearney Hub* and the *Omaha Herald*, January
1891. Elaine Goodale Eastman to Mari Sandoz, 15 December 1942.
(Elaine Goodale was supervisor of Indian education in the Dakotas
at the time of the battle; she later married the famous Sioux physician and author Charles Eastman.)

16. Mary Louise Jeffery, "Young Radicals of the Nineties," *NH* 38, no. 1
(March 1957): 25–42; Herbert S. Schell "American Leviathan: A
Historical Review," *NH* 38, no. 4 (December 1957): 259–76; John D.
Hicks, *The Populist Revolt*, pp. 82, 84; Yasua Okada, *Public Lands
and Pioneer Farmers: Gage County, Nebraska, 1850–1900*.

17. Interviews with Helen Bixby and Mae Peters Manion. John and
Henry Peters, quoted in the *Green Bay* (Wis.) *Journal*, 30 January
1936; *Lincoln State Journal*, 21 January 1909; *Rushville Standard*,
21 July 1916 and 17 July 1925. Jules Sandoz to Dr. A. E. Sheldon,
NSHS, 28 February 1925. *Old Jules*, pp. 172–73, 186, 195.

18. Interviews with the Sandoz family; Mari Sandoz to Leo Katcher, 18
May 1954.

19. *Old Jules*, p. 185.

20. Interviews with Jule and James Sandoz.

21. Johnny Jones to his daughter, 11 January 1936, UN-L Arch.; interview with Mae Peters Mannion.

22. I have oversimplified names here for clarity. The daughter was
called Mary later at school.

23. Caroline Pifer to Caroline Bancroft, 21 May 1969, Denver Public
Library.

24. Interviews with the Sandoz family.

25. Mari Sandoz's autobiographical notes, 1953–54; interviews with
the Sandoz family.

26. Max Rothpletz to Mari Sandoz, 29 May 1936.

27. The family does not recall whether Mari actually participated in the
delivery or was only an observer, but she implies in several of her
writings that she assisted (see "Murky River"). Interview with Flora
Sandoz.

28. Mari's relationship with her mother is most clearly suggested in her

early writing. A more mellow view is given in "The Neighbor" and "Martha of the Yellow Braids," both written around 1945. In "A New Frontier Woman" (*Country Gentleman*, September 1936), she praises Mary's qualities of endurance but does not discuss her as a mother. Ethel Forburger, who knew her in Lincoln, recalls that she spoke of her concern about her father's treatment of her mother (interview with author).

29. Sandoz family recollections and pictures; interview with Mae Peters Manion; Mari Sandoz, "Dumb Cattle," *PrS* 3, no. 4 (Winter 1929): 38–46. "Author Meets Teacher," *Madison* (Wis.) *Capital Times*, 17 July 1951.

30. Interview with Jule Sandoz; Gary Brackhen interview with Jule Sandoz, October 1975.

31. Mari Sandoz to Edward Weeks, 14 November 1935; interview with Rudolph Umland.

32. Mari Sandoz, *These Were the Sioux*; interviews with the Sandoz family. James recalled details of Indian dress, April 1976.

33. Marguerite Young, "An Afternoon with Mari Sandoz," MS, ca. 1949, Sandoz Collection, UN-L Arch.

34. The sandhills are still well populated with raconteurs. The people there just naturally rely on the vignette or short tale; their conversation is colorful, picturesque in the literal sense.

35. Mari Sandoz, "Look of the West, 1854," *NH* 35, no. 4 (December 1954): 243–54.

36. Kathleen O'Donnell Walton, "Mari Sandoz: An Initial Critical Appraisal" (Ph.D. diss., University of Delaware, 1970); Mari Sandoz's autobiographical notes; interviews with Mae Peters Manion, Caroline Bancroft, and Louise Fitzell.

37. Mari Sandoz to Charlotte Curtis, *Columbus Citizen*, 11 March 1956; to Mrs. George C. Schmid, 6 February 1937. See also the quotation in the headnote to autobiographical sketch, *Hostiles and Friendlies*, p. xv.

38. See Marie Surber Hare, "Pioneer Teaching," *Recollections of Sheridan County, Nebraska*, pp. 77–80; see also Charley O'Kieffe, *Western Story: Recollections of Charley O'Kieffe, 1884–1898*, chaps. 3, 4.

39. Celia Peters Reid to Mari Sandoz, 18 November 1931; Mae Peters Manion to Mari Sandoz, 30 January 1935; interview with Caroline Pifer.

40. John Peters in the *Green Bay Journal*, 30 January 1936; *Old Jules* notebook no. 1; interview with Caroline Pifer; Gary Brackhan interview with Jule Sandoz.

41. Mari Sandoz's autobiographical notes; Mari Sandoz's address to Kearney State College.

42. Mari Sandoz to H. L. Mencken, 28 May 1931.

43. Mary S. Sandoz, "The Broken Promise," Junior Writers' Page, *Omaha Daily News*, 26 April 1908.
44. Mari Sandoz to Jacques Chambrun, 12 April 1941; Roger Langenheim, "Turning Points," *Nebraska Alumnus*, June 1957; "Murky River"; Mari Sandoz's autobiographical notes. See also Mari Sandoz's acceptance speech, Distinguished Achievement Award, *Westerners' Brand Book* (Chicago Corral), January 1956, cited in *Hostiles and Friendlies*, p. xvii. In later years Mari tended to discount the effect of her father's punishment on her, but her early writings indicate that he punished her severely and that she dreaded the cellar even more than a beating.
45. *Rushville Standard*, 17 January 1910. Variations of the advertisement appeared in later papers.
46. C. Barron McIntosh, "Forest Lieu Selections in the Sand Hills of Nebraska," *Annals of the Association of American Geographers* 64, no. 1 (March 1974): 87–89. Ranchers sometimes secured government forest land in a distant area such as Oregon or Washington and then traded those tracts for private land more suitably located. Ranchers in the sandhills often traded for land around water sources.
47. Interviews with Jule and James Sandoz. Mari Sandoz refers in "The Kinkaider" to the sandhills as "Jotunheim"—the "outer world" in Scandinavian mythology.
48. The muskrat was the subject of an article, "Musky, the Narrative of a Muskrat," *Nature* 22, no. 5 (November 1933). The prairie fire appeared in several works.
49. Caroline Pifer, *The Making of an Author*; interviews with the Sandoz family.

Chapter 2
Breaking the Ties

For information about Lincoln and Nebraska during the 1920–40 period I have used the following: James C. Olson, *History of Nebraska*; Bruce Nicoll, comp., *Nebraska: A Pictorial History*; Addison E. Sheldon, *Nebraska, Old and New*; Bruce H. Nicoll and Ken R. Keller, *Know Nebraska*; Neale Copple, *Tower on the Plains*.

1. Mari Sandoz, *Hostiles and Friendlies*, p. xviii.
2. Mari Sandoz, *Old Jules*, p. 366. The episode is treated in much greater detail in "Murky River."
3. "Sandhill Sundays," *Sandhill Sundays*, p. 136.
4. *Sandhill Sundays*, pp. 129–30.
5. Teacher candidates could take tests for separate subjects in order to upgrade their certificates. They received an individual grade for

each subject. According to the Sheridan County school records, Mari Sandoz taught the following schools in these years: 1913–14, District 163; 1915–16, District 163; 1917–18, District 163; 1918–19, Spade School, District 131. For Mari Sandoz's early years in the sandhills, see Judith McDonald's "Antaeus of the Running Water: A Biographical Study of the Western Nebraska Years of Mari Sandoz, 1906–1922" (unpublished paper, University of Denver, 1972), although my dates do not always agree with hers.

6. Jules Sandoz to *Rushville Standard*, 27 March 1914 and 24 March 1916; *Standard* editorial comments, 27 March 1914 and 27 June 1915.

7. Interviews with the Sandoz family.

8. Interviews with Rudolph Umland, Helen Bixby, and Martha Sandoz Peterson.

9. The county records show that Mari signed a contract to teach in District 112 in 1919–20, but she was in Lincoln at that time, after an argument with the county superintendent. She apparently left just weeks after the district school started. Interview with Martha Sandoz Peterson.

10. The date of her departure is given in *Old Jules* black notebook no. 1. The school is now the Lincoln School of Commerce.

11. Kay Rogers to author, 30 March 1978; interview with Raymond Latrom; Dorothy Nott Switzer, "Mari Sandoz's Lincoln Years," *PrS* 45, no. 2 (Summer 1971): 107–15.

12. Mari Sandoz to Mrs. Babcock, 21 January 1936; to Mamie Meredith, n.d. 1936; *Hostiles and Friendlies*, p. xii; interview by Bernard Kalb in *Saturday Review*, 21 August 1954, referred to in *Hostiles and Friendlies*, p. xviii.

13. Interviews with Rosalie Sandoz Martin and with Alberta Sheehan; Mari Sandoz to A. E. Sheldon, 16 December 1933; to Jasper Hunt, 1 March 1940.

14. Caroline Pifer, "Mari Sandoz," *Recollections of Sheridan County*, p. 570.

15. Interviews with James Dalton and with the Sandoz family.

16. Pifer, *Making of an Author*, p. 22.

17. Sheridan County records do not show that Mari taught the Hunzicker School in the spring 1923 term, but family scrapbooks and recollections clearly establish that she did. Both the Spade and Hunzicker schools were sod structures.

18. Mari Sandoz's bitterness is clear in early writing such as "The Vine," "Dumb Cattle," and "Murky River." All are fiction, but disclose the author's intense involvement with and sympathy for the protagonists. The incidents are easily verified as those experienced by the author.

19. Interview with Helen Bixby.

20. Interview with Mrs. Clayton Adee.
21. The map is in the Sandoz Corporation archives.
22. Mari Sandoz, *Hostiles and Friendlies*, p. 30.
23. Interview with Anna Bishop Wentz.
24. Interviews with Anna Bishop Wentz and with Caroline Bancroft. Many of Mari's friends mention this aspect of her nature; many others were unaware of it.
25. Penciled notebook dated 17 April 1943.
26. A typical condensation is in Mari Sandoz's *Hostiles and Friendlies*, p. xvii. On her later skill at impersonal and detached narration, see Walton, "Mari Sandoz," passim.

Chapter 3
New Horizons

1. Mari Sandoz to Rose Pflug, 11 March 1936.
2. Mari Sandoz to Rebecca Burrows, 24 January 1940. Fling introduced at the University of Nebraska the concept of scientific history as taught in the German universities. Pioneering in the source approach—the examination of historical proof—he developed the so-called Nebraska method for high school history teachers, which became a model for the whole country. Concerned that his students learn to separate fact from hearsay, he wrote ("Information versus Method in Education," *University Journal*, January 1908, pp. 59–60): "Perhaps no subject would be more transformed in its teaching by the introduction of the study of proof than history. The logic of history, historical proof, these are sealed books to the majority of history teachers. How can they teach historical proof, how can they tell historical fact from fiction when the only process of investigation that they are acquainted with is the natural science method of experiment and generalization?"
3. Mari Sandoz to Thomas W. Wright, 6 November 1939. Fling's method of indexing appears to be so abstruse that no one at the University of Nebraska–Lincoln today understands it. However, the archivists have worked out a retrieval system. The UN-L Arch. collection contains a wealth of source materials Mari Sandoz had garnered from research in archives, interviews, privately published booklets and memoirs, as well as correspondence and autobiographical notes. Mari Sandoz stated that she had kept notes since she was very small, often had dated them, even though she was not doing much writing at that time (interview with Mrs. Clayton Adee).
4. Mari Sandoz to Helen Grace, 4 May 1936.
5. Pifer, *Making of an Author*, pp. 46–47.
6. Mari Sandoz to Margaret Christie, 6 January 1930.

7. Dorothy Thomas Buickerood to author, 6 July 1972; Helen Alcorn to author, 18 October 1977; interviews with Dorothy Nott Switzer, with Mrs. Clayton Adee, with Leonard Thiessen, with Anna Bishop Wentz, and with Rudolph Umland.

8. R. E. Dale, "Back to Normal," *NH* 38, no. 3 (September 1957): 179–206.

9. Interviews with Mrs. Clayton Adee; with Anna Bishop Wentz; and with Ethel Forburger. Dorothy Nott Switzer, "Mari Sandoz's Lincoln Years," *PrS* 45, no. 2 (Summer 1971): 107–15.

10. Dorothy Thomas Buickerood to author, 12 August 1972; W. H. Werkmeister to author, 1 October 1972; Ruth Pike to author, 25 August 1976; Ruth Pike, unpublished MS, corrected by Mamie Meredith, 11 July 1966, NSHS; interview with Anna Bishop Wentz. Mrs. Wentz remarked, "To live in the world, some feel they must be cozy with people, but Mari Sandoz had no coziness that I could see."

11. Mari Sandoz, *Ossie and the Sea Monster and Other Stories*, p. 88. Mari Sandoz's correspondence contains almost no allusions to poetry, but her lifelong interest in it is evident in her active participation in poetry societies in Denver and New York.

12. Helen Alcorn to author, 18 October 1977.

13. Kay Rogers to author, 30 March 1978.

14. Mari Sandoz's name change included a change in the spelling of her first name, which she had varied throughout the years. When she was a youngster it was spelled variously *Mary* or *Marie*. She asserted that her teacher misunderstood her "thick tongued" pronunciation when she first started school. Panhandle newspapers spelled it *Mary* in several accounts. Her first short story published in the *Omaha Daily News* Junior Writers' Page was signed Mary S. Sandoz. Family letters were usually addressed to Marie, occasionally to Mary. Her family and her friends in Lincoln usually pronounce her name *Marie*. She said the spelling was European, the name to be pronounced with equal accent on both syllables, and a letter from Max Rothpletz, a Swiss, spells her mother's name *Mari*. Since she had no birth certificate, she was free to choose the spelling she preferred. Although she never formally legalized it, her constant use established it socially and legally as well as professionally.

15. Mari Sandoz to *Twentieth Century Authors*, 5 September 1939.

16. Mari Sandoz to Peggy Benjamin, 18 January 1937.

17. Ruth Pike to author, 25 August 1976; Pike MS, NSHS.

18. Mari Sandoz, "I Remember Lincoln," *Lincoln Journal*, 8 May 1959; interviews with Leonard Thiesson, with Rudolph Umland, with Raymond Latrom, and with Wilbur Gaffney.

19. Lowry C. Wimberly, "The Best Known of All Lincolns in the World," in *Roundup: A Nebraska Reader*, comp. and ed. Virginia Faulkner, p. 249.
20. Interviews with Allie Sandoz, with Wilbur Gaffney, with Helen Bixby, with Caroline Pifer, and with Flora Sandoz.
21. Mari Sandoz to Fr. Peter J. Powell, 27 June 1960; Pifer, *Making of an Author*, p. 65.
22. The scrapbook is in the Mari Sandoz museum in Gordon, Nebraska.
23. Mari Sandoz to the editor, *Forum*, 1 January 1929; Mari Sandoz to Jay Barrett, 4 February 1936.
24. Executive Minutes, NSHS, 1926–35. Dorothy Nott Switzer stated ("Lincoln Years" and interviews with author) that she met Mari while the latter was working at the Historical Society in the fall of 1924, but no records extant verify this. Mari may simply have been there doing her own research. Mari said she worked several times for A. E. Sheldon, but verified records indicate only two occasions. NSHS records for the 1920s seldom list names of part-time employees.
25. Mari Sandoz to Jay Barrett, 4 February 1936. Barrett, a former archivist at the society and very knowledgeable in his field, thought her undoubtedly the best-posted person in the world on the Niobrara country (Barrett to Mari Sandoz, 9 January 1936).
26. Dorothy Nott Switzer, "Lincoln Years"; Ruth Pike MS, NSHS. Anna Bishop Wentz said, "Mari Sandoz had every reason to be concerned that if she did not preserve her stories of the west they would be gone for all time" (interview with Anna Bishop Wentz).
27. Frederick L. Allen, editor of *Harper's Monthly*, to Mari Sandoz, 16 July 1926. He noted that "Fearbitten," or "Hounds of Fear," was one of only nine stories selected from eighty-four colleges, entries from which had already been chosen in rigorous local competition. Nevertheless, although sent out at least eight times, it was never published in Mari Sandoz's lifetime. One version is in Pifer, *Making of an Author*.
28. *Old Jules*, p. viii; Mari Sandoz's speech at Kearney State College, October 1964.
29. Paul J. Stewart, *Prairie Schooner Story*, pp. 22–23.
30. Sandoz-Pound correspondence; Pike MS, Mamie Meredith Collection, NSHS; *Cornhusker* (UN-L annual), 1918–35; *Alliance Spud*, 18 June 1935; interviews with Caroline Pifer and with Caroline Bancroft.
31. Mari Sandoz to Frank Hanighan, 31 May 1933.
32. Although "The Smart Man" was admired in Nebraska, it was not published until 1959, in *PrS* 33, no. 1 (Spring 1959): 32–43, and in *Hostiles and Friendlies*. One of the few stories Mari did not destroy,

it was she felt, a "sort of transition stage" into *Old Jules* (Mari Sandoz to Virginia Faulkner, 8 August 1957, quoted in *Hostiles and Friendlies*, p. 126).

33. Mari Sandoz to Joseph Conrad Fehr, 1 January 1930; to Dr. Aiken, 21 January 1936.

34. Quill Minutes, NSHS.

Chapter 4
Discouragement and Success

1. Margaret Christie to Mari Sandoz, 27 June 1929. See the Sandoz-Christie correspondence, 1929–30. Since Margaret Christie was also a beginner in the business, her ability to help her client publish is a moot point.

2. Mari Sandoz, unpublished MS, Sandoz Corporation Archives.

3. Margaret Christie to Mari Sandoz, 22 March 1930.

4. To "My Dear Lady" [Opal Paap?], 3 November 1929.

5. Interviews with Flora Sandoz and with Caroline Pifer.

6. Mari Sandoz to N. C. Abbott, 9 June 1945.

7. B. A. Botkin to Mari Sandoz, 24 March 1931.

8. Lowry C. Wimberly to Mari Sandoz, 22 March 1930.

9. Mari Sandoz to Eleanor Hinman, 10 January 1930.

10. Schell, "American Leviathan," pp. 259–75.

11. Mari Sandoz to A. R. Modisett, 22 May 1930.

12. Editorial, *Omaha Bee News*, 28 March 1930.

13. Publisher's Preface, *A Pictographic History of the Oglala Sioux*, drawings by Amos Bad Heart Bull, text by Helen Blish, pp. vii–viii; Jean Blish (Mrs. Neville) Joyner to author, 11 August 1972 and 4 February 1973.

14. Mari Sandoz to Kenneth Wilcox Payne, editor, *North American Review*, 21 June 1930.

15. Mari Sandoz, "junket notes." Eleanor Hinman's interview notes, NSHS, were published as "Oglala Sources on the Life of Crazy Horse," *NH* 57, no. 1 (Spring 1976): 1–52. Interview with Eleanor Hinman.

16. Interview with Eleanor Hinman.

17. Helen Blish to Eleanor Hinman, 30 June 1930, UN-L Arch.

18. A version of "The Great Council" was published posthumously by Caroline Pifer, but as she points out, there were over two hundred sheets scrambled together—three completed versions and two partially completed. Whether the published version is the one Mari herself would consider best is uncertain. There are several structural anomalies as well as some ambiguous characterization.

19. In a tape made for KUON-TV, 26 April 1962, Mari stated that

whenever she had saved fifty dollars she would quit her job to write. She gave various figures at different times.

20. Mari Sandoz to Information Bureau, University of Mexico, 26 November 1930.

21. Mari Sandoz to Gold Co., 23 April 1931.

22. Mari Sandoz to Nebraska Credit Co., 12 July 1933. The store was Moeller's.

23. NSHS annual reports; A. E. Sheldon correspondence file, NSHS; A. E. Sheldon to the Whitmans, 3 July 1934, NSHS.

24. Jules Sandoz to A. E. Sheldon, 8 February 1925, NSHS.

25. Mari Sandoz to B. A. Botkin, n.d., and 13 May 1932; to Tyler Buchaneau, 6 December 1933.

26. Interviews with Leonard Thiessen and with Raymond Latrom. The Cornhusker management took a personal pride in the author, sending her congratulations on several occasions. The booth was the setting for at least one short story, unpublished.

27. Edward Weeks to Mari Sandoz, 18 May 1933; *Lincoln Journal*, 23 June 1935.

28. Mari Sandoz to Watson "Doc" Bidwell, 8 July 1946; Mari Sandoz to Mamie Meredith, 17 July 1933; Hinman-Sandoz letters; interview with Anna Bishop Wentz.

29. Mari Sandoz to Frank Hanighan, Dodd Mead, 31 January 1933; Mari Sandoz to Atlantic Press, 8 May 1933.

30. Mari Sandoz to Fred Howard, *Clay County Sun*, 31 August 1936.

31. Mamie Meredith, unpublished MS, NSHS; Marie Cronley to Caroline Pifer, n.d., Sandoz Corporation archives; Mari Sandoz, *Hostiles and Friendlies*, p. xix; Bruce Nicoll, "Mari Sandoz: Nebraska Loner,"*American West* 2, no. 2 (Spring 1965): 32–36.

32. Mari Sandoz to Buck [Buchaneau], 6 December 1933.

33. Eleanor Hinman to Mari Sandoz, 18 November 1933.

34. Mari Sandoz to Eleanor Hinman, 7 November 1933.

35. Eleanor Hinman to Mari Sandoz, 18 November 1933.

36. Mari Sandoz to Buck, 6 December 1933.

37. During the depression years, the Nebraska State Historical Society was almost without state tax funds. The federal government provided money for personnel, and Mari was one of three hired with funds appropriated under New Deal relief legislation. Eventually her work became so heavy the society supplemented her Federal Emergency Relief Administration salary of forty-one cents an hour with twenty dollars a month from their own funds. When A. E. Sheldon and A. T. Hill were out of town she was in charge of the office, actually of all Lincoln branches of the society. Sheldon's book was published in 1936 as Nebraska State Historical Society Publication 22. Mari had a major part in its completion, particularly

with organization of material relating to the period before 1930. Months after she had left, Sheldon asked her to approve certain portions, for she was, he said, more knowledgeable about that material than anyone else (NSHS Minutes).

38. Kay Rogers to author, 30 March 1978.
39. Mari Sandoz to Tyler Buchaneau (telegram), n.d.; Mari Sandoz to Buck, n.d.; Tyler Buchaneau to Mari Sandoz, Thursday, n.d.; Mari Sandoz to Tyler Buchaneau, 30 April 1934.
40. Sandoz-Caxton Printers correspondence, 8 August–11 November 1934; reader's evaluation, n.d.
41. Caxton Printers to author, 25 July 1976.
42. Mari Sandoz to Glenn McFarland, 1 February 1936.
43. Mari Sandoz to Edward Weeks, 8 August 1935. The letter used as foreword was similar in many details to the one she sent with her 1932 MS. Her lapse of memory concerning the letter's use remains a minor mystery.
44. Interviews with Raymond Latrom and with Ethel Schaible.
45. Mari Sandoz to Volta Torrey, 8 April 1965.

Chapter 5
Old Jules

1. Edward Weeks to Mari Sandoz, 20 June 1935.
2. *St. Louis Post-Dispatch*, 27 November 1935, reprinted in PrS 48, no. 2 (Summer 1967): 173.
3. C. B. Palmer, "Writers, Books, and People," *Boston Transcript*, 2 November 1935.
4. Yvonne Umland Smith to author, 26 September 1976.
5. Mari Sandoz–Paul Hoffman correspondence, Syracuse University; interviews with James Carr and with Walter Frese.
6. Edward Weeks to Mari Sandoz, 19 August 1935.
7. Mari Sandoz to Edward Weeks, 15 October 1935.
8. *Alliance* (Neb.) *Spud*, 18 June 1935; Meredith MS, NSHS; Pike MS, NSHS.
9. Mari Sandoz to Mrs. Ray Wiles, 29 October 1959.
10. Mari Sandoz variously identified the book as fictionalized biography, novelized biography, fictionalized history, novel, and biography: "Should the book go as biography or fiction?" (Mari Sandoz to Frank Hanighan, Dodd, Mead Co., 31 May 1933).
11. Mari Sandoz to Frank Hanighan, 31 May 1933: "Everyone mentioned actually existed, every event is authenticated by the account in some newspaper, my mother or in my own recollection."
12. "Mari Sandoz Discusses Creative Writing," series of seven lectures, April–May 1959, Nebraska ETV Network.
13. Ibid.

14. Wallace Stegner, "On the Writing of History," *The Sound of Mountain Water*, p. 204.
15. L. R. H., *Winnipeg Free Press*, 8 February 1936.
16. William Soskin, "Reading and Writing," *New York Journal*, 2 November 1935.
17. Arthur Maurice, "Book of the Day," *New York Sun*, 31 October 1935.
18. "A Violent, Fighting Pioneer," *Saturday Review of Literature*, 2 November 1935, p. 5.
19. Dorothy Thomas Buickerood to author, 7 August 1972.
20. By 1935, Mari Sandoz had 121 hours of the 125 required, but in no recognizable program (Registrar's Office, University of Nebraska–Lincoln, to author, 28 September 1977).
21. *Nebraska State Sunday Journal-Star*, 10 November 1935.
22. *Hartington* (Nebr.) *News*, 18 December 1935.
23. Mari Sandoz to Herbert Cushing, 6 January 1936.
24. Walton, "Mari Sandoz," passim. For a good general analysis of the Sandoz canon, this is a most helpful work. Switzer, "Mari Sandoz's Lincoln Years," pp. 107–15; Eva Mahoney, *Omaha World-Herald*, 26 November 1939; James Sandoz interview with author, May 1973.
25. Mari Sandoz, "Writing Serious Books," unpublished MS, n.d., Sandoz Corporation archives.
26. W. Keith Peterson to Mari Sandoz, 7 January 1936; Mari Sandoz to Peterson, 22 January 1936; *Hartington* (Neb.) *News*, 5 February 1936; *Alliance* (Neb.) *Times*, 7 February 1936.
27. E. E. Sturgeon to Mari Sandoz, 16 December 1935; Mari Sandoz to Sturgeon, 24 December 1935.
28. For examples of historians' belief in her accuracy, see *Sweet Medicine* by Father Peter J. Powell; *General George Crook: His Autobiography*, ed. Martin F. Schmitt; *The Life and Times of Frank Grouard* by Joe Debarthe, ed. Edgar I. Stewart; and *With Crook at the Rosebud* by J. W. Vaughn. Father Peter J. Powell to Mari Sandoz, n.d. [Easter] 1961.
29. Mari Sandoz to Karl Spence, 21 December 1935.
30. Typed MS, F. L. Williams, *Nebraska State Journal*, n.d.
31. Vardis Fisher, "The Western Writer and the Eastern Establishment," *WAL* 1, no. 4 (Winter 1967): 245.
32. Walton, "Mari Sandoz," p. 142.
33. Interviews with Flora Sandoz and with Edward Weeks.

Chapter 6
Two Thematic Novels

1. Mari Sandoz to Paul Hoffman, 15 October 1935; Mari Sandoz to

Edward Weeks, 14 November 1935; Otho K. DeVilbiss, "I Dare Say," *Lincoln Star*, 22 November 1935.

2. Otho DeVilbiss to author, 2 March 1978.
3. Mari Sandoz, "Writing Serious Books," Sandoz Corporation Archives; Mari Sandoz to Paul Hoffman, 15 October 1935; to Russell Gibbs, 30 March 1939; to Richard Thruelson, *Saturday Evening Post*, 16 January 1939; to Jacques Chambrun, 22 May 1941.
4. Mari Sandoz to Paul Hoffman, 15 October 1935.
5. Mari Sandoz to Collier Young, Brandt and Brandt, 20 July 1935; Collier Young to Mari Sandoz, 1 August 1935. Elizabeth Nowell (Thomas Wolfe's agent) sent Mari a thirteen-page single-spaced analysis of its strengths and weaknesses (Nowell to Sandoz, n.d. [1935]); Mari Sandoz to Elizabeth Nowell, 25 August 1935.
6. Mari Sandoz to George Grimes, *Omaha World-Herald*, 7 February 1936.
7. Mari Sandoz to Mrs. C. E. Doner, 13 December 1935.
8. Mari Sandoz to Anne Ford, 23 March 1938; to John Fisher, 8 June 1938; interviews with Leonard Thiessen, with Anna Bishop Wentz, and with Helen Bixby; Otho DeVilbiss to author, 2 March 1978.
9. Mari Sandoz to *Harper's Monthly*, 19 October 1932, responding to an article in the November 1932 issue, "Sex in Biography," by Earnest Boyd, probably hoping her letter would be published.
10. Mari Sandoz to "Pete," 29 March 1930; interviews with Mrs. Carl Wolforth, with Caroline Bancroft, with Caroline Pifer, with Alberta Sheehan, and with Helen Bixby.
11. Mari Sandoz to Paul Hoffman, 2 August 1935.
12. Mari Sandoz to Edward Weeks, 19 September 1936.
13. Mari Sandoz's admiration of the Man Afraid of His Horse family never ceased. Although she never wrote the biography, members of the family appear, sometimes as peripheral characters, in several books and articles, including *Crazy Horse, These Were the Sioux*, and *Hostiles and Friendlies*. Jules first met descendants of this family, along with other Oglalas such as the White Eye, Young Ghost, and He Dog families, when he arrived at Mirage Flats the summer of 1884.
14. Mari Sandoz to Edward Weeks, 12 August 1936.
15. Mari Sandoz to W. M. Heckler, 28 February 1936.
16. Mari Sandoz to Lila Katherine [Kryger], 5 October 1936.
17. Interviews with Caroline Pifer and with Flora Sandoz.
18. Mari Sandoz to Alfred McIntyre, 22 March 1937.
19. Louise Stegner to Mari Sandoz, 1 January 1937.
20. Edward Weeks to Mari Sandoz, 17 September 1937.
21. Mari Sandoz to Jacques Chambrun, 11 May 1937; to Harold Ober, 8 January 1937 and 11 January 1937; Ober to Sandoz, 29 January

1937; Mari Sandoz to Edward Weeks, 17 May 1937; to Paul Hoffman, 10 October 1937.

22. Howard Spring in the *Evening Standard*, 1 July 1937; H. M. Tomlinson in the *London Observer*, 11 July 1937.

23. Speech to Chi Delta Phi, published in *Quill*, June 1937.

24. Speech to Nebraska Writers Guild, 15 May 1937, published in the *Lincoln Journal and Star*, 23 May 1937.

25. Mari Sandoz to Grace Morrow, 1 January 1936; to Mrs. John Selder, 9 September 1937; interview with Helen Bixby.

26. Howard Mumford Jones, "Hunger for Land," *Saturday Review of Literature*, 27 November 1937, p. 6; Eva Mahoney in the *Omaha World-Herald*, 26 November 1939.

27. Dan Butler, quoted in the *Omaha World-Herald*, 18 January 1938.

28. John Peters and Elmer Sturgeon quoted in the *Hay Springs News*, n.d., quoted in the *Omaha World Herald*, 6 February 1938.

29. Mari Sandoz to Lincoln Chief of Police, 10 December 1937; to Helen Bixby, 17 December 1937; interviews with Helen Bixby and with others.

30. Both Flora Sandoz and Kay Rogers stated that Mari's concern for the poor condition and inaccurate filing of old western archives led to the new accommodations for them. Mari discussed the situation with Senator George W. Norris, who was instrumental in getting appropriations for adequate new buildings. Mari felt this was one of her greatest contributions to historical preservation.

31. Mari Sandoz to Edward Weeks, 22 June 1938.

32. Mari Sandoz to Harry Hansen, 9 August 1939.

33. Mari Sandoz to G. A. Kinster, 11 December 1951.

34. Mari Sandoz to Jule, 15 January 1938; to Harold Ober, 23 March 1938; to Paul Hoffman, 12 November 1940.

35. Mari Sandoz to Wilbur Schramm, 14 January 1939; "Mari Sandoz Discusses Creative Writing."

36. Interview with Ron Hull.

37. Robert Gatewood to "Doll," 18 July 1939; Mari Sandoz to Gatewood, 5 August 1939; Gatewood to Sandoz, 12 September 1939; interview with Leonard Thiessen.

38. Mari Sandoz to Edward Weeks, 19 October 1938; Fred Ballard to Mari Sandoz, 18 December 1939.

39. "Mari Sandoz Discusses Creative Writing"; Mari Sandoz to Mrs. Eugene Thorpe, 5 April 1940.

40. Mari Sandoz to Frank L. Williams, 9 November 1933.

41. Mari Sandoz to daughter of Jay Manahan, 24 October 1936; to Edward Weeks, 10 August 1939; to editor of *Time*, 15 September 1941; interviews with Raymond Latrom, with Helen Bixby, and with Rudolph Umland.

42. Mrs. Anita Bohner to her daughter Janet Kirby, fall 1975 (author's files).
43. Mari Sandoz to Blanche Blackmer Gould, 23 March 1938.
44. Mari Sandoz to Vida Belk, 20 January 1941.
45. The best description of her intent is in Mari Sandoz to Edward Weeks, 3 December 1938.
46. Mari Sandoz to Vida Belk, 20 January 1941.
47. Mari Sandoz to Edward Weeks, 10 September 1939; Edward Weeks to Mari Sandoz, 15 August 1939 (telegram).
48. Mari Sandoz to C. E. Holen, 27 March 1940.
49. Helen Mary Hayes, review of *Capital City*, *Lincoln Evening Journal*, 10 December 1939.
50. Robert L. Ferguson to Mari Sandoz, 30 July 1940.
51. Caroline Pifer to Art Vetter, 17 October 1966, Sandoz Collection, Chadron State College, Chadron, Nebraska; *Lincoln Journal*, 7 April 1940.
52. Marie Cronley to Caroline Pifer, n.d., Sandoz Corporation Archives; interviews with Rudolph Umland, with Helen Bixby, and with Virginia Faulkner; *Omaha World-Herald*, 1 April 1940.

     In 1959 one of the university regents moved that the scripts for Mari Sandoz's television series be submitted to the regents for approval before she recorded them, and raised the question of the university's liability for her statements. He was voted down. University Regents Minutes, March 1959, UN-L Arch. For an editorial response, see William O. Dobler, "A Discouraging Episode," *Lincoln Star*, 13 March 1959.

Chapter 7
Denver

1. *Omaha World-Herald*, 30 June 1940.
2. Helen Blish to Mari Sandoz, 13 December 1939; Mari Sandoz to Helen Blish, 1 March 1940.
3. Edward Weeks to Max Schuster, 5 February 1940; Quincy Howe to Edward Weeks, 7 February 1940; Edward Weeks to Mari Sandoz, 2 May 1940.
4. Mari Sandoz to Edward Weeks, 2 February 1940; to Jacques Chambrun, 22 February 1940; to Paul Eldridge, 5 April 1940.
5. Mari Sandoz to Edward Weeks, 14 July 1938; to Eleanor Hinman, 1 March 1940; to Helen Blish, 16 June 1941; interview with Eleanor Hinman.
6. Mari Sandoz to Rebecca Knowles, 2 May 1944.
7. Mari Sandoz to C. E. Holen, 27 March 1940; A. J. Burkhart to Mari Sandoz, 12 February 1940; Mari Sandoz to Jacques Chambrun, 3

March 1940; to A. E. Sheldon, 7 December 1940; A. E. Sheldon to Mari Sandoz, 26 March 1940 and 20 April 1940.

8. *Omaha World-Herald*, 30 June 1940; Mari Sandoz to Theresa Fitzpatrick, 9 July 1940; to Fred Ballard, 27 December 1941.

9. Mari Sandoz to Fred B. Daniels, 26 June 1940; to Bob Ferguson, 16 July 1940.

10. Interviews with Rudolph Umland, with Leonard Thiessen, with Gladys Douglass, with Helen Bixby, and with Virginia Faulkner.

11. Mari Sandoz to Helen Bixby, 16 July 1940; to Hazel Hendricks, 1 August 1940; to Helen Blish, 16 June 1941; to Louise Bechtel, 7 August 1941; interview with Caroline Bancroft.

12. Mari Sandoz to Leonard Thiessen, 25 September 1940.

13. For details of Mari's life in Denver, I have depended on interviews with Caroline Bancroft, with Lenore Fitzell, with Thomas Hornsby Ferril, with Fred Rosenstock, and with Ruth Beebe Hill. Also, Caroline Bancroft's and Lenore Fitzell's MSS intended for a *Festschrift* for Mari Sandoz edited by James Carr but not published; Thomas Hornsby Ferrill daily journals, 1940–42.

14. Interview Ron with Ron Hull.

15. Mari Sandoz to Helen Mary Hayes, 28 August 1940.

16. Interview with Caroline Bancroft. Although Caroline Bancroft had been a columnist for some time, she had not concentrated on serious writing, but Mari urged her to try fiction. She sold only one short story, but under Mari's influence turned to writing history and eventually published several historical pamphlets about Colorado personages, many articles, and *Gulch of Gold*, a book about Central City.

17. Unfortunately, this map has disappeared, as has her even larger map for *Cheyenne Autumn*.

18. Mari Sandoz to the Sandoz Chemical Co., 27 September 1940; to the Evan Stegers, 11 October 1940 and 5 April 1941.

19. James M. Adamson, Commanding Officer, Fort Robinson, to Mari Sandoz, 27 April 1940.

20. Mari Sandoz to Robert Gatewood, 5 August 1939; to Paul Hoffman, 12 November 1940; interviews with Caroline Bancroft and with Leonard Thiessen.

21. Mari Sandoz to James Poling, Doubleday Doran, 22 March 1940; to Paul Hoffman, 15 October 1940.

22. Rosenstock, an avid historian and inveterate reader, was awarded an honorary doctorate in history by Brigham Young University. Although he argued against the use of direct dialogue in *Crazy Horse*, he felt Mari's *Battle of the Little Bighorn* was accurate and one of the first works to suggest that Custer's political ambition drove him to his attack on the Sioux and Cheyennes.

23. Mari Sandoz to Jacques Chambrun, 25 September 1940.
24. Mari Sandoz to Charles Kerr, Atlantic Press, 9 September 1940; to Atlantic Press, 14 December 1940; to Van [Melvin Van den Bark], 23 December 1940 and 5 April 1941.
25. Mari Sandoz to Paul Hoffman, 12 November 1940.
26. Mari Sandoz to the Evan Stegers, 5 April 1941.
27. "Mari Sandoz Discusses Creative Writing."
28. Mari Sandoz to Helen Blish, 16 June 1941.
29. Charles Kerr to Mari Sandoz, 22 September 1941; "The Cheyenne Trek Back to the Black Hills," newspaper clipping, n.d.
30. Henry Barnard, author of *Eagle Forgotten* (1938), a biography of John Peter Altgeld, governor of Illinois, 1892–96, sued Fast and his publishers, claiming that Fast's novel *The American* (1945) was taken largely from his work. Settling out of court, Fast's publishers, Duell, Sloane and Pearce made a cash settlement and agreed to reprint Barnard's book (*New York Herald-Telegram*, 13 January 1948).
31. Mari Sandoz to Mrs. Gertrude Grant, 21 October 1941; to C. A. Kroening, 11 September 1946.
32. Mari Sandoz to Paul Hoffman, 22 October 1940; to Janet Hague, Authors Guild, 12 December 1944; to Mrs. Susan Bettelyoun, 22 November 1940.
33. Mari Sandoz to Agnes Wright Spring, 15 December 1941; to Fred Ballard, 27 December 1941.
34. Eleanor Hinman to Mari Sandoz, n.d.
35. Eleanor Hinman to Mari Sandoz, n.d.
36. Eleanor Hinman to Mari Sandoz, n.d. Eleanor is the young woman John G. Neihardt refers to in his introduction to *Black Elk Speaks*, who had come to visit the holy man a week before Neihardt, in August 1930. Black Elk told her he did not want to talk to her about such things. Mari sent a note to Eleanor, consoling her for her lack of success with the interview (holograph pencil copy, n.d., Sandoz Corporation archives).
37. Eleanor Hinman to Mari Sandoz, 16 January 1947.
38. Mari Sandoz to Paul Hoffman, 31 May 1942, 9 June 1942, and 7 August 1942; Paul Hoffman to Mari Sandoz, 10 June 1942; Mari Sandoz to Eli Hinman, 15 September 1942; interviews with Caroline Bancroft.
39. Paul Hoffman to Mari Sandoz, 10 June 1942.
40. Interview with Caroline Bancroft.
41. Mari Sandoz to Paul Hoffman, 16 September 1942; Paul Hoffman to Mari Sandoz, 5 October 1942.
42. Mari Sandoz to Bill Bueno, 21 July 1942; to Helen Blish, 16 June 1942.
43. Mari Sandoz to Paul Hoffman, 17 January 1942.

44. Mari Sandoz to Stuart Rose, *Saturday Evening Post*, 6 November 1942.

45. Newspaper clipping, n.d., UN-L Arch.

46. Clifton Fadiman, review of *Crazy Horse, New Yorker*, 5 December 1942, p. 100.

47. *Rocky Mountain Herald*, 19 March 1966, p. 1.

48. Daniel J. Elazer, review of *Crazy Horse, Colorado* 39, no. 2 (April 1962): 156–57. This review was written at the time the University of Nebraska Press reissued the book in the Bison Book edition.

49. Wallace Stegner to Mari Sandoz, 2 December 1942.

50. M. I. McCreight to Mari Sandoz, 19 December 1942. See also the Sandoz-Harold Conklin correspondence, 1943, and the correspondence between Sandoz and Wyoming senator Fred Toman, 1946.

51. Chief Standing Bear to Mari Sandoz, 16 May 1943; Lone Eagle to Mari Sandoz, 2 February 1955.

52. Mari Sandoz to Helen Mary Hayes, n.d. [1944?].

Chapter 8
New York

1. Mari Sandoz to Jackson Demary, 4 May 1943. Mari Sandoz, "Outpost in New York," *PrS* 37, no. 2 (Summer 1963): 96; interviews with Caroline Bancroft and with James Carr.

2. Interview with Caroline Bancroft.

3. Mari Sandoz to Mrs. McCanns, 21 February 1949; interview with Marguerite Young.

4. Sandoz, "Outpost"; interview with Ruth Beebe Hill.

5. Interview with Caroline Bancroft; Bancroft *Festschrift* MS.

6. Mari Sandoz to Blanche Knopf, Alfred A. Knopf, 15 March 1944.

7. Sidnee Livingston to author, 11 May 1976; Kay Rogers to author, 30 March 1978 and 9 May 1978.

8. Kay Rogers to Mari Sandoz, 15 April 1965; Kay Rogers to author, 16 August 1978.

9. Interview with Polly Spence Richardson.

10. Mari Sandoz to Tyler Buchaneau, 6 December 1933; to Martha Deane, 3 November 1947; Mamie Meredith to Mari Sandoz, 6 November 1951; interview with Polly Richardson.

11. Mari Sandoz to Miss Auls, 12 January 1944; to Will M. Derig, 19 October 1947; to Doc Bidwell, 19 December 1945.

12. Mari Sandoz to Dwight Griswold, 10 November 1944.

13. Mari Sandoz to Blanche Knopf, Alfred A. Knopf, 15 March 1944.

14. Orin Stepanek to Mari Sandoz, 8 May 1945; Mari Sandoz to Orin Stepanek, 10 May 1945.

15. Mari Sandoz to E. A. Brininstool, 21 May 1945.

16. Mari Sandoz to Mrs. Richard E. Brennaman, 17 September 1945.

17. Mari Sandoz to Ralph L. Collins, Indiana University, 4 April 1946.
18. Mari Sandoz to Mamie Meredith, 27 March 1947.
19. Unpublished MS, Sandoz Corporation archives.
20. Interview with Caroline Bancroft.
21. Walton, "Mari Sandoz," p. 145; *New York Herald Tribune*, 7 September 1947, p. 6; *Time*, 8 September 1947, p. 112.
22. At this time the photo-offset process had not been developed. Once the plates were melted down a book could not be reprinted unless it was entirely reset.
23. Mari Sandoz to John Walker McCain, 27 February 1948. This is the first mention of postponement of *Cheyenne Autumn* because of World War II. Mari Sandoz to Elizabeth Otis, 12 December 1950; to Joseph Balmer, 20 September 1952 (a discussion of the relationship of the book to the Korean War); to Kay, 17 November 1948 (decision to stay in the East).
24. Interview with Ruth Beebe Hill.
25. Mari Sandoz to Edward Weeks, 25 October 1949.
26. Mari Sandoz to Fr. Peter J. Powell, 12 September 1959.
27. Mari Sandoz to Neckyoke Jones (F. H. Sinclair), 12 October 1964.

Chapter 9
The Middle Years

1. Mari Sandoz to Maurice Frink, 23 February 1953; interview with Dorothy Nott Switzer.
2. Louise Pound to Mari Sandoz, 29 April 1950; *Lincoln Journal and Star*, 6 June 1950.
3. Carl Sandburg to Mrs. Gibbons, 6 July 1950, UN-L Arch.
4. Mari Sandoz to Charlie [Morton], 11 October 1950; to David Leherman, Duell, Sloan and Pearce, 11 October 1950; to Ted [Weeks], 13 October 1950.
5. Mari Sandoz to Judge Roscoe C. South, 28 April 1952.
6. Mari Sandoz to Greer Garson, 8 December 1950; to Elizabeth Otis, 11 December 1951.
7. Mari Sandoz to Brummett Echohawk, 9 June 1952.
8. Mari Sandoz to Sybil Davis, 31 August 1953.
9. Mari Sandoz to Alice Palmer, McGraw-Hill, 21 April 1953.
10. Mari Sandoz to Elizabeth Otis, 22 January 1953; to Don Beckman, 24 January 1958.
11. Mari Sandoz to Mary Abbot, 20 December 1953.
12. *Cheyenne Autumn*, pp. v–vi.
13. Mari Sandoz to the American Council of Learned Societies (typed draft), 9 January 1950.
14. Mari Sandoz to Joe DeYong, 19 February 1951.
15. Mari Sandoz to Doc Wimer, 19 April 1958.

16. Mari Sandoz to Ed, 28 March 1959.
17. *Saturday Review of Literature*, 12 December 1953, pp. 26–27.
18. Helen Mary Hayes to Mari Sandoz, 12 December 1953.
19. Mamie Meredith to Mari Sandoz, 12 January 1954.
20. Mari Sandoz to Fr. Powell, 27 June 1960.

Chapter 10
The Harvest Years

1. Mari Sandoz to Henry Alsberg, 14 March 1954.
2. Henry Alsberg to Mari Sandoz, 11 March 1954.
3. Autobiographical notes, 6 June [1954]; *Lincoln Journal and Star*, 23 June 1954.
4. Autobiographical notes, 6 June [1954].
5. Interview with Sidnee Livingston. The novelette, sent to the *Saturday Evening Post*, was not published; editors thought its slight story did not justify the length. Caroline Pifer published it as a pamphlet, "Ossie and the Sea Monster and Other Stories," (Rushville, Neb.: *News-Star*, 1974).
6. Mari Sandoz to Daniel Willner, 28 September 1962.
7. Fred Cassidy to Mari Sandoz, 29 March 1954.
8. Mari Sandoz to Colonel Theo. C. Wenzlaff, 16 June 1956.
9. Orin Stepanek to Mari Sandoz, 12 February 1955.
10. Mari Sandoz to Tess Mase, 7 October 1954.
11. Published in *NH* 35, no. 4 (December 1954): 243–54.
12. Mari Sandoz to Flora Kicken, 16 October 1954.
13. Paul Engle to Mari Sandoz, 17 August 1954.
14. Mari Sandoz to Elizabeth Otis, 15 December 1954.
15. Ida Mae Taliaferro to Mari Sandoz, 29 October 1953; Fred Bullard to Mari Sandoz, 24 June 1953; Mari Sandoz to Helen Mary Hayes, 24 December 1954; to Annie Laurie Williams, 27 October 1954 and 15 December 1954; to Cecil B. De Mille, 26 April 1938.
16. Mari Sandoz to A. L. Williams, 29 June 1954.
17. E. A. Brininstool to Mari Sandoz, 30 May 1954 and 7 February 1955; Mari Sandoz to Brininstool, 5 June 1954 and 7 February 1955; to Helen Mary Hayes, 20 July 1954; to Don Beckman, 12 March 1955.
18. Helen Mary Hayes to Mari Sandoz, n.d. [1954] (Friday nite).
19. Marvin Borowsky to Mari Sandoz, 28 January 1954 [1955].
20. Mari Sandoz to John R. Frame, 16 April 1955.
21. Mari Sandoz to Norma Kidd Green, 27 August 1955; to Mamie Meredith, 24 September 1955.
22. Mari Sandoz to Edward N. Wentworth, 13 February 1956.
23. *New York Times Book Review*, 20 November 1955, p. 49; Barbara McKinzie, "Region and the World: The Achievement of American

Woman Writers of Fiction since 1930" (Ph.D. diss., Florida State University, 1963), p. 17.

24. Walton ("Mari Sandoz") makes a similar point in her dissertation.

25. Mari Sandoz to Caroline Sauer, McIntosh and Otis, 19 September 1955; to Harold McGraw, Jr., 20 November 1955; to Edward Aswell, 29 November 1955; Edward Aswell to Mari Sandoz, 5 December 1955; Mari Sandoz to Bill and Marie Steuber, 15 December 1955.

Chapter 11
Ties to the West

1. *Omaha World-Herald*, 16 December 1956, Midlands section. The local sleuth was Harry B. Allen of Cozad. Details of Mari Sandoz's access to the material came from an interview with Leonard Thiessen.

2. Mari Sandoz to *Harper's*, 11 March 1956.

3. Mari Sandoz to Elizabeth Otis, 24 September 1956.

4. Mari Sandoz to Virginia Faulkner, 25 December 1956.

5. Walton, "Mari Sandoz," p. 166.

6. Mari Sandoz to Virginia Faulkner, 8 August 1957.

7. Mari Sandoz to Virginia Faulkner, 18 May 1957 and 10 August 1957.

8. Mari Sandoz to *Chicago Tribune*, 1958.

9. Mari Sandoz to "Boss" Van Vleet, 14 May 1955.

10. Mari Sandoz to Sonia Leventhal, 3 January 1956; Westerners *Brand Book* (New York Posse), Fall 1956.

11. Interviews with Caroline Bancroft, with Marguerite Young, and with James Carr.

12. Mari Sandoz to H. L. Mencken, 13 February 1933; to Clarence Trued, 3 March 1941.

13. Mari Sandoz to William D. Aeschbacher, NSHS, 28 June 1958.

14. Mari Sandoz to Mary Abbot, 23 June 1958 (not sent) and 4 August 1958.

15. Virginia Faulkner, Introduction to *Hostiles and Friendlies*, p. xi.

16. Mari Sandoz to Virginia Faulkner, 22 January 1959.

17. *San Francisco Chronicle*, 12 June 1959; *Library Journal*, 15 June 1959.

18. Interview with Mrs. Gladys Douglass.

19. Mari Sandoz to Bruce Nicoll, 12 June 1960.

20. Mari Sandoz to Mildred Bennett, 3 November 1954; to Carlton F. Wells, 11 November 1935.

21. Ed Kuhn to Mari Sandoz, 4 April 1959; Mari Sandoz to Mary Abbot, 27 March 1959 and 28 March 1959.

22. Henry S. "Tom" Smith to Mari Sandoz, 27 December 1958; Mari Sandoz to Tom Smith, 12 January 1959; Catherine E. Lucas, Library

Director of Riverside City and County Public Library, to author, 20 January 1978.

Chapter 12
Battles Won and Lost

1. Mari Sandoz to Mary Abbot, 17 January 1960.
2. Clarkson Potter to Mari Sandoz, 14 January 1960; Mari Sandoz to Mary Abbot, 2 May 1960, 27 May 1960, 1 June 1960, and 30 September 1960.
3. Mari Sandoz to Caroline Sauer, 14 May 1960.
4. McKinzie, "Region and the World," p. 53.
5. Caroline Bancroft, review of *Son of the Gamblin' Man, Colorado Magazine*, October 1960, pp. 303–4.
6. *Time*, 2 May 1960, p. 99.
7. "Childe Herald," *Rocky Mountain Herald*, 28 May 1960, p. 1.
8. Mari Sandoz to Caroline Bancroft, 3 January 1963; interview with Caroline Bancroft.
9. Walton, "Mari Sandoz," pp. 98, 156.
10. Mari Sandoz to Lester G. Wells, Syracuse University Library, 14 August 1960, notes sent with MS, Syracuse University archives.
11. Mari Sandoz to Mary Abbot, 22 September 1960.
12. Hanson Baldwin to Mari Sandoz, 26 May 1960; Mari Sandoz to Baldwin, 13 June 1960 and 20 June 1960.
13. Donald Danker to Mari Sandoz, 28 May 1960 and 20 December 1960; Mari Sandoz to Danker, 31 May 1960 and 28 December 1960.
14. Mari Sandoz to Mary Abbot, 5 August 1960 and 16 October 1960.
15. Mari Sandoz to Mary Abbot, 1 June 1960 and 18 August 1960; *New York Times*, 22 June 1960.
16. Mari Sandoz to copy editor, n.d. [1961].
17. Mari Sandoz's address to Kearney State College, October 1964.
18. The portrait is in the Sandoz Room, UN-L Arch.
19. Mari Sandoz to Buz Wyeth, 6 September 1961.
20. *New York Herald Tribune*, 12 November 1961, p. 4.; "From a Bookman's Notebook," *Omaha World-Herald*, UN-L Arch.
21. Mari Sandoz to Buz Wyeth, 31 December 1961.
22. R. C. Nelson, in the *Christian Science Monitor, 13 December 1961*, p. 9; *Kirkus Review*, 1 August 1961, p. 724.
23. Mari Sandoz form letter, n.d. [1961].
24. Mari Sandoz to Robert W. Lewis, 3 December 1961.
25. Collected in Howard W. Ottoson, ed., *Land Use Policy and Problems in the United States*, also in *Sandhill Sundays and Other Recollections*.
26. Mari Sandoz to Buz Wyeth, 3 August 1962.

27. Mari Sandoz to Adele DeLeeuw, 18 April 1962; to Mary Abbot, 15 August 1962; to Arnold Cayser, 11 November 1962.
28. Mari Sandoz to Bruce Nicoll, 27 April 1959.
29. Bruce Nicoll to Mari Sandoz, 30 November 1961; Joslyn Museum to Mari Sandoz, 22 January 1962; *Lincoln Journal*, 8 July 1962.
30. Mari Sandoz to Mark Miller, 23 October 1961.
31. Public law 280, passed in 1953, extended state jurisdiction over offenses committed by or against Indians on reservations in a number of western states, including Nebraska.
32. Mari Sandoz to Neckyoke Jones (F. H. Sinclair), 11 November 1953, 10 November 1956, 30 January 1960, and 12 October 1964; Jones to Mari Sandoz, 24 June 1953, 28 January 1960, and n.d. [1964]; Hila Gilbert to Mari Sandoz, 1 January 1959, 2 December 1959, and 17 April 1960; Mari Sandoz to Hila Gilbert, 25 May 1959 and 21 January 1965.
33. Mari Sandoz to John S. DuMont, 16 April 1953. See also her 1953–54 correspondence with DuMont and John Parsons. Mari Sandoz to Harvey Little Thunder, 12 November 1961.
34. Mari Sandoz to the Editorial Board, *Westerners Brand Book* (New York Posse), 22 August 1962.
35. E. A. Brininstool to Mari Sandoz, 25 May 1945.
36. Mari Sandoz to Walter Frese, 27 February 1963.
37. Mari Sandoz to Mary Pfeiffer, Westminster Press, 25 October 1962.
38. Mary Abbot to Mari Sandoz, 30 March 1963; Mari Sandoz to Caroline Sauer, 23 August 1963.
39. Mari Sandoz to Lavinia Russell, 6 March 1963; to J. L. Smith, 12 May 1963.
40. Mari Sandoz to Annie Laurie Williams, 31 January 1955.
41. Mari Sandoz to Ron Hull, 8 January 1964; to Mary Abbot, 20 January 1964; to James Webb, 28 June 1964 and 25 July 1964; Webb to Mari Sandoz, 20 July 1964.
42. Mari Sandoz to John E. Parsons, 26 December 1957; to Donald Danker, 28 December 1960; Savoie Lottinville, University of Oklahoma Press, to Mari Sandoz, 30 July 1963 and 13 September 1963; Mari Sandoz to Lottinville, 31 August 1963; to Pendleton Garrison, 16 August 1964 and 26 September 1964.
43. Mari Sandoz to Roger Grange, Jr., 3 November 1956.
44. Mari Sandoz to Hanson Baldwin, 23 February 1964; to Mamie Meredith, 16 April 1964.
45. Author's notes, UN-L Arch.
46. Mari Sandoz to Walter Frese, 16 November 1962; to Mamie Meredith, 8 January 1964, NSHS.
47. Mari Sandoz to Bruce Nicoll, 14 June 1964.
48. Mari Sandoz to Mary Abbot, 8 November 1964; to Irene Baur-

Sandoz, 18 January 1965; to Bruce Nicoll, 28 December 1964; interview with Allie and Gail Sandoz.

49. Bruce Nicoll to Mari Sandoz, 9 July 1963 and 10 December 1964; Mari Sandoz to Nicoll, 28 December 1964; to Donald Danker, 6 April 1965.
50. Mari Sandoz to Norma Kidd Green, 26 April 1965.
51. Mari Sandoz, "The Grisly Epilogue," *American Heritage*, April 1966, p. 73; Mari Sandoz to Elizabeth Otis, 14 November 1965.
52. Mari Sandoz to Dr. Ernst Hammerschlag, 13 April 1965; to Mary Towner, 27 April 1965; Mari Sandoz's memo notes, n.d.
53. Donald Danker to Mari Sandoz, 6 January 1965.
54. *New York Times*, 8 May 1965; Mary Ann Pifer Anderson to author, 16 September 1976.
55. Eleanor Hinman to Mari Sandoz, 13 September 1965.
56. Pifer, *Making of an Author*; interviews with James Carr, Sidnee Livingston, and Marguerite Young.
57. Mari Sandoz to Donald Danker, 6 April 1965; to Hanson Baldwin, 26 June 1965; Baldwin to Mari Sandoz, 3 August 1965; Mari Sandoz to Mary Abbot, 1 August 1965 and 13 October 1965; to Carolyn Blakemore, Lippincott, 17 November 1965.
58. Interview with Ron Hull.
59. Mari Sandoz, "The Homestead in Perspective."
60. Mari Sandoz, *Old Jules*, p. 354.

Chapter 13
Epilogue

1. Walton, "Mari Sandoz," p. 243; Alvin M. Josephy, Jr., in *WAL* 1, no. 4 (Winter 1967); idem, *New York Times Book Review*, 3 July 1966, p. 6.
2. Rudolph Umland, review of *The Battle of the Little Bighorn*, *Kansas City Star*, 8 July 1966; interview with Rudolph Umland.

Mari about the time she went to Lincoln

Bibliography

Chronological Bibliography of Mari Sandoz's Works

The first date given is the date of composition, where that is known. (Not included are newspaper articles and book reviews.)

1908 "The Broken Promise" (short story, signed Mary S. Sandoz), Junior Writers' Page, *Omaha Daily News*, 26 April 1908.

1924 "The Prairie Fire" (essay, signed Marie Macumber), *Freshman Scrapbook*, University of Nebraska, 1 (1924): 19.

1925? "College in Capsules" (essay, signed Marie Macumber). In *The Making of an Author: From the Mementoes of Mari Sandoz*, edited by Caroline Sandoz Pifer. Gordon, Neb.: Gordon Journal Press, 1972, pp. 44–47.

1925 "Fearbitten" (short story, signed Marie Macumber). Honorable mention, Harper's Intercollegiate Short Story Contest, 1926. Collected in *The Making of an Author; From the Mementoes of Mari Sandoz*, edited by Caroline Sandoz Pifer. Gordon, Neb.: Gordon Journal Press, 1972, pp. 49–59.

1925 "The Vine" (short story, signed Marie Macumber), *PrS* 1 no. 1 (January 1927): 7–16.

1926 "Old Potato Face" (short story, signed Marie Macumber), *PrS* 2 no. 1 (January 1928): 29–35.

1926. "Dumb Cattle" (short story, signed Marie Macumber), *PrS* 3, no. 1 (January 1929): 38–46.

1928 "The Smart Man" (short story), *PrS* 33, no. 1 (Spring 1959): 32–43.

1927–30 "The Kinkaider Comes and Goes" (article), *North American Review*, April 1930, pp. 422–31; May 1930, pp. 576–83.

1929 "Victorie" (short story). Winner of Omaha Women's Press Club Award, 1929. Unpublished.

1927–29 "Murky River" (novel), unpublished.

1927–30 "Sandhill Sundays" (article). In *Folksay: A Regional Miscellany*. Edited by B. A. Botkin. Norman: University of Oklahoma Press, 1931, pp. 291–303.

1931–35 *The Great Council*. Compiled by Caroline Sandoz Pifer for the Sandoz Corporation, Gordon, Neb.: Gordon Journal Press, 1970.

1932   "What Should Be Considered When Choosing a Profession?" (essay, signed Marie Macumber), *Daily Nebraskan*, 3 April 1932.

1932   "Pieces to a Quilt" (short story), *North American Review*, May 1933, pp. 435–42.

1930–32 "Musky, the Narrative of a Muskrat" (article), *Nature*, November 1933, pp. 199–202.

1928–35 *Old Jules* (biography). Boston: Little, Brown, 1935.

1933   "White Meteor" (short story), *Ladies' Home Journal*, January 1937, pp. 12–13.

1934–35 "The Birdman" (short story), *Omaha Sunday World-Herald Magazine of the Midlands*, 10 February 1935, pp. 7–8.

1935   "I Wrote A Book" (article), *Nebraska Alumnus*, November 1935, pp. 6–7.

1935   "River Polak" (short story), *Atlantic Monthly*, September 1937, pp. 300–308.

1935–36 "The New Frontier Woman" (article), *Country Gentleman*, September 1936, p. 49.

1936   "Mist and the Tall White Tower" (short story), *Story*, September 1936, pp. 41–50.

1937   "Stay Home, Young Writer" (article), *Quill*, June 1937, pp. 8–9.

1933–37 *Slogum House* (novel). Boston: Little, Brown, 1937.

1937–38 "The Devil's Lane" (short story), *Ladies' Home Journal*, April 1938, p. 17.

1938   "Foreword from a Friend." In *Tales of Pioneer Days in North Platte Valley*, edited by A. B. Wood. Gering, Neb.: Courier Press, 1938, pp. 2–3.

1938–39 "The Girl in the Humbert" (short story), *Saturday Evening Post*, 4 March 1939, pp. 16–17.

1938–39 *Bone Joe and the Smokin' Woman* (novella), *Scribner's Magazine*, March 1939, pp. 20–24.

1939   "The Far Looker" (Indian tale), *The Sight-Giver*, February 1939, n.p.

1938–39 *Capital City* (novel). Boston: Little, Brown, 1939.

1939   "The Peachstone Basket" (short story), *PrS* 17, no. 3 (Fall 1943): 125–36.

1940–42 *Crazy Horse: The Strange Man of the Oglalas*. New York: Alfred A. Knopf, 1942.

1943   "To a Woman Who Made a Beautiful Garden" (paragraph), *NH* 23 (April–June 1942).

1943   "Anybody Can Write" (article), *The Writer* 57, no. 4 (April 1944): 99–101.

1944   "Sit Your Saddle Solid" (short story), *Saturday Evening Post*, 10 February 1945, pp. 26–27.

1945   "The Spike-earned Dog" (short story), *Saturday Evening Post*, 11 August 1945, pp. 24–25.

1945   "Martha of the Yellow Braids" (article), *PrS* 21, no. 2 (Summer 1947): 139–44.

1945   "The Neighbor" (article), *PrS* 30, no. 4 (Winter 1956): 340–49.

1947–49 "Foal of Heaven" (short novel), unpublished.

1943–47 *The Tom-Walker* (novel). New York: Dial Press, 1947.

1947   "Yuletide Saga of a Lone Tree" (allegory), *Philadelphia Inquirer Book Review Supplement*, 7 December 1947.

1948   "There Were Two Sitting Bulls" (article), *Blue Book*, November 1949, pp. 58–64.

1950–51 *The Lost School Bus* (novella), *Saturday Evening Post*, 19 May 1958, pp. 24–25.
        Winter Thunder. Unabridged version of *The Lost School Bus.* Philadelphia: Westminster Press, 1954.

1951   "What the Sioux Taught Me" (article), *Empire*, 24 February 1952, reprinted in *Reader's Digest*, May 1952, pp. 21–24.

1952   "To a Special Group of Blue Birds Who are Soon to Become Camp Fire Girls" (letter), *Camp Fire Girl*, December 1952, p. 11.

1936–39;
1949–53 *Cheyenne Autumn* (biography). New York: McGraw-Hill, 1953.

1954   "Some Notes on Wild Bill Hickok" (article), *Westerners Brand Book* (New York Posse), Winter 1954, p. 8.

1954   "The Indian Looks at His Future" (article), *Family Weekly*, 11 April 1954.

1954   "Ossie and the Sea Monster" (short story). In *Ossie and the Sea Monster and Other Stories.* Compiled and published by Caroline Sandoz Pifer for the Sandoz Corporation. Rushville, Neb.: News/ Star Press, 1974.

1954   *The Buffalo Hunters: The Story of the Hide Men.* New York: Hastings House, 1954.

1954   "Search for the Bones of Crazy Horse" (article), *Westerners Brand Book* (New York Posse), Autumn 1954, pp. 4–5.

1954   "The Look of the West, 1854" (speech, article), *NH* 35, no. 4 (December 1954): 243–54.

1954   "Some Oddities of the American Indian" (article), *Westerners Brand Book* (Denver Posse), 1955, pp. 17–28.

1952–55   *Miss Morrissa: Doctor of the Gold Trail* (novel). New York: McGraw-Hill, 1955.
Acceptance Speech, Distinguished Achievement Award, *Westerners Brand Book* (Chicago Corral), January 1956, pp. 81–83.

1956   "Nebraska" (article), *Holiday*, May 1956, pp. 103–14.

1956   "December 2006 A.D." (article), unpublished. Enclosed in cornerstone of KETV building, Omaha, Nebraska, to be opened in fifty years.

1956   *The Horsecatcher* (novel). Philadelphia: Westminster Press, 1957.

1958   "How I Came to Write" (article), *Baltimore Bulletin of Education* 35 (May–June 1958): 19–24.

1954–58   *The Cattlemen: From the Rio Grande across the Far Marias* (history). New York: Hastings House, 1958.
"Tyrant of the Plains" (article; section of *The Cattlemen*), *Saturday Evening Post*, 7 June 1958, pp. 48–49.
Hostiles and Friendlies: Selected Short Writings of Mari Sandoz (recollections, short stories, articles, a novella). Lincoln: University of Nebraska Press, 1959.

1942–60   *Son of the Gamblin' Man: The Youth of an Artist* (novel). Clarkson N. Potter, 1960.

1960–61   "Look of the Last Frontier" (article on artist Harvey Dunn), *American Heritage*, June 1961, pp. 42–53.

1961   *These Were the Sioux* (nonfiction). New York: Hastings House, 1961.

1958–61   *Love Song to the Plains* (nonfiction). New York: Harper and Row, 1961.
"Climber of Long's Peak" (article), *Westerners Brand Book* (New York Posse), 1961, pp. 70–71.
"The Daughter: A Recollection" (tale), *Midwest Review*, Spring 1961, pp. 29–30.
"Fly Speck Billie's Cave" (folktale). In *Legends and Tales of the Old West*, edited by S. Omar Barker. New York: Doubleday and Co., 1962, pp. 37–39.
"The Buffalo Spring Cave" (folktale). In *Legends and Tales of the Old West*, edited by S. Omar Barker. New York: Doubleday and Co., 1962, pp. 97–98.
"Unavailable Documents" (article), *Westerners Brand Book* (New York Posse), 1962, p. 47.

1962   "Outpost in New York" (article), *PrS* 37 (Summer 1963): 95–106.

1962   "The Homestead in Perspective" (article). In *Land Use Policy and Problems in the United States*, edited by Howard W.

Ottoson. Lincoln: University of Nebraska Press, 1963, pp. 47–62.

Introduction to *The Cheyenne Indians: Their History and Ways of Life*, by George Bird Grinnell. New York: Cooper Square Publishers, 1962.

1959–62 *The Story Catcher* (novel). Philadelphia: Westminster Press, 1963.

1962–64 *The Beaver Men: Spearheads of Empire* (history). New York: Hastings House, 1964.

Old Jules Country: A Selection from Old Jules and Thirty Years of Writing since the Book Was Published (includes previously uncollected pieces: "Evening Song," "Coyotes and Eagles," and "Snakes"). New York: Hastings House, 1965.

1963–66 *The Battle of the Little Bighorn* (history). Philadelphia: J. B. Lippincott Co., 1966.

1965 *The Christmas of the Phonograph Records* (recollection). Lincoln: University of Nebraska Press, 1966.

1965–66 Introduction to *A Pictographic History of the Oglala Sioux*, by Amos Bad Heart Bull and Helen Blish. Lincoln: University of Nebraska Press, 1967.

1966 "Letter for a Seventh Birthday," *PrS* 40 (Winter 1966): 285–88.

Posthumous Publications, Collections

Sandhill Sundays (selected articles). Lincoln: University of Nebraska Press, 1970.

Ossie and the Sea Monster and Other Stories (previously unpublished stories and articles, except for "The Daughter" [1961]. Compiled and published by Caroline Sandoz Pifer for the Sandoz Corporation. Rushville, Neb.: News / Star Press, 1974.

Contents:

1954 "Ossie and the Sea Monster" (story).
Untitled poem.

1941 "Junket through the Indian Country" (article).
"The Grubline Rider" (recollection).

1944 "Lineup at 39 Whitehall" (article).

1933 "Catching Eagles" (story).
"The Daughter" (story).

1920s "Music" (poem).

The Cottonwood Chest and Other Stories (previously unpub-

lished short stories and articles). Edited by Caroline Sandoz
Pifer, Mari Sandoz Corporation. Crawford, Neb.: Cottonwood
Press, 1980.
Contents:
"Handy Andy" (recollection).

1920s	''Youth Rides into the Wind'' (story).
1920s	"Face of the Dying Monk" (story).
1958	"Boy Trail Drivers of Texas" (article).
1920s	"The Cottonwood Chest" (story).
1940–42	"The Road of the Strong Young Men" (story).
1920s	"The Woman in Grey" (story).

Selected Sources

Published sources relating to Mari Sandoz are very scarce. Most references are to be found in contemporary newspaper articles and book reviews. Mari Sandoz kept a collection of this material, which is now in the University of Nebraska–Lincoln Archives in Love Library. I have used it extensively. These articles have been clipped from newspapers and sometimes are only partially identified; dates and page numbers are often missing. In listing my sources I have made no attempt to trace the original publication data if it was not recorded in the Sandoz Collection, nor have I recorded every reference used, whether having to do with Mari Sandoz or her own use of materials. She claimed to have read "everything" published on the subjects of western history, the frontier, and the Plains Indians. I make no such claim, but I am aware of several collections of material she must have seen but which would make my bibliography unwieldy. I have made no attempt to list later editions of the books I have used.

Since to date so little substantial writing has been published about Mari Sandoz and her work, my most valuable sources were those who knew her.

Author's Interviews

Adee, Mrs. Clayton, summer 1975.
Bancroft, Caroline, 17 October 1972; 6 July 1976; 7 July 1976.
Bixby, Helen, 10 August 1972.
Carr, James F., 10 August 1975, 28 December 1977.
Dalton, James, 20 May 1976.
Danker, Donald, 28 June 1973.
Diedrich, Sam, 22 September 1977.
Douglass, Gladys, 24 July 1976.
Faulkner, Virginia, 1974–80.
Ferril, Thomas Hornsby, 8 July 1976.

Fitzell, Lenore, 7 July 1976.
Forburger, Ethel, 22 April 1980.
Frese, Walter, August 1975.
Gaffney, Wilbur, June 1979.
Hill, Ruth Beebe, 13 April 1979.
Hinman, Eleanor, 17 August 1970, July 1980.
Hull, Ron, 7 June 1972, 10 July 1980.
Koshland, William, 7 August 1975.
Latrom, Raymond, 24 July 1976.
Little Thunder, Trudy, 3 August 1972.
Livingston, Sidnee, December 1976.
Madison, Erma (Jean Gries), fall 1972.
Manion, Mae, April 1976.
Martin, Rosalie Sandoz (Mrs. Ralph), summer 1972.
Moor, Emogene, 27 September 1977.
Neihardt, John G., 30 January 1972.
Olson, James, 15 April 1972.
Peterson, Martha Sandoz, 24 June 1978.
Pifer, Caroline Sandoz, 1971; 24–26 May 1972; 20–21 April 1976; 9–10
    October 1980.
Richardson, Polly, 1 April 1976.
Rosenstock, Fred, 7 May 1977.
Sandoz, Allie and Gail, 1 February 1972.
Sandoz, Flora, 11 May 1973, 21 April 1976.
Sandoz, James, 11 May 1973, 23 April 1976.
Sandoz, Jules, 22 April 1976.
Schaible, Ethel, 24 July 1976.
Sheehan, Alberta Cheney, 1 February 1978.
Switzer, Dorothy Nott, 6 June 1972, 12 July 1972.
Thiessen, Leonard, 21 January 1976.
Towner, Mary, 7 August 1975.
Umland, Rudolph, 21 January 1976.
Weeks, Edward, 5 August 1975.
Wentz, Anna Bishop, 21 January 1976.
Wimer, H. D. "Doc," 18 July 1975.
Wolforth, Mary (Mrs. Carl), 1 August 1972.
Young, Marguerite, 7 August 1975.

Other Interviews

Gary Brackhan's interviews with the Sandoz family, October 1975.
Scott Greenwall's interviews with Anna Bishop Wentz.

Letters to Author

Abbot, Mary Squire, 18 February 1977, 18 October 1977.

Alcorn, Helen, 18 October 1977.
Alexander, Hubert, 5 February 1976.
Aly, Lucile, 1978.
Anderson, Mary Ann Pifer, 8 October 1976.
Bancroft, Caroline, 8 June 1972, 6 October 1972.
Binderup, Margaret, 7 March 1978.
Bohner, Nita, to Janet Kirby, Fall 1975 (sent to me by Janet
    Kirby).
Buchenau, Tyler, 27 April 1978.
Buickerood, Dorothy Thomas, 7 August 1972, 13 August 1972, 24
    August 1972, 19 December 1977, December 1977.
Caxton Printers (Gordon Gipson), 27 July 1975.
DeVilbiss, Otho, 2 March 1978.
Diffendal, Anne, 19 January 1976, 21 April 1976.
Eiseley, Loren, 21 January 1976.
Fairfield, Joseph W., 2 May 1976.
Faulkner, Virginia, 1974–80.
Ferril, Thomas Hornsby, 20 April 1976.
Frese, Walter, 21 August 1975.
Gressly, Gene, Director of Western History Research Center, University
    of Wyoming, 19 April 1972.
Hill, Ruth Beebe, 18 July 1980, September 1980.
Hoffman, Carola, 22 April 1976, 3 May 1976.
Hull, Ron, 19 April 1972, 7 June 1972.
Jones, Donald J., Superintendent of Schools, Sheridan County, 8 May
    1976.
Joyner, Jean Blish (Mrs. Neville), 11 August 1972, 4 February 1973.
Koshland, William, 18 July 1972, 7 August 1973, 1 November 1973, July
    1975.
Lawrence, Richard, 8 August 1975.
Livingston, Sidnee, 15 September 1975, 11 May 1976.
Lucas, Catherine E., Library Director, Riverside City and County Li-
    brary, 20 January 1978.
McDonald, Judith, 12 April 1972, 26 April 1972, 22 September 1972, 16
    January 1973.
McGraw-Hill Publishing Co. (Jonathan Gillett), 1 August 1975.
Manion, Mae, 20 April 1976, n.d. (1975).
Merrill, Kenetha Thomas (Mrs. R. H.), 17 August 1972.
Myrer, Patricia S. (McIntosh and Otis), 11 December 1975.
Nelson, Vance, June 1972, 20 October 1972.
Otis, Elizabeth, 17 July 1973, 21 July 1975.
Paul, John, 13 August 1975.
Pence, Paul, 23 January 1976.
Pifer, Caroline Sandoz, 1971–81.
Pifer, Caroline Sandoz, to Caroline Bancroft, 31 January

1968, 17 September 1969, 20 August 1969 (Denver City Library).
Pike, Ruth, 1 August 1973, 25 August 1976.
Powell, Father Peter J., 9 September 1972, 4 September 1974, 20 November 1974, 4 December 1974.
Rice, Minnie, 25 May 1972.
Rogers, Kay, 8 March 1978 to 10 June 1979.
Rosenstock, Fred, 30 April 1977.
Sandoz, Flora, 17 March 1976.
Savery, Gil, *Lincoln Journal*, 3 July 1980.
Schrier, C. L., Mayor of Verdigre, 11 September 1975.
Schoene, Lester, Mrs., 2 March 1978.
Slote, Bernice, 17 July 1975.
Smith, Yvonne Umland, 26 September 1976.
Snell, Joseph W., 31 July 1973, 8 August 1973.
Stegner, Wallace, 1 August 1973, 6 September 1974.
Thomas, Macklin, 9 September 1972.
Umland, Rudolph, 22 April 1976, 26 August 1976.
Weeks, Edward, 10 July 1975, 10 September 1975.
Werkmeister, W. H., 1 October 1972.

Archives

UNIVERSITY OF NEBRASKA–LINCOLN
Board of Regents Correspondence, University of Nebraska, 1966–68.
"How to Write a Novel by the Mari Sandoz Method . . . As Told to an Old Friend . . . ," n.d.
Sandoz, Mari. "Nebraska's Place in the New Literature," MS for speech, n.d.
Sandoz, Mari Collection. Includes correspondence for the years 1926–66; card files for all her historical research (except for some Indian interviews and other privileged matter) and miscellaneous information; research notes; map collection (over 250 pieces); Indian pictures; photographs; newspaper articles; memorabilia; her personal library of over 1,000 volumes; voluminous historical research material; MSS for her books.

KEARNEY STATE COLLEGE
"Depopulation of Sheridan County and the Relation of the Migratory Habits of the Oglala Sioux to the Economic Survival of the Northern Communities," MS, n.d., no author.

NEBRASKA STATE HISTORICAL SOCIETY
Crazy Horse Oglala Indian File ca. 1842–77. MS 179, series 1, folder 1. Correspondence about Crazy Horse for 1930–40; folders of plats; typed and annotated copy of Eleanor Hinman's interviews with

Indians on the Rosebud and Pine Ridge reservations in 1930.

Hinman, Eleanor. See above, "Crazy Horse" entry.

Lemmon, G. MS 959, series 2.

Meredith, Mamie. Correspondence MS 565, box 1.

Ricker Interviews. MS 8, 30 MS boxes, 8 series. Interviews, letters, treaties, newspaper articles relating to the Indians.

Area newspapers, 1884–1912. *Kearney Hub, Rushville Standard, Sidney Telegraph, Omaha Bee,* Lincoln and Chicago papers.

SANDOZ CORPORATION

Sandoz, Mari. "Ungirt Runner" ("Murky River") MS, novel.

———. "Foal of Heaven," unpublished MS, novel.

———. Unpublished short stories, some untitled.

Unpublished Manuscripts

Bancroft, Caroline. *Festschrift* essay for James Carr, May 1967.

Clark, Felie Woodrow. "Mari Sandoz, Daughter of Old Jules." Master's thesis, University of Florida, 1956.

DeVilbiss, Otho. *Festschrift* essay for James Carr, 26 January 1967.

Ferril, Thomas Hornsby. Diaries, 1940–41, Denver, Colorado.

Fitzell, Lenore. *Festschrift* essay for James Carr, 21 January 1967.

McDonald, Judith Louise. "Mari Sandoz: "An Educational History." Ph.D. dissertation, University of Nebraska–Lincoln, 1980.

———. "Antaeus of the Running Water: A Biographical Study of the Western Nebraska Years of Mari Sandoz, 1906–1922." Unpublished paper, Denver University, 1972.

McKinzie, Barbara, "Region and the World: The Achievement of American Women Writers of Fiction since 1930." Ph.D. dissertation, Florida State University, 1963.

Meldrum, Helen Struble. "Great Plains Women: Fact and Fiction." Master's thesis, University of Wyoming, 1962.

Overing, Robert. "Willa Cather and Mari Sandoz: Differing Viewpoints of the Early West." Master's thesis, University of South Carolina, 1971.

Stauffer, Helen Winter. "Mari Sandoz: A Study of the Artist as Biographer." Ph.D. dissertation, University of Nebraska–Lincoln, 1974.

Walton, Kathleen O'Donnell. "Mari Sandoz: An Initial Critical Appraisal." Ph.D. dissertation, University of Delaware, 1970.

Journal Articles Relating to Mari Sandoz

Auberjonois, F. "French Swiss Review." Review of *Old Jules. Gazette de Lausaun,* January 1936.

Canfield, Dorothy. Review of *Old Jules. Book-of-the-Month Club News,* October 1935.

————. Review of *Crazy Horse. Book-of-the-Month Club News,* January 1943.

Danker, Donald. "The Eli Ricker Tablets." *Prairie Scout,* 1973, pp. 22–30. (Article giving the history and uses of the Ricker Collection at the NSHS.)

Decker, Pete. "The Hitching Post." *Westerners Brand Book* (New York Posse), 1961, p. 79.

De Voto, Bernard. "The Easy Chair," *Harper's,* April 1949, pp. 52–55.

————. "Violent, Fighting Pioneer," *Saturday Review,* 2 November 1935, pp. 5–6. (Review of *Old Jules.*)

Doane, Gilbert H. "A Bookman's Notes." *Nebraska Alumnus,* November 1935, p. 20. (Review of *Old Jules.*)

Elazer, Daniel J. Discussion of *Crazy Horse. Colorado* 39, no. 2 (April 1962): 156–57.

Fadiman, Clifton. Review of *Old Jules. New Yorker,* 2 November 1935, p. 83.

————. Review of *Crazy Horse. New Yorker,* 5 December 1942, pp. 100–102.

Faulkner, Virginia. Review of *Old Jules Country. WAL* 1, no. 3 [Fall 1966): 223–27.

"*Flair* Personified: Mari Sandoz." *Flair,* June 1950, p. 67. (Sketch of Mari Sandoz.)

Green, Norma Kidd. "Book Notes." *Nebraska Alumnus,* February 1954, p. 26. (Review of *Cheyenne Autumn.*)

Hahn, L. A. Review of *Love Song to the Plains. WAL* 2, no. 1 (Spring 1967): 72–73.

Hanna, Archibald. *Westerners Brand Book* (New York Posse), n.d., p. 11.

Harper's, August 1926, p. 395. (List of winners of intercollegiate short story contest.)

Huff, Elizabeth. "Mari Sandoz, a Living Legend." *Outdoor Nebraska,* February 1964, pp. 6–9, 40.

Hutchens, John K. *Book-of-the-Month Club News,* July 1966, p. 11, quoted in *WAL* 1, no. 3 (Fall 1966): 227. (Eulogy of Mari Sandoz.)

Irwin, Virginia. "Mari Sandoz: 1935." *St. Louis Post-Dispatch,* 27 November 1935, quoted in *PrS* 41, no. 2 (Summer 1967): 173. (Interview with Mari Sandoz.)

Kielty, Bernardine. "Authors between Books." *Book-of-the-Month Club News,* February 1954, p. 11. (Review of *Cheyenne Autumn.*)

Knoll, Robert. Review of *Love Song to the Plains. NH* 43, no. 2 (June 1962): 131–32.

LaFarge, Oliver. "Last Noble Gasps." *Saturday Review,* 12 December 1953, pp. 26–27. (Review of *Cheyenne Autumn.*)

Langenheim, Roger. "Turning Points." *Nebraska Alumnus,* June 1957, n.p. (Essay on Mari Sandoz.)

Lowe, David. "A Meeting with Mari Sandoz." *PrS* 42, no. 1 (Spring 1968): 21–26. (Memoir of Mari Sandoz.)

McIntosh, C. Barron. "One Man's Sequential Land Alienation on the Great Plains." *The Geographical Review* 71, no. 4 (October 1981): 427–445.

MacCampbell, Donald. "Mari Sandoz Discusses Writing." *The Writer*, November 1935, pp. 405–6. (Interview with Mari Sandoz.)

Mattes, Merrill. Review of *Cheyenne Autumn*. *NH* 35, no. 2 (June 1954): 147–49.

Meredith, Mamie. Review of *The Horsecatcher*. *NH* 38, no. 2 (June 1957): 165–67.

"Nebraskan." *Saturday Evening Post*, 4 March 1939, p. 88. (Biographical sketch of Mari Sandoz.)

Needham, Arnold E. Reference to Mari Sandoz's work. *WAL* 2, no. 4 (Winter 1967): 299.

Nicoll, Bruce H. "Mari Sandoz, Nebraska Loner." *American West*, Spring 1965, pp. 32–36.

Olson, Paul. "Some Books about Nebraska." *PrS* 41, no. 2 (Summer 1967): 261–64. (Reference to Mari Sandoz's work.)

"O Pioneers." *Time*, 29 November 1937, p. 69. (Review of *Slogum House*.)

"Out of Old Nebraska." *Nebraska Farmer*, 6 April 1957, p. 35.

Rister, Carl Coke. "Harvesting the Bison." *Saturday Review*, 21 August 1954, pp. 11–12. (Review of *The Buffalo Hunters*.)

Sergeant, Elizabeth Shepley. Review of *Crazy Horse*. *American Indian*, Spring 1944, pp. 26–27.

Saturday Review, 21 August 1954, cover picture.

Sheldon, Addison E. "New Books." *NH* 16, no. 1 (January–March 1935): 62. (Review of *Old Jules*.)

Sidey, Hugh. "The Presidency." *Life*, 6 February 1970, p. 2. (Reference to Mari Sandoz.)

South Pass Pete. "The Hitching Post." *Westerners Brand Book* (New York Posse), 1959, p. 36.

Stegner, Wallace. "Crazy Horse." *Atlantic Monthly*, January 1943, p. 140. (Review of *Crazy Horse*.)

Stewart, Edgar I. Essay on Mari Sandoz's work. *Montana Magazine of History*, Fall 1954.

Switzer, Dorothy Nott. Letter to the Editor. *Nebraska Alumnus*, June 1940. (Memoir of Mari Sandoz.)

———. "Mari Sandoz's Lincoln Years." *PrS* 45, no. 2 (Summer 1971): 107–15. (Article on Mari Sandoz as a student.)

Time, 2 May 1960, p. 99. (Review of *Son of the Gamblin' Man*.)

Vestal, Stanley. "Chief of the Oglalas." *Saturday Review*, 12 January 1943, p. 20. (Review of *Crazy Horse*.)

Weeks, Edward. "Mari Sandoz." *Book-of-the-Month Club News*, October 1935. (Article on Mari Sandoz and *Old Jules.*)

Westerners Brand Book (Chicago Corral), November 1954, n.p. (Westerners Achievement Award to Mari Sandoz.)

White, William Allen. "First Five Readers." *Saturday Review,* 5 October 1935, pp. 3–4. (Review of *Old Jules.*)

———. "The Bookshelf." *Atlantic Monthly,* November 1935, pp. 16, 18. (Review of *Old Jules.*)

Williams, Stanley T. Review of *Old Jules. Yale Review* 25, no. 2 (December 1935): 391–93.

Newspapers

Alderman, Harriet. "*Old Jules* by Mari Sandoz." *Alliance* (Neb.) Spud, 13 January 1936. (Review of *Old Jules.*)

Allen, Tom. "It's Springtime in the Sand Hills." *Omaha World-Herald,* 10 April 1970, p. 31. (Story about Mari Sandoz.)

Allen, William. *Pittsburgh Press,* 5 June 1955.

Alliance Spud, 18 June 1935. (Story about Mari Sandoz and Louise Pound.)

Anderson, LaVere. "Under the Reading Lamp." *Tulsa World,* 24 January 1954, p. 20. (Review of *Cheyenne Autumn.*)

"The Artist as Biographer." *London Times Literary Supplement,* 12 October 1962. (Article on biography.)

"Author Again Meets Teacher Who Opened Door to Literary World for Her." *Madison* (Wis.) *Capital Times,* 17 July 1951. (Story about Mari Sandoz.)

Bancroft, Caroline. "Book Week." *Denver Post,* n.d. (Review of *Son of the Gamblin' Man.*)

Beckman, Don. "The Pen Goes Dry." *Gordon* (Neb.) *Journal,* 7 February 1968. (Story about Mari Sandoz's last years.)

———. "Two Old Friends and a Shelf of Books." *Gordon* (Neb.) *Journal,* 24 January 1968. (Story about Beckman's friendship with Mari Sandoz.)

Bentley, John. "After-thoughts." *Lincoln Journal and Star,* 29 May 1965.

Brogan, Hugh. "Mari Sandoz: An English Opinion." *Manchester Guardian,* 29 September 1966. Review of *Love Song to the Plains;* (reprinted in *PrS,* Spring 1969, pp. 288–89.)

Burnett, W. R. "Frozen Flight of Little Wolf and His People." *New York Times Book Review,* 22 November 1953, p. 6. (Review of *Cheyenne Autumn.*)

Butcher, Fanny. "This Biography Has Frankness That Intrigues." *Chicago Daily Tribune,* 2 November 1935, p. 21. (Review of *Old Jules.*)

Coffey, Marilyn, *Daily Nebraskan,* 8 April 1959. (Interview with Mari Sandoz.)

"Cromie Looks at Authors and Books." *Chicago Tribune,* 8 March 1965.

Davis, Richard S. "Big Hollander Tells Truth about Old Jules." *Green Bay Journal,* 30 January 1936. (Interview with neighbors of Old Jules.)

Derleth, August. "Finely Told Tale of a Sioux Chieftain." *Chicago Sun Book Week,* 6 December 1942, p. 20. (Review of *Crazy Horse.*)

DeVilbiss, Otho. "I Dare Say." *Lincoln Star,* 22 November 1935. (Article about Mari Sandoz.)

Dobie, J. Frank. "When the Cheyennes Went Home." *New York Herald-Tribune Book Review,* 13 December 1953, p. 1. (Review of *Cheyenne Autumn.*)

Erickson, Saare. "Mari Sandoz Lived Frontier Life." *Lincoln Sunday Journal and Star,* 23 June 1935, sec. C-D, pp. 2–3. (Story about Mari Sandoz.)

Ferril, Thomas Hornsby. "Ideas and Comment." Childe Herald, *Rocky Mountain Herald,* 12 December 1953, pp. 1–2. (Review of *Cheyenne Autumn.*)

———. "Ideas and Comment." Childe Herald, *Rocky Mountain Herald,* 23 May 1960, p. 1. (Review of *Son of the Gamblin' Man.*)

Foell, Earl W. "An Indian Viewpoint." *Christian Science Monitor,* 14 January 1954. (Review of *Cheyenne Autumn.*)

Fox, William. *Boston Transcript,* 27 November 1937, p. 1.

Gannett, Lewis. *New York Herald-Tribune,* 3 December 1942. (Review of *Crazy Horse.*)

Gordon (Neb.) *Journal,* 18 May 1966. (Article about material moved from Mari Sandoz's apartment to University of Nebraska.)

Gordon (Neb.) *Journal,* 16 August 1967 to 6 January 1971. (Some of Mari Sandoz's letters published.)

H. L. R. *Winnipeg Free Press,* 8 February 1936. (Review of *Old Jules.*)

Hansen, Harry. "The First Reader." *New York World-Telegram,* 30 November 1942. (Review of *Crazy Horse.*)

Hass, Victor P. "From a Bookman's Notebook." *Omaha World-Herald,* 20 January 1942. (Review of *Crazy Horse.*)

———. "From a Bookman's Notebook." *Omaha World-Herald,* 23 May 1965. (Article about Mari Sandoz.)

Havighurst, Walter. "Nebraska Girl Goes Fondly Home." *New York Herald-Tribune,* 12 November 1961. (Story about Mari Sandoz.)

Hayes, Helen Mary. "Story of Cheyennes, a People Betrayed Is 'Great Achievement' for Mari Sandoz." *Lincoln Sunday Journal and Star,* 20 December 1953, p. 4D. (Review of *Cheyenne Autumn.*)

"Historic Tour of Sandoz Land." *Box Butte County* (Neb.) *Ledger,* 13 July 1967. (Article on tour of Sandoz country.)

Hughes, Elizabeth. "Move to Denver Will Free Mari Sandoz of Crank Calls." *Omaha World-Herald,* 30 June 1940, p. 1. (Story about Mari Sandoz.)

Jordan, Philander. *Omaha World-Herald,* 21 January 1906. (Story about the surrender of Crazy Horse at Fort Robinson, Nebraska.)

Josephy, Alvin M., Jr. "Soldiers and Indians." *New York Times Book Review,* 3 July 1966, sec. 7, p. 6. (Review of *The Battle of the Little Bighorn.*)

Kearney (Neb.) *Hub,* 6 January 1891. (Story of the court-martial of Col. Forsythe after the battle at Wounded Knee.)

Lawrence, J. E. "Personal Views of the News." *Lincoln Journal and Star,* 2 May 1948. (Reference to Mari Sandoz.)

Lincoln State Journal, 21 January 1909. (Story about Jules Sandoz.)

Lincoln State Journal, 23 June 1935. (Story about *Old Jules* as prize winner in Atlantic contest.)

Mahoney, Eva. "An Interview with the Author." *Omaha World-Herald,* 26 November 1939. (Interview with Mari Sandoz.)

"Mari Sandoz's College Essay Reflects Style of *Old Jules.*" *Daily Nebraskan,* 13 February 1936. (Essay on Mari Sandoz, republication of essay.)

Maurice, Arthur. "Book of the Day." *New York Sun,* 3 October 1935. (Review of *Old Jules.*)

Neihardt, John G. "Crazy Horse, Who Led the Sioux at Custer's Last Fight." *New York Times Book Review,* 20 December 1942, sec. 6, p. 4, col. 1. (Review of *Crazy Horse.*)

New York Herald-Tribune, 13 December 1953. (Review of *Cheyenne Autumn.*)

"Mari Sandoz, Arthur, 65, Dies. Historian of Nebraska Plains." *New York Times,* 11 March 1966.

Omaha Herald, 6 September 1877. (Article about the death of Crazy Horse.)

Omaha Weekly Bee, 12 September 1877. (Article about the death of Crazy Horse.)

Palmer, C. B. "Writers, Books, and People." *Boston Transcript,* 2 November 1935. (Story about Mari Sandoz in Boston.)

Perkins, Robert L. "One Man's Pegasus." *Rocky Mountain News,* 29 November 1953. (Review of *Cheyenne Autumn.*)

Prescott, Orville. "Books of the Times." *New York Times Book Review,* 2 December 1942, p. 31, col. 3. (Review of *Crazy Horse.*)

———. "Books of the Times." *New York Times Book Review,* 18 November 1953. (Review of *Cheyenne Autumn.*)

Propp, Len. *Omaha World-Herald,* 15 September 1971. (Story of marriage of Mari Sandoz and Wray Macumber.)

Rushville (Neb.) *Standard,* 21 July 1916; 17 July 1925. (Jules's letters to the editor.)

"Saga of the Sandhills and Adventures of Kinkaiders." *Omaha Bee-News*, 28 March 1930. (Editorial about Mari Sandoz's writing and research.)

"Society's Inherent Symbolism Theme of Mari Sandoz." *Daily Cardinal* (University of Wisconsin), 28 July 1955. (Interview with Mari Sandoz.)

Soskin, William. "Reading and Writing." *New York Journal*, 2 November 1935. (Review of *Old Jules*.)

"Surrender and Death of Chief Crazy Horse." *Omaha Daily Herald*, n.d. (Story about death of Crazy Horse.)

Taylor (Neb.) *Clarion*, 20 February 1936. (Editorial about *Old Jules*.)

Tomlinson, H. M. *London Observer*, 11 July 1937. (Review of English edition of *Old Jules*.)

Voiles, Jane. *San Francisco Chronicle*, 12 December 1942. (Reference to Mari Sandoz.)

Williams, F. L. "More or Less Personal." *Lincoln Journal and Star*, 24 May 1935. (Story about Mari Sandoz and *Old Jules*.)

"Wimberly Thinks Regionalism Passe; Mari Sandoz Defends Such a Theme." *Lincoln Journal and Star*, 23 May 1937. (Essays by Lowry Wimberly and Mari Sandoz.)

"Woman of the Plains." *Christian Science Monitor*, 13 December 1961. (Article about Mari Sandoz.)

Television, Public Addresses

Dick Cavett–John Neihardt interview, 28 April 1971, ABC (KHOL-TV Lincoln, Neb).

Lois Weaver–Mari Sandoz, "Mari Sandoz Day," 19 May 1958, KOLN-TV (Lincoln, Neb.).

"Mari Sandoz Discusses Creative Writing," April–May 1959, series of seven presentations, NETV (Lincoln, Neb.). Ron Hull, producer and director. Transcribed.

"Mari Sandoz Looks at the Old West," April–May 1959, series of seven presentations, NETV (Lincoln, Neb.). Ron Hull, producer and director. Taped.

Mary Sandoz, "How I Became a Writer," address to Kearney State College, 26 October 1964. Taped.

"Mari Sandoz, Her Life and Work," n.d., KUON-TV (Lincoln, Neb.).

Rita Shaw–Mari Sandoz, "Mari Sandoz, Past, Present, Future," n.d., KUON-TV (Lincoln, Neb.).

Ron Hull–Mari Sandoz interview, 26 April 1972 (repeat), KUON-TV (Lincoln, Neb.).

"Song of the Plains," 1978 (biography of Mari Sandoz), NETV (Lincoln, Neb.).

Secondary Sources

Aeschbacher, W. A. "Development of the Sandhills Lake Country." *NH* 27, no. 3 (September 1946): 205–21.

Bad Heart Bull, Amos. *A Pictographic History of the Oglala Sioux.* Lincoln: University of Nebraska Press, 1967.

Blish, Helen H. "The Ceremony of the Sacred Bow of the Oglala Dakota." *American Anthropology*, April–June 1934, pp. 180–87.

———. "Ethical Conceptions of the Oglala Dakota." *University of Nebraska Studies* 26, nos. 3, 4 (1926).

Boswell, James. *Boswell on the Grand Tour: Germany and Switzerland.* Edited by Frederick A. Pottle. New York: McGraw Hill, 1928, 1953.

Botkin, Ben A., ed. *Folk-Say I.* Norman: University of Oklahoma Press, 1931.

———. *Folk-Say II.* Norman: University of Oklahoma Press, 1932.

Boyd, Ernest. "Sex in Biography." *Harper's Monthly*, November 1932, pp. 752–59.

Brininstool, E. A., et al. "Chief Crazy Horse: His Career and Death." *NH* 12, no. 4 (December 1929): 14–77.

Brill, Charles. *Conquest of the Southern Plains.* Oklahoma City: Golden Saga Publisher, 1938.

Bronson, Edgar Beecher. *Reminiscences of a Ranchman.* 1910. Reprinted Lincoln: University of Nebraska Press, 1962.

Butcher, S. H., trans. and ed. *Aristotle's Theory of Poetry and Fine Art.* New York: Dower Publishing, 1951.

Clark, William Philo. *The Indian Sign-Language.* 1885. Reprinted San Jose: Rosicrucian Press, 1959.

Cook, James H. *Fifty Years on the Old Frontier.* 1923. Reprinted Norman: University of Oklahoma Press, 1954.

Copple, Neale. *Tower on the Plains: Lincoln's Centennial History, 1859–1959.* Lincoln: Lincoln Centennial Commission Publishers (*Lincoln Sunday Journal and Star*), 1959.

Crofton, Nebraska, 1892–1967. Crofton: *Crofton Journal,* 1967.

Dale, R. E. "Back to Normal." *NH* 38, no. 3 (September 1957): 179–206.

Danker, Donald, ed. *Man of the Plains: Recollections of Luther North 1856–1882.* Lincoln: University of Nebraska Press, 1961.

DeBarthe, Joe. *Life and Times of Frank Grouard.* Edited by Edgar I. Stewart. Norman: University of Oklahoma Press, 1958.

De Voto, Bernard. *Across the Wide Missouri.* New York: Houghton Mifflin, 1947.

Dick, Everett. *Conquering the Great American Desert.* Lincoln: Nebraska State Historical Society, 1975.

Eckholt, A. Marbro. *The Capitols of Nebraska.* Edited by Beth Robbins Cowgill. Lincoln: Nebraska State Historical Society, 1969.

Fast, Howard. *The Last Frontier.* New York: Duell, Sloan and Pearce, 1941.

Faulkner, Virginia, ed. *Roundup: A Nebraska Reader.* Lincoln: University of Nebraska Press, 1957.

Fisher, Vardis. "The Western Writer and the Eastern Establishment." *WAL* 1, no. 4 (Winter 1967): 244–59.

Fling, Fred M. "Historical Synthesis." *American Historical Review,* October 1903.

———. "Information versus Method in Education," *University Journal,* January 1908, pp. 59–60.

Gleed, Charles S. "The True Significance of Western Unrest." *Forum,* October 1893, pp. 251–60. Collected in *Farmer Discontent, 1860–1900,* edited by Vernon Carstensen, pp. 155–65. New York: John Wiley and Sons, 1974.

Grange, Roger, Jr. *Fort Robinson: Outpost on the Plains.* Lincoln: Nebraska State Historical Society, 1972. Reprinted from *NH* 39, no. 3 (September 1958).

Hicks, John D. *The Populist Revolt.* Minneapolis: University of Minnesota Press, 1931.

———. "The Legacy of Populism in the Western Middle West." *Agricultural History,* October 1949, collected in *Farmer Discontent, 1865–1900,* edited by Vernon Carstensen, pp. 149–55. New York: John Wiley and Sons, 1974.

———. "Our Pioneer Heritage." *PrS* 2, no. 1 (Winter 1928): 16–28.

Hinman, Eleanor. "Oglala Sources on the Life of Crazy Horse." *NH* 57, no. 1 (Spring 1976): 1–52.

Jeffery, Mary Louise. "Young Radicals of the Nineties." *NH* 38, no. 1 (March 1957): 25–42.

Jones, Howard Mumford, and Ludwig, Richard. *Guide to American Literature and Its Backgrounds since 1890.* Cambridge: Harvard University Press, 1964.

Kollmorgan, Walter. "The Woodmen's Assaults on the Domain of the Cattleman." *Annals of the Association of American Geographers* 59, no. 2 (June 1969): 215–39.

——— and Kollmorgan, Johanna. "Landscape Meteorology in the Plains Area." *Annals of the Association of American Geographers* 63, no. 4 (December 1973): 424–41.

Kunitz, Stanley, Jr. *Twentieth Century Authors. First Supplement: A Biographical Dictionary of Modern Literature.* New York: H. W. Wilson, 1955.

Lennon, Florence. *Lewis Carroll: Victoria through the Looking Glass.* New York: Simon and Schuster, 1945.

Lockman, Carl. *The Years of Promise.* N.p., 1971. (Personal history of Sheridan County, Nebraska.)

McGillycuddy, Julia. *McGillycuddy Agent*. Stanford: Stanford University Press, 1941.

McIntosh, C. Barron. "Forest Lieu Selections in the Sand Hills of Nebraska." *Annals of the Association of American Geographers* 64, no. 1 (March 1974): 87–89.

Manley, Robert. *Centennial History of the University of Nebraska. Vol. I, Frontier University, 1869–1919*. Lincoln: University of Nebraska Press, 1969.

Marriott, Alice. "Beowulf in South Dakota." *New Yorker*, 2 August 1952, pp. 42–45.

Meredith, Mamie. "Mari Sandoz." *Roundup: A Nebraska Reader*. Edited by Virginia Faulkner. Lincoln: University of Nebraska Press, 1957, pp. 382–86.

Nebraska History 22, no. 1 (January–March 1941). (Sioux memorial issue.)

Nebraska State Capitol Building. Nebraska State Building Division. (Pamphlet.)

Neihardt, John G. *Black Elk Speaks*. 1932. Reprinted Lincoln: University of Nebraska Press, 1967.

————. *Cycle of the West*. 1949. Reprinted Lincoln: University of Nebraska Press, 1965.

Nicoll, Bruce H., comp. *Nebraska: A Pictorial History*. Lincoln: University of Nebraska Press, 1967.

———— and Keller, Ken R. *Know Nebraska*. Lincoln: Johnsen Press, 1961.

O'Brien, Edward J., ed. *Best Short Stories of 1927 and the Yearbook of the American Short Story*. New York: Dodd, Mead, 1928.

————. *Best Short Stories of 1928 and the Yearbook of the American Short Story*. New York: Dodd, Mead, 1928.

Okada, Yasua. *Public Lands and Pioneer Farmers: Gage County, Nebraska, 1850–1900*. Tokyo: Keico Economic Society, 1971; New York: Amo Press, 1979.

O'Kieffe, Charley. *Western Story: Recollections of Charley O'Kieffe, 1884–1898*. Lincoln: University of Nebraska Press, 1960.

Olson, James C. *History of Nebraska*. 2d ed. Lincoln: University of Nebraska Press, 1966.

————. *Red Cloud and the Sioux Problem*. Lincoln: University of Nebraska Press, 1965.

————. "Literary Tradition in Pioneer Nebraska." *PrS* 24 (Summer 1950): 161–70.

Ottoson, Howard W., ed. *Land Use Policy and Problems in the United States*. Lincoln: University of Nebraska Press, 1963.

Paine, Bayard H. "Decisions Which Have Changed Nebraska History." *NH* 16, no. 4 (October–December 1935): 195–219.

Pifer, Caroline Sandoz, ed. *The Making of an Author*. Gordon, Neb.:

Pifer, Caroline Sandoz, ed. *The Making of an Author.* Gordon, Neb.: Gordon Journal, 1972.

Pound, Louise. *Selected Writings of Louise Pound.* Lincoln: University of Nebraska Press, 1949.

Powell, Peter J. *Sweet Medicine.* 2 vols. Norman: University of Oklahoma Press, 1969.

Reynolds, A. R. "The Kinkaid Act and Its Effects on Western Nebraska." *Agricultural History,* 1949, pp. 20–29.

Rice, John Andrew. *I Came Out of the Eighteenth Century.* New York: Harper and Row, 1942.

Sawyer, R. McLaran. *Centennial History of the University of Nebraska. Vol. II, Modern University, 1920–1969.* Lincoln: Centennial Press, 1973.

Schell, Herbert S. "The American Leviathan: A Historical View." *NH* 38, no. 4 (December 1957): 259–76.

Schmitt, Martin F., ed. *General George Crook: His Autobiography.* Norman: University of Oklahoma Press, 1960, 1964.

Scarlet and Cream, 12 December 1901, pp. 3–4. No title, no author. (Article about Professor Fling's system of collecting and filing historical information.)

Sheldon, Addison E. *Land Systems and Land Policies in Nebraska.* Lincoln: Nebraska Historical Society, 1936.

———. *Nebraska, Old and New: History, Stories, Folklore.* Chicago: University Publishing Co., 1937.

———. *Semi-Centennial History of Nebraska: Historical Sketch.* Lincoln: Lemon Publishing Co., 1904.

Sheridan County Historical Society, comp. *Recollections of Sheridan County.* N.p., Iron Man Industries, 1976.

Shumway, Grant Lee, ed. *History of Western Nebraska and Its People.* Lincoln: Western Publishing Co., 1921.

Stegner, Wallace. *The Sound of Mountain Water.* New York: Doubleday, 1969.

———. *The Writer in America.* Folscroft, Pa.: Folscroft Press, 1959.

Stewart, Paul R. *The Prairie Schooner Story.* Lincoln: University of Nebraska Press, 1955.

Turner, Frederick Jackson. *The Frontier in American History.* New York: Henry Holt, 1920.

Vaughn, J. W. *With Crook at the Rosebud.* Harrisburg, Pa.: Stackpole Press, 1956.

Weeks, Edward. *My Green Years.* Boston: Little, Brown, 1973.

Western Writers of America. *Legends and Tales of the Old West.* New York: Doubleday, 1962.

Westbrook, Max. "Conservative, Liberal, and Western: Three Modes of American Realism." *Literature of the American West,* edited by J. Golden Taylor. Boston: Houghton Mifflin Co., 1971.

Wimberly, Lowry C., ed. *MidCountry: Writings from the Heart of*

America. Lincoln: University of Nebraska Press, 1945.

————. "The Best Known of All Lincolns in the World." *Roundup: A Nebraska Reader*, edited by Virginia Faulkner. Lincoln: University of Nebraska Press, 1957.

Wood, A. B. *Tales of Pioneer Days in North Platte Valley*. Gering, Neb.: Carrier Press, 1938.

Woodress, James, ed. *American Literary Scholarship: An Annual, 1966*. Durham, N.C.: Duke University Press, 1968.

Wylder, Delbert E. Editorial on eastern publishers and western authors. *WAL* 1, no. 4 (Winter 1967): 241–43.

Mari at the height of her career

PHOTOGRAPHIC CREDITS
Sandoz Family Corporation:
frontispiece, pp. x, xiii,
xiv, 10, 34, 48, 96, 180,
196, 262, 288, 312
Nebraska State Historical
Society: pp. 228, 311
Lincoln Journal: p. 257
Omaha World Herald: p. 258

The Sandoz place on the Niobrara

Index